Diplomats Without a Country

Diplomats Without a Country

Baltic Diplomacy, International Law, and the Cold War

James T. McHugh and James S. Pacy

Contributions to the Study of World History, Number 86

GREENWOOD PRESS
Westport, Connecticut • London

Dedicated to the Courageous Members of
the Estonian, Latvian, and Lithuanian Diplomatic
Services: Past, Present, and Future

Library of Congress Cataloging-in-Publication Data

McHugh, James T.
 Diplomats without a country : Baltic diplomacy, international law, and the Cold
War / James T. McHugh and James S. Pacy.
  p. cm.—(Contributions to the study of world history, ISSN 0885–9159 ; no. 86)
 Includes bibliographical references and index.
 ISBN 0–313–31878–6 (alk. paper)
  1. Baltic States—International status. 2. Diplomatic and consular service,
Baltic States. I. Pacy, James S. II. Title. III. Series.
KZ4216.M34 2001
341.2'9—dc21   00–049089

British Library Cataloguing in Publication Data is available.

Library of Congress Catalog Card Number: 00–049089
ISBN: 0–313–31878–6
ISSN: 0885–9159

First published in 2001

Greenwood Press, 88 Post Road West, Westport, CT 06881
An imprint of Greenwood Publishing Group, Inc.
www.greenwood.com

Printed in the United States of America

The paper used in this book complies with the
Permanent Paper Standard issued by the National
Information Standards Organization (Z39.48–1984).

10 9 8 7 6 5 4 3 2 1

Contents

Preface

The genesis of this book was a seminar at the University of Vermont entitled "The Craft of Diplomacy," taught by Professor Jim Pacy. One of his undergraduate students, Jim McHugh, wrote a ten-page critical research essay as an assignment for that seminar, during the 1982-1983 academic year, on the topic of Baltic diplomacy. The subject of the essay had been inspired by a brief passage in an encyclopedia entry he had read, as a child, declaring the fact that some Western countries continued to recognize diplomatic representatives of the formerly–independent Baltic states, despite their annexation by the Soviet Union. Professor Pacy was fascinated by this essay topic, and professor and student kept in contact, concerning this general subject, during the years when the undergraduate student became a graduate student, then a doctoral candidate, and then, eventually, a professional colleague. This book is the ultimate product of the ongoing scholarly dialogue that began with that particular undergraduate seminar assignment.

In a seminar on diplomacy, it is important to direct attention to such novel cases as presented by the three Baltic states of Estonia, Latvia, and Lithuania. Independent through the inter-war period, they were absorbed by the Soviet Union, during World War II, and remained under Moscow's control until becoming independent, again, by 1991. It is remarkable that citizens of three, once-independent states, which had their sovereignty suppressed by the Soviet Union, managed to maintain some form of diplomatic representation, for varying lengths of time, in assorted countries, world-wide. One must appreciate the fact that the actual continuation of these legations and consulates was managed by some very creative people who, without a sovereign state, without a government, without instructions from a foreign ministry, carried on their duty, nonetheless—albeit in a most incredible diplomatic circumstance.

Indeed, one can ponder the oddness of it when contemplating such incidents as the Soviet ambassador in London needing to visit the British Foreign Office for a most unique reason: to demand the removal of the names of the Baltic diplomats from the London *Diplomatic List*. British officials moved these Baltic diplomats to a special section of the list, but not out of the list. We can reflect, also, upon a Baltic minister in Berlin who, ordered to relinquish his legation to Soviet authorities, placed his country's flag on a flag-pole in such a manner that Soviet officials needed to request the help of the Berlin Fire Department to remove it. The recounting of these incidents is not intended to make light of the Baltic tragedy, but to render a small observation that, for diplomats, the years of Baltic statelessness were, indeed, diplomatically unnatural, if not, sometimes, bizarre.

In this book, you can read about these determined people. You also can read about those courageous Baltic diplomats who were home when the Soviet Army invaded their country and who were, then, deported to the Soviet Union and never heard or seen, again. Every effort has been made to include in this book *all* of the *ministers* of the Baltic states—that is, those diplomats who were officially titled "envoy extraordinary" and "minister plenipotentiary." We also cover Baltic diplomats not ranked as minister who had been assigned duty as the principal officer of a mission—some of them as chargé d'affaires. Legations and ministers have all but disappeared from diplomacy. The world now deals with ambassadors—"ambassadors extraordinary and plenipotentiary," to be precise. Henceforth, we also mention, in this book, the ambassadors of the Baltic states accredited to the United States since the restoration of their independence.

We would appreciate correspondence from readers concerning our coverage of these Baltic diplomats, welcoming any comments on the information we have provided about their careers. As nearly as we can determine, this book is the only work in the English language which presents such a detailed account of the former ministers, and some other diplomats, of the three Baltic foreign services. We also wish to acknowledge the very regrettable absence of a treatment of women diplomats from the Baltic states. We have searched, in vain, for women who have served at the ministerial rank as representatives of Estonia, Latvia, or Lithuania, prior to 1991. We feel confident that many women *have* served, bravely and effectively, the cause of Baltic independence, diplomatically and otherwise, both at home and abroad, especially during the period of the Cold War. Indeed, we have encountered, and been assisted by, Estonian, Latvian, and Lithuanian women whose hard work and scholarship have advanced the cause of Baltic sovereignty and the completion of this book. Unfortunately, their official, pre-1991 diplomatic efforts at the ministerial level, in Baltic legations abroad, have remained obscured to our scholarship, so we encourage, particularly, any information on this matter that will permit us to correct this lamentable omission, especially for the purpose of any future editions of this book.

Acknowledgments

We are indebted to many persons in writing this book. At the apex of the list of persons deserving our utmost appreciation are *Maira Bundža*, librarian of the Latvian Studies Center Library in Kalamazoo, Michigan, and *Mara R. Saule*, library associate professor at the University of Vermont. We have been most fortunate to have been accorded such exemplary assistance! *Dr. Olga Berendsen, Olev Berendsen*, and *Juri Viiroja* of the Estonian Archives in the United States, Inc., Lakewood, New Jersey, also gave exceptional help to us, repeatedly. They, too, are remembered for defining the meaning of "reliability" to us. *Arunas Zailskas*, director of research services, Lithuanian Research and Studies Center, Chicago, and *Heini Vilbiks*, librarian, Estonian Foreign Ministry, Tallinn, are included in this memorable group of persons who were crucially important to us. Despite our many requests, all of them rendered continually invaluable service, and always with pronounced cordiality.

Elina Wetterstrand, librarian, Finnish Foreign Ministry, Helsinki, and *Kirsten Ostenfeld*, librarian, Danish Foreign Ministry, Copenhagen, very kindly and perceptively did far more than we dared to expect; we cannot thank them, enough. We express our gratitude to *Rita Aars-Nicolaysen* and *Anne-Gry Skonnord*, librarians, Norwegian Foreign Ministry, Oslo and, likewise, *Kai Bøe*, archivist, National Archives of Norway. We also are beholden to *Bertil Johansson*, senior archivist, Swedish National Archives, Stockholm. In sum, all of these people were more helpful than they will ever imagine.

We were privileged to have been granted interviews with the following ambassadors: *Vincas Balickas*, Lithuania (London); *Dr. Anatol Dinbergs*, Latvia (Washington); *Ernst Jaakson*, Estonia (New York [United

Nations] and Washington); *Jānis Lūsis*, Latvia (London); and *Riivo Sinijärv*, Estonia (London). We also appreciate the cooperation extended by those diplomats who engaged in detailed correspondence with us, particularly the distinctive efforts of Ambassador *Jaakson*. Also, Ambassador *Kalnins*, an alumnus of Roosevelt University (which he attended when he came to Chicago as a displaced person following World War II), offered particularly noteworthy information and support.

We want to recognize, as well, the various aid and support offered in the form of interview, correspondence, telephone conversation, translation, written material, and other means. These people include *Stasys Bačkis*, Lithuanian chargé d'affaires, Washington; *Julie Charron*, Canadian Mission to the United Nations, New York; *Kathleen Dana*, Northfield, Vermont; *Kenneth Heger*, archivist, National Archives, College Park, Maryland; *Ilmar Heinsoo*, Estonian honorary consul general, Toronto; *Ivars Indans*, Latvian Academic Library, Riga; *Vaiki Laurimaa Kreckovič*, Burlington, Vermont; *Grazina Lappas*, consular secretary, Lithuanian Honorary Consulate General, Toronto; *Haris Lappas*, Lithuanian honorary consul general, Toronto; *Okke Metsmaa*, Estonian vice consul, New York; *Victor Nakas*, political and press officer, Lithuanian Embassy, Washington; *Arvydas Naujokaitis*, acting head, Information and Press Department, Lithuanian Foreign Ministry, Vilnius; *K. A. Neil*, Foreign and Commonwealth Office, London; *Professor Janis Penikis*, Department of Political Science, Indiana University, South Bend; *A. Michele Powell*, librarian, Department of State, Washington; *Andrew Silski*, Office of Nordic and Baltic Affairs, Department of State, Washington, D.C.; *Guntis Treijs*, Latvian Studies Center Library, Kalamazoo, Michigan; *Professor Gretchen van Slyke*, Department of Romance Languages, University of Vermont, Burlington; *Marie-Ann Zarins*, Latvian Embassy, London.

The assistance we received from the dedicated, and eminently genial, staff of the University of Vermont Library was, unquestionably, outstanding. We also received support and assistance from *Mary Beth Riedner*, head librarian, Roosevelt University Library, Chicago, and other members of that staff. We are grateful to the libraries of Dartmouth College, Hanover, New Hampshire, Harvard University, Cambridge, Massachusetts, McGill University, Montreal, and Princeton University, Princeton, New Jersey for permission to pursue research among their holdings. Special thanks are rendered to *Bill Rodney* of the University of London Library for the time he expended on our behalf.

We express further appreciation, as well, to the staffs of the British Public Record Office, Kew, London, and the United States National Archives, Washington and College Park, Maryland. Additional support was provided by the administrative staff of the School of Policy Studies, Roosevelt University, Chicago, including *Paule Bernadel, Jerlean Fleming*, and *Bonnie Wedington*. Invaluable technical advice and assistance for preparing the final copy of this manuscript was provided by *Dr. Gary Langer*, vice provost for academic technology at Roosevelt University. The patient assistance, encouragement, and supervision of the staff of Greenwood Press also has proven to be critical to the success of this book, especially from *Dr. Heather Ruland Staines*, senior editor for history and military studies, and our production editor, *Nina Duprey*. Finally, the patience and encouragement of our families have been, always, crucial to our success. We are grateful for all of the assistance and support we have received, in this endeavor.

Abbreviations

Public Records

FO

Material from the Public Record Office [PRO] in London is identified with the PRO designation FO (for Foreign Office) preceding a series of numbers and one or more letters, *e.g.*, FO371/17255-N739/120/38. In order to know immediately the city of origin of a document, citations offer the city first, in the following format:

Moscow, January 27, 1933, Sir Esmond Ovey, FO371/17255-N739/120/38.

The preceding citation indicates that Sir Esmond Ovey sent this item from Moscow to the Foreign Office in London on January 27, 1933. It should be noted that a British diplomat, who has been listed for years as, for example, Esmond Ovey, will be designated in documents differently, after having been knighted, for example, Sir Esmond Ovey. Thus, in one document, we find a diplomat cited with the title "Sir," and, in another document, we find the same diplomat cited without a title, as this example illustrates.

USNA

Material from the National Archives and Records Administration, in Washington and College Park, Maryland, is identified with the designation USNA (for U. S. National Archives), preceding a series of numbers and a letter, for example, USNA701.60P 61/18. In order to know immediately the city of origin of a document, citations offer the city first, in the following format:

Riga, November 24, 1936, Arthur Bliss Lane, USNA701.60P 61/18.
This citation indicates that Arthur Bliss Lane sent this item from Riga, Latvia to the State Department in Washington on November 24, 1936.

Other Citations

ENE-1
Eesti nõukogude entsüklopeedia [Estonian Soviet Encyclopedia] 1st ed. 9 vols. Tallinn: Valgus, 1968–1978.

ENE-2
Eesti nõukogude entsüklopeedia [Estonian Soviet Encyclopedia]. 2d ed. 10 vols. Tallinn: Valgus, 1985– . From vol. 5 (1990), title changed to *Eesti Entsüklopeedia* [Estonian Encyclopedia].

ELI
Encyclopedia Lituanica. Simas Sužiedélis, ed. 6 vols. Boston: Juozas Kapočius, 1970–1978.

EVP
Es viņu pazīstu: Latviešu biografiskā vārdnīca [I Know Him: Latvian Biographical Dictionary], 2nd ed., Žanis Unāms, ed. Grand Haven, MI: "Raven Printing" Spiestuvē, 1975. Reprint of 1st ed. Riga: Biografiskā archiva apgāds, 1939.

FOLD
Great Britain. Foreign Office. *The Foreign Office List and Diplomatic and Consular Year Book.* London: Harrison and Sons, 1920–1965. Since 1966, it has been titled *The Diplomatic Service List.*

HVL
Unpublished list of Estonian ministers of foreign affairs, ministers, and chargés d'affaires, the latter two groups being classified by country of assignment, in chronological order of service, 1919–1940. Prepared for the authors by Heini Vilbiks, librarian, Estonian Foreign Ministry, Tallinn, February 23, 1995.

LAM
Latvia. Ārlietu Ministrija [Foreign Ministry]. *Le corps diplomatique en Lettonie, 1918–1938*. Riga: Ministère des affaires étrangères de Lettonie, novembre 1938.

LEA
Latvju enciklopēdia [Latvian Encyclopedia], *1962–1982*. 4 vols, Edgars Andersons, ed. Rockville, MD: American Latvian Association, 1983–1990.

LEN
Lietuvių Enciklopedija [Lithuanian Encyclopedia]. 37 vols. Vaclovas Biržiška, et al., eds. South Boston: Lietuvių enciklopedijos leidykla, 1953–1985.

LES
Latvju enciklopēdija [Latvian Encyclopedia]. 3 vols., Arvēds Švābe, ed. Stockholm: Trīs Zvaigznes, 1950–1955. Supplements, Lidija Svābe, ed. Stockholm: Trīs Zvaigznes, 1962.

LKV
Latviešu konversācijas vārdnīca [Latvian Conversational Dictionary], 21 vols., Arvēds Švābe, A. Būmanis, and K. Dišlērs, eds. Riga: A. Gulbis, 1927–1940.

RHA
Eero Medijainen, "Tartu Ülikool kogub teateid Eesti Välisministeeriumi töötajate kohta" [University of Tartu collects information about the workers of the Estonian Foreign Ministry], (1918–1940), *Rahva Hääl* [The People's Voice], (Tallinn), February 8, 1995.

USDL
U. S. Department of State. *Diplomatic List*. Washington, DC: U. S. Government Printing Office, 1919–.

USRD
U. S. Department of State. *Register of the Department of State*. Washington, DC: U. S. Government Printing Office, 1922–1931.

Chapter 1

Introduction:
The Paradox of Baltic Diplomacy

Prior to the restoration of political independence for the Baltic states of Estonia, Latvia, and Lithuania, in 1991, these three states were "republics" of the Union of Soviet Socialist Republics, with a political structure that aped the systemic appearance of a federal subunit of government, such as an American state or a Canadian province. The Soviet Union was, however, a highly centralized country. Its political structure was de jure federal, but it was de facto unitary; all ecomomic, political, and military power and decision making emanated from the Kremlin, particularly via the Communist Party of the Soviet Union.[1] The conditions experienced within the Baltic states at this time differed little, in this respect, from the conditions experienced by the other Soviet "republics" (such as Ukraine, Belarus, Armenia, Moldova, Kazakhstan) with the exception of the Russian Federated Soviet Socialist Republic, which formed the infrastructural and ethnic nucleus of the Soviet "empire" that had replaced the Russian Empire of the czars.[2]

However, one formal difference distinguished the three Baltic states from the other parts of the Soviet Union. It was, essentially, an external difference that really was more meaningful for Estonian, Latvian, and Lithuanian expatriates (and, arguably and to a limited extent, for certain Western governments) than it was for the members of these nations who continued to occupy this territory while enduring Soviet rule. It was a difference that was little known or noticed, although it was a source for potential anti-Soviet propaganda. Nonetheless, despite its relative obscurity, this difference was not entirely unappreciated. Separate entries for each of the Baltic states were maintained between 1940 and 1991 (the years of Soviet occupation) within certain source books, including the *World Book Encyclopedia*. Within that particular source, a curious fact was mentioned as an aside within each of the three relevant entries.

> Estonia [/Latvia/Lithuania] is a land on the Baltic Sea in northern Europe. It was an independent country for twenty-two years. But, in 1940, Russia [sic] seized Estonia [/Latvia/Lithuania] and made it a state of the Union of Soviet Socialist Republics. It is now called the Estonian [/Latvian/Lithuanian] Soviet Socialist Republic. Many countries, including the United States, do not recognize the Russian [sic] seizure of Estonia [/Latvia/Lithuania]. Such countries recognize Estonian [/Latvian/Lithuanian] diplomats and consuls who still function in many countries in the name of their former government.[3]

This fact may seem quaint (perhaps, even poetic) on the surface; within the context of traditional diplomacy and international law, it appears to be remarkable or even absurd. None of these states had their claims to independence fostered, during this period, by governments-in-exile. These "diplomats and consuls" were representatives of nonexistent sending states—a situation that defies any logical structure that purports to guide and unify the fragile system of modern international law. Perhaps, it makes more sense when it is contemplated within the context of the Cold War, when symbol and substance frequently were confused as political actions became submerged within, and subservient to, a larger "struggle." The conflicts that emerged from the Cold War resulted from a more abstract confrontation between the United States and the Soviet Union (as the most recent representatives of a perceived Western tradition of idealized bipolar conflicts, extending back as far as the romanticized struggle between Athens and Sparta), the North Atlantic Treaty Organization and the Warsaw Pact, "democracy" and "dictatorship," "freedom" and "tyranny," "good" and "evil." The Baltic states were pawns, as well as victims, of that grand confrontation. Therefore, the diplomatic representatives of these states, regardless of their true status, were well placed to become characters (albeit minor ones) upon the stage of this international, and often skewed, morality play.[4]

The origins of this specific diplomatic situation are very understandable. During World War II, many occupied countries continued to be represented abroad by diplomats who had been appointed by governments that subsequently were defunct. In some cases, these governments maintained a de jure existence as governments-in-exile until their respective countries were liberated, so that the formal relationship between foreign ministries and diplomatic missions could be maintained—thus satisfying the necessary legal conditions which these missions needed (even if only symbolically) to fulfill. For other countries, however, there were no governments-in-exile to maintain "appearances." In some cases, the diplomatic missions of these countries actually assumed many of the functions and responsibilities that normally would be expected of a government-in-exile. Regardless of the circumstances, World War II had made international law, understandably, a more malleable tool of foreign and military policy than it normally was accepted to be—and that acceptance was relatively high during times of relative peace and international stability. Independent diplomats and diplomatic missions, like those of the Baltic states, were an accepted, and even expected, consequence of this most awesome and terrible global conflagration. They became unique and very peculiar only after the Allies won the war.[5]

The vast majority of those countries that had been occupied during World War II regained their independence by the time of its conclusion. Indeed, within a few years of the end of that war, several colonies of the victorious Allied powers achieved political liberation, too. Even the countries of Eastern Europe that had a political system and government imposed upon them through the dominant influence of the Soviet Union maintained their independent status within the international community and, therefore, also maintained a conventional diplomatic presence throughout the world. The Baltic states represented an exception to that trend.[6]

Estonia, Latvia, and Lithuania were annexed and "incorporated" into the Soviet Union. These countries maintained a politically distinct status under Soviet rule, but they were not sovereign, so these "soviet socialist republics" were not represented abroad. The international status of these three states ceased to exist, despite the objections of the United States and other Western countries. However, their diplomatic presence as known prior to World War II continued to be represented by those same diplomats who had been appointed by the former Baltic governments prior to, or (in a few cases) during, 1940. Under normal circumstances, the various host governments simply would have revoked their acceptance of the credentials of these officials and, if necessary, declared them persona non grata, granted them political asylum, or had them deported. The Cold War hardly qualified, however, as "normal" circumstances; the principles of international law could be "reinterpreted" in order to accommodate broader political objectives, just as moral principles could be manipulated by, or even surrendered to, rationalizations in support of these same objectives.[7]

It is unfair to be too cynical about this situation, for many politicians and other officials who defended the legitimacy of these Baltic missions were motivated, at least in part, by a sincere (though occasionally naive) commitment to the values of freedom and self-determination that were exhorted on their behalf. However, given the tentative presence and quality of democracy within the Baltic states (especially Lithuania) prior to the World War II, a defense of the differing policies regarding the diplomatic recognition of the Baltic missions upon the basis of a support for the "restoration" of democracy might reasonably be treated with at least a modicum of scepticism.

But the politics of power, within the context of a "realist" approach to international relations, does not, necessarily, offer a more plausible explanation of one of the most imaginative anomalies in the history of diplomacy.[8] Obviously, Estonian, Latvian, and Lithuanian diplomats could not perform most of the normal functions of their formal positions under these circumstances. At the same time, they could not lay claim to the status of governments-in-exile or even revolutionary movements aimed at the restoration of political independence, since their diplomatic claims (and the diplomatic immunity that would accompany the recognition of those claims) would preclude such political activities as being inconsistent with the diplomatic status they sought and occasionally (in varying forms) achieved. It is not easy to find a satisfying theoretical characterization of Baltic diplomacy, but its obvious lack of practicality and the imagination that sustained it could suggest, to the casual observer, an "idealist" approach to this international relations issue.[9]

There are two ways that this episode of diplomatic history and international law could be characterized (at least, superficially) as "idealist."[10] First, it was based upon a genuine desire to restore democratic sovereignty to the peoples of this region, despite the seemingly insurmountable obstacle of Soviet control. Second, its apparent impracticality contradicted the normal pattern of Western foreign policy (especially American foreign policy), which emphasized feasible strategies for isolating and containing the communist superpower.[11] However, these goals were shared by many people throughout the West (including Americans), and not just advocates of a "utopian" vision of international affairs.

Realist approaches dominated the conduct of American foreign policy during most of the Cold War era.[12] The underlying assumption that power and the promotion of national interests offer the only valid motive of governments in their interactions with the international community would suggest that the maintenance of a Baltic diplomatic presence was, at best, a relatively minor distraction from the pragmatic strategy of "containing," or, later, reaching a practical accommodation with, Soviet military and political strategies.[13] It seemed nearly impossible that the Soviet hegemony over the Baltic states or any other part of its "domestic empire" would be shaken, even during the late 1980s. Expending any effort in support of this cause certainly might have been perceived by many observers, understandably, to be based upon rather romantic assumptions or, perhaps, even a Wilsonian ideal of self-determination.

Of course, realist strategies can be engaged to support the dominant ideals of a particular society. The continued support of Baltic diplomats throughout the West was a source of annoyance to Soviet officials, as well as being embarrassing. In that way, it contributed to the general aim of keeping Soviet influence "contained," in the broad sense of the term. Furthermore, national identity and democratic development have been objects of genuine respect and desire by American politicians and foreign policy strategists throughout American history, including the Cold War era.[14] But, understandably, an observer could have concluded that the support of diplomatic missions that did not represent even a tangible government-in-exile must have appeared to be a counter-intuitive exercise in symbolic futility that could not justify any expense that might detract from much more feasible tactics. Nonetheless, these Baltic diplomats did receive political and, in certain cases, limited financial support for their seemingly impossible quest, especially (but not exclusively) from the United States. The restoration of full independence to Estonia, Latvia, and Lithuania and the continuity of their respective diplomatic representation to various Western governments that greeted this event offer an extraordinary exception to the normal pattern of Western international relations during the late twentieth century.

This phenomenon also defied the generally accepted expectations regarding public international law. Political theorists such as Alberico Gentili and Hugo Grotius identified the essential source of international law as a basic human self-interest that replaced Christian strictures. All sovereign states would agree to obey these laws because their enforcement guaranteed the stability that they needed for securing their own prosperity. Since each country wanted to feel certain that its diplomatic representatives could conduct relations in safety, the mutual interest of observing principles of diplomatic immunity would be assured. There could be no gain from violating that principle, since a violating country would be mistrusted and, therefore, effectively cut off from that international intercourse that was vital to their own physical security and economic prosperity. [15] Indeed, it is possible to argue that realism found its first effective expression within international law, just as it found its earliest theoretical expression within the writings of Niccolò Machiavelli.[16]

The extension of diplomatic recognition to representatives of defunct governments defies these underlying principles. Indeed, such action could be counterproductive, since it would expose the offending state to the possibility of retaliation and create the potential for undermining the entire diplomatic order. It certainly will be argued that the continued recognition of Baltic diplomats long after the demise of the governments that appointed them did not violate the letter of international law, especially as interpreted through multilateral treaties, such as the Vienna Convention on Diplomatic and Consular Relations. However, it is equally arguable that the spirit of international law may have been offended by this practice, especially since it did not appear to serve even the overt self-interest of the countries that engaged in it, including the acceptance of representatives (also encompassing honorary representatives) who were appointed by other diplomats, rather than by the governments of recognized, sovereign states. Nonetheless, certain Western governments allowed this unique interpretation of international law to persist, despite the fact that it seemed to offer no real hope of bearing results that would warrant the process or further the aims of these countries as in their pursuit of power and self-interest within a global context.

This book identifies, and makes sense of, this unusual incident of diplomatic history and the unusual consequences that it offered for international law, in particular, and international relations, in general. It does it through an analysis of empirical evidence relating to Baltic diplomacy, including pre–World War II and Cold War era documents, interviews, notes, and published sources. The book also offers normative explanations for this unusual development, placing the evolution of modern Baltic diplomacy within the theoretical constructs of international relations, international law, and comparative politics. From this perspective, it is hoped that this event of diplomatic history can be regarded as a model for future imaginative policies and developments (where such policies are applicable and appropriate), rather than merely as an isolated and, arguably, bizarre exception to the conventional procedures of modern diplomacy.

Chapter 2 examines the historical and political context from which Baltic diplomacy originally emerged. It provides a brief outline of the rich and often volatile evolution of the Baltic region and the peoples who would emerge as the modern nations of Estonia, Latvia, and Lithuania. It provides insight into the conditions that made the historical role of Baltic diplomats both difficult and precarious, and it offers an appreciation of the recuring theme of the Baltic states as cultural and political entities trapped between larger, competing forces and ideals of international politics. Chapter 3 returns to this historical perspective by focusing upon the specific evolution of Estonian, Latvian, and Lithuanian diplomacy. It emphasizes the diplomats and their missions, focusing upon prominent individuals, the extensiveness of Baltic diplomatic efforts throughout the world, and the difficult task of representing countries that frequently were overwhelmed by the larger struggles of great powers. This difficulty is particularly apparent in relation to Europe during the period between the world wars and Baltic relations with Nazi Germany, the Soviet Union, and the major Western Allies during the World War II.

Chapter 4 focuses upon the relationship between the emergence of a separate Estonian, Latvian, and Lithuanian diplomatic presence following the annexation of these countries by the Soviet Union. It examines the various approaches of the major powers to the continued presence of Baltic diplomats and missions in the absence of Baltic governments. In doing so, it evaluates the competing normative theories of international law that provided justifications for these different policies, especially the positions of the United States, the United Kingdom, and the Soviet Union. Chapter 5 engages in a more specific analysis of the actual functioning and perpetuation of Baltic diplomats and missions after World War II. It places this development within the broader context of international relations, including in relation to certain general theoretical explanations regarding the policy approaches of different governments toward this unusual brand of Baltic diplomacy. It also places this development within the context of the foreign policies of the United States, the United Kingdom, and the Soviet Union toward Estonia, Latvia, and Lithuania, as well as their respective domestic policies regarding Baltic nationals (whether as refugees or as citizens) within their respective sovereign territories.

Chapter 6 focuses upon the approach to this issue that was developed by successive Canadian governments. It evaluates the special, and different, relationships of Canada with the United Kingdom and the United States, considerations of Canada's evolving presence in world affairs, and domestic concerns regarding the politics of multiculturalism. In particular, this chapter considers the status, within international law, of honorary consuls and consulates, as well as the historical circumstances and the political strategy behind Canada's decision to pursue that alternative approach to the issue of Baltic diplomacy during the Cold War era. Chapter 7 examines the Australian approach to this issue, especially in terms of that country's ultimate ambivalence toward Baltic diplomatic representatives within that country. It evaluates Australia's domestic considerations regarding Estonian, Latvian, and Lithuanian émigrées, Australia's foreign policy within the context of the Cold War and the emerging significance of the Pacific rim region, and its ambivalence regarding the legal status of these diplomats and missions.

Chapter 8 evaluates the remarkable transition to independence of the Baltic states and its implications for those Estonian, Latvian, and Lithuanian diplomats and their missions who had persisted in their efforts, despite the fact that it appeared to have been a "lost cause" until the end of the 1980s. The Baltic states, unlike other, newly independent former Soviet republics, already had a limited diplomatic base for reestablishing their respective diplomatic and foreign relations. This chapter considers some of the practical advantages and difficulties, as well as the repercussions, of Baltic Cold War diplomacy for the countries that had recognized that effort—particularly the United States.

Finally, Chapter 9 concludes the overall study by offering some lessons that may be derived from this historical development. It briefly considers the possibility that diplomatic activity on behalf of nonindependent peoples, even in the absence of any sort of effective political body that claims to represent such peoples, can be emulated from the experience of Estonia, Latvia, and Lithuania. It reevaluates the theoretical applications of this unusual approach to diplomacy, in terms of both abstract considerations of international law and the viable considerations of international relations and broad political conflict. While the lessons learned from this episode of diplomatic history should be applied to other contexts with extreme care or outright skepticism, it might prove to be useful for a world community that pursues greater global cooperation while grappling increasingly with problems of militant nationalism, political decentralization, and various forms of economic, cultural, and ethnic conflict.

A group of aging Baltic diplomats maintained, for 42 years, an extremely tentative existence within their own, unique legal and political "limbo." They endured enormous tragedy and defied conditions that might have reduced other people to a state of hopelessness. Their remarkable persistence was matched only by the remarkable events that resulted in the ultimate demise of the Soviet Union and the restoration of the independence of Estonia, Latvia, and Lithuania.[17] A phenomenon that appeared to be a quaint anachronism during the early 1980s was regarded as being remarkably prophetic by the end of that decade. It served as a vindication of a seemingly impossible dream for Baltic nationalists, Western advocates of self-determination, and "true believers" everywhere. It may also serve as a model for other, extraordinary events and causes that are made inevitable by the machinations of political competition and the struggles for human dignity that have consistently resisted them throughout history.

It was understandable that many people may have felt sorry for these diplomats, who seemed to cling to a desperate, but apparently hopeless, cause. It is equally understandable that their efforts were often overlooked or underappreciated, in terms of both their positive effect upon the restoration of a viable sovereignty for Estonia, Lithuania, and Latvia and for its effect upon the way that many relevant people and institutions might come to understand and appreciate the creative possibilities that diplomacy can offer. This appreciation can be practically useful, especially when it is removed from the parochial, theoretical limits that have traditionally been imposed upon this realm of political endeavor. Certainly, it merits critical consideration.

Notes

1.   John N. Hazard, *The Soviet System of Government* (Chicago: University of Chicago Press, 1957), pp. 74–88; Ronald J. Hill, *Soviet Politics, Political Science, and Reform* (Oxford: Martin Robertson, 1980), pp. 63–84.

2.   For an assessment of this Soviet "empire" and its consequences, see Geoffrey Hosking, *The Awakening of the Soviet Union* (Cambridge: Harvard University Press, 1990), pp. 76–111.

3.   Francis J. Bowman, entries on Estonia, Latvia, and Lithuania, *World Book Encyclopedia* (Chicago: Field Enterprises Educational, 1961), vol. 5, p. 288, vol. 11, pp. 108, 346.

4.   A contemporary overview of the pragmatic manifestations of these alllegorical comments is provided in Hubert S. Gibbs, "The American Alliance System," in *Problems in International Relations*, Andrew Gyorgy and Hubert S. Gibbs, eds. (Englewood Cliffs, NJ: Prentice-Hall, 1962), pp. 121–140.

5.   These missions often served as extensions of governments-in-exile that were established during World War II. An overview of these contingency governments and an indirect assessment of their diplomatic relationships are offered in George V. Kacewicz, *Great Britain, the Soviet Union, and the Polish Government in Exile* (The Hague: Martinus Nijhoff, 1979), pp. 215–225.

6.   Nonetheless, Eastern European diplomatic and foreign policy and institutions (like the respective political and economic systems as a whole) were directed by a "foreign policy orthodoxy" imposed by the Soviet Union throughout the Cold War era, as noted in William A. Welsh, "Towards an Empirical Typology of Socialist Systems," in *Comparative Socialist Systems: Essays on Politics and Economics*, Carmelo Mesa-Lago and Carl Beck, eds. (Pittsburgh: University of Pittsburgh Center for International Studies, 1975), pp. 54–56.

7.   An evaluation of these inconsistencies can be found in Hans J. Morgenthau and Kenneth W. Thompson, *Politics among Nations* (New York: Alfred A. Knopf, 1985), pp. 243–278.

8.   A good summary of the realist approach to international relations is offered in James E. Dougherty and Robert L. Pfaltzgraff, Jr., *Contending Theories of International Relations* (New York: Harper and Row, 1981), pp. 84–127.

9.   The need for flexibility, if not imagination, in addressing changing circumstances within the international legal order is considered in Wolfgang G. Friedmann, *The Changing Structure of International Law* (New York: Columbia University Press, 1964), pp. 67–71.

10.   An overview of idealism and its relation to foreign policy is provided in Charles W. Kegley, Jr. and Eugene Wittkopf, *American Foreign Policy: Pattern and Process* (New York: St. Martin's Press, 1987), pp. 72–74.

11.   The seminal expression of this policy was offered by one of the most influential American Cold War statesmen in "X" [George F. Kennan], "The Sources of Soviet Conflict," *Foreign Affairs* 25 (July 1947), especially in his adoption of the term "containment," p. 514.

12.   These realists argued that worthy idealist goals could be achieved only through the application of realist strategies, especially regarding the building of Western armed power (including a nuclear arsenal), George F. Kennan, *Russia, the Atom, and the West* (New York: Harper and Row, 1958), pp. 41–45.

13.   The most famous proponent of this approach to American foreign policy was the scholar, diplomat, and Secretary of State, Henry Kissinger. An overview of this aspect of his approach is offered in Peter W. Dickson, *Kissinger and the Meaning of History* (Cambridge: Cambridge University Press, 1978), pp. 20–22.

14.   This understanding is suggested in Raymond Aron, *Peace and War* (New York: Doubleday, 1966), pp. 591–594.

15.   Peter Haggenmacher, "Grotius and Gentili: A Reassessment of Thomas E. Holland's Inaugural Lecture," in *Hugo Grotius and International Relations*, Hedley Bull, Benedict Kingsbury, and Adam Roberts, eds. (Oxford: Clarendon Press, 1992), pp. 133–176.

16.   Steven Forde, "International Realism and the Science of Politics: Thucydides, Machiavelli, and Neorealism," *International Studies Quarterly*, 39, no. 2 (June 1995), pp. 141–160.

17.   The success of this final Baltic transition to sovereignty and its implications for international relations are recorded in Cynthia Kaplan, "Estonia: A Plural Society on the Road to Independence," in *Nation and Politics in the Soviet Successor States*, Ian Bremmer and Ray Taras, eds. (Cambridge: Cambridge University Press, 1993), pp. 212–218; Richard Krickus, "Lithuania: Nationalism in the Modern Era," in Bremmer and Taras, eds., pp. 174–178; Nils Muiznieks, "Latvia: Origins, Evolution, and Triumph," in Bremmer and Taras, pp. 192–201.

Chapter 2

The Context of Baltic History

Reference often is made to the Baltic states and their respective citizens, but the term does not refer to a homogeneous culture, people, or political system. Despite the frequent application of the term, its use should be understood as a convenience rather than as a statement of collective identity. In order to appreciate specific controversies and successes of the politics and history of this region, it is important to gain an understanding of its rich and diverse background, as well as significant aspects of that background that *do* unite the people of this region within a common historical experience.[1]

A general evaluation of Baltic history and culture tends to produce a superficial division of that region into two parts. Nonetheless, that division is convenient as a starting point for exploring this subject. Therefore, it will be useful to examine Latvia and Lithuania separately from Estonia—at least in terms of gaining an appreciation of some of the basic anthropological events and trends that shaped these societies and their relationship to the rest of the world. It then will be useful to examine the political development of Lithuania separately from the development of Estonia and Latvia, especially in terms of the emergence, expansion, and decline of Lithuania as a prominent European power during the late medieval and early modern periods. This process proves to be most useful in terms of gaining an elementary understanding of the anthropological origins of the Baltic people which initially shaped that relationship—one which has, in certain respects, persisted until the present and continues to guide the destinies of these three countries.

Ethnic Latvians and Lithuanians are descendants of, as some anthropologists denote, "true Balts." The ancient Letts and Lithuanians were a tribal people who gradually absorbed other groups living in present Northeastern Europe, including the area bordering upon the Baltic Sea. The Balts absorbed tribes such as the Kurs, Zemgals, and Selonians; the Slavs to the east gradually absorbed other groups, such as the Belarus. They originally emerged from the steppes of central Russia, but the Balts tended to be more oriented toward the West than their Slavic neighbors, who tended, along with the Prussians, to pressure them in that direction.[2] During the ancient period, these people developed a relatively sophisticated local civilization that traded with German tribes and the Roman Empire. However, the pressures of migrating groups posed a continuously disruptive influence upon the Balts, who, eventually, occupied the sites of modern Latvia and Lithuania sometime before the beginning of the tenth century.[3]

The Estonians are descended of the Finno-Ugric group. More specifically, they were part of the southern branch of the Baltic Finns, which included tribes such as the Livs and the Votes. They also traded with Germans and Romans, although they appear to have been less subjected to the pressures of migration than their Baltic neighbors to the south. They also were well established in the area that is modern Estonia by the tenth century. However, in many respects they differed markedly from the Balts, with whom they would become geographically, economically, historically, and politically associated.[4]

In some ways, it appears that the people of the Baltic region may have been influenced by the Celts who passed through Central Europe in ancient times. Certainly, the religious practices of these people strongly resemble the cyclical, nature–oriented beliefs that have been more conspicuously associated with the Druids of the British archipelago. Regardless of the origins of their religious customs, the Baltic people shared a broad system of beliefs that proved to be resistant to the inroads made by Christian missionaries during the medieval period.[5]

Vikings overran western parts of the region from both the north and the sea during the eleventh and twelfth centuries. Meanwhile, to the east, the East Slavs were making territorial gains of their own. Danish missionaries were especially active throughout the region, and their aggressive efforts were indicative of a larger desire on the part of the Church to spread the Faith—if necessary, by force. In their wake came another wave of invasions by the Danes, as well as considerable pressure from the Saxons. By the end of the thirteenth century the lands of the Estonians and Latvians had been largely overrun.[6]

Much of this Saxon effort was led by a mercenary Christian movement organized by Bishop Albert of Buxhoevden. The Brothers of the Sword were typical of those knights who were empowered by Rome to spread the faith through territorial acquisition that they would possess and rule on behalf of the church. The Brothers of the Sword were successful in their efforts throughout much of present Estonia and Lithuania, from which base they directed their efforts towards the east and south. However, their strength and effectiveness were badly shaken after their defeat by Lithuanians at the Battle of Saule in 1236. The Brothers of the Sword were reorganized as the Livonian Order and formed an alliance with the better—known Order of the Teutonic Knights, with the help of whom they were able to retain much of their territory within the Baltic region.[7]

Despite the persistent presence of these orders, there was no truly dominant force that could unite the people of the area that became modern Estonia and Latvia. During the latter part of the thirteenth century, the Danes occupied much of northern Estonia, the Livonian Order dominated southern Estonia and much of Latvia, and there also were four ecclesiastical states in the area, as well as the independent city of Riga. In some respects, this situation resembled the decentralized, and often weak, condition of the later stages of the Holy Roman Empire. The largely German—dominated feudal divisions of this area made it difficult to impose real stability, yet the indigenous people lacked the means to oppose their overlords effectively. Therefore, the cultural development of Estonia and Latvia would become influenced by German culture and practices long after those foreign forces ceased to control the region.[8]

The Lithuanians were more fortunate than their northern neighbors, for the terrain that they inhabited (which was inundated with marshes and dense forest) was largely inhospitable to invasion and easy to defend. They retained their independence, but the Lithuanians were a disunited people throughout the ancient and early medieval periods. However, a movement toward greater unity resulted in the emergence of a strong tribal leader named Mindaugas. In 1236, he united the various Lithuanian tribes and established Lithuania as an autonomous political unit. Under the influence of missionaries, he initiated social and political reforms in order to strengthen this union, and, in 1251, he accepted conversion to Roman Catholicism and promoted it among his people. The papacy took advantage of this conversion to draw Lithuania into the larger religious and political association of Europe; in 1253, Mindaugas was crowned king of the Lithuanians by a papal legate.[9]

Despite this enforced unity, the Lithuanian political system remained unstable. In 1263, King Mindaugas was assassinated, and intertribal conflict was renewed. A further result of the death of Mindaugas was the abandonment of Catholicism in Lithuania (as well as its formally recognized status as a kingdom) and a reversion to former religious beliefs and practices. The political struggle that followed this event eventually produced another dominant tribal leader, Traidenis, who founded another Lithuanian dynasty. This dynasty took its name from Gediminas, who acceded to the throne in 1315. Lithuania achieved both greater internal stability and increased external expansion under his leadership. A series of military moves enabled King Gediminas to embark upon a policy of conquest and consolidation that was remarkable for a non-Christian country in fourteenth-century Europe, especially one as small, pressured, and internally divided as Lithuania had been during the latter part of the previous century. In his capacity as grand prince, Gediminas converted Lithuania from a small princely state into, essentially, an empire that included such diverse Slavic territories as Ukraine and Belarus. This trend continued after his death with such great success that, in 1370, Grand Prince Algirdas was threatening to occupy Moscow.[10]

However, despite both domestic and military successes, internal conflict continued to pose a problem for Lithuanian rulers. Following the death of Algirdas, his brother, Kestutis, and his nephew, Vytautas, challenged the ascendancy of his son, Jogaila, at a time when the Teutonic Knights again were menacing the Lithuanian frontiers. The dual threat of an internal power struggle and territorial intrusions convinced many Lithuanian leaders that the country needed to secure an alliance with a foreign power that would provide for greater external security, as well as a new focus for domestic politics that could promote internal stability.[11]

One alternative strategy was forming an alliance with the princely state of Muscovy, which had managed to free itself from the domination of the Mongol Empire and was emerging as a potentially formidable power in Eastern Europe. However, Lithuanians were more favorably inclined westward. Therefore, the second alternative strategy of an alliance with Poland was cultivated. An alliance with Muscovy would necessitate an adoption of Orthodox Christianity within Lithuania, while an alliance with Poland would necessitate the readoption of Roman Catholicism. Lithuania already possessed historical ties to Rome and the West, and the Catholic faith was already familiar to its people. So, the alliance with the Poles appeared to be more attractive and feasible than one with the Muscovites. Polish leaders also appeared to be favorably inclined toward such an arrangement for reasons of the country's own domestic security and foreign ambitions, including the continuing threat of the Teutonic Knights.

Therefore, upon this basis of mutual advantage, negotiations between the two countries began.[12]

Throughout this period, the territory that now constitutes modern Estonia and Latvia continued to be dominated by various feudal authorities. Riga was relatively prosperous as an independent city-state, while trade persisted throughout the area. The German rulers of the area continued to dominate politically the Estonians and Latvians. However, attempts at Germanic cultural dominance proved to be unsuccessful, so the area remained divided, and internal struggles for power were frequent. Foreign authorities were unable to subjugate the area entirely, and Estonians and Latvians were unable to promote desires for greater indigenous control and autonomy.[13]

Grand Prince Jogaila's negotiations with Polish leaders produced an agreement whereby he married the newly crowned, 12–year–old Queen Jadwiga and ascended the Polish throne. He became King Wladislaw II Jagiello in 1385 and transferred direct rule of Lithuania to his cousin, Vytautas. Although this alliance would remain informal at first, the personal union of the two countries through Jogaila made the relationship between them as significant (if not more so) than the famous de facto union of the crowns that occurred when King James VI of Scotland also became King James I of England. The Polish–Lithuanian alliance produced a coordinated foreign policy that proved to be enormously advantageous to both Poland and Lithuania.[14]

The military successes of Grand Prince Vytautas the Great removed the threat posed by Slavs and Mongols from the east. The defeat of a Lithuanian army at the Battle of Vorskla River at the hands of the army of the Golden Horde ended Vytautas' policy of eastward expansion in 1399. But his country's dominance within that region remained secure.[15] In the meantime, the armies of both members of this new alliance were turned, with even greater success, toward the problem of the Teutonic Knights. A joint Polish and Lithuanian campaign against this aggressor in 1410 resulted in an overwhelming victory for them at the Battle of Grünwald. In fact, the defeat of the Teutonic order was so crushing that it was never able to recover sufficiently to pose a threat to either country, and the order's final decline can be traced to this particular battle.[16]

This military cooperation proved to be so successful that leaders in both countries became increasingly inclined toward making this alliance more formal. Besides accepting Roman Catholicism, once again, the Lithuanian nobility became increasingly influenced by Polish culture and ideas. This trend tended to alienate the Lithuanian masses from their leaders in much the same way as the Latvian and Estonian masses had become alienated from their Germanic overlords, or the Anglo-Saxon population of England became estranged from the Norman nobility. However, it also produced closer ties between Lithuania and the Roman Catholic countries of western Europe, while distancing it from the Slavic regions, which increasingly came under the Orthodox influence of Muscovy. Therefore, the creation of a more formal union between Lithuania and Poland became an increasingly attractive goal that leaders within both countries gradually accepted and fostered.

The movement toward establishing a more formal union culminated in the meeting of a joint parliament at Lublin in 1569. As a result of the deliberations of that session the Polish–Lithuanian alliance was transformed into the Commonwealth of Two Peoples on July 1, 1569. This arrangement (also known as the Union of Lublin) united the two countries under a common elected monarch and joint parliament. However, each country retained its own military, administrative, and legal structure and, thus, a degree of autonomy and separate identity. Despite the fact that the Union of Lublin did not result in complete incorporation, this Polish–Lithuanian arrangement proved to be both stable and successful. Economic, political, and military success was enjoyed by the union for the next two centuries, and cities such as the Lithuanian capital of Vilnius (now strongly influenced by the advances of the late Renaissance period) enjoyed financial and cultural prosperity.[17]

Although the Estonians and Latvians did not enjoy equal success as independent entities, those territories did experience a period of stability and prosperity, particularly while under the domination of Sweden. Initially, pressure from the emerging Russian realm destabilized the area, and it became divided into the duchies of Estland, Livonia, and Courland. However, control of the area ultimately became a struggle between Sweden in the north, the Polish-Lithuanian Union in the south, and certain indigenous forces in between. By the early seventeenth century, both Estland and most of Livonia came under Swedish domination, while Courland became semi-autonomous, under limited Lithuanian control. Swedish rulers introduced many enlightened reforms within the Baltic territories (especially those policies that benefited the peasantry) that resembled similar reforms in Sweden, including educational improvements. Lithuanian authorities allowed trade and industry to develop in Courland without interference, so the duchy began to flourish, economically.[18]

However, Russian expansion eventually disrupted the stability and prosperity of the Baltic region. Both Sweden and Lithuania lost much of this territory to that expansion during the latter part of the seventeenth century. Both countries managed to regain some of that land (especially as a result of the Peace of Andrusovo in 1667), but Russian dominance within the region increasingly appeared inevitable. This trend was confirmed during the Swedish invasion of 1655–1660 and the Great Northern War of 1700–1721. The Polish–Lithuanian Union joined the broad alliance, which opposed the military expansion of Sweden under King Charles XII. Sweden's final defeat following the Battle of Poltava resulted in a significant loss of territory, including the Baltic territories. Although part of the winning coalition, the Polish–Lithuanian Union did not fare well as a result of the war. It did not lose any territory, but its internal stability and hold upon its land was irrevocably weakened, especially following the drain upon its resources that the Great Northern War imposed upon it.[19]

Part of this decline was the result of the growing domination of the Polish–Lithuanian Union's internal politics by German nobles, including those rulers of Saxony who also arranged for their elections as kings of the union. These rulers tended to involve the union in the larger political and military struggles that were occurring within the Holy Roman Empire (especially among Saxony, Prussia, and Austria) and between German–speaking states and the Russian Empire. These struggles not only were expressed in terms of warfare but in terms of diplomatic maneuvering, which often placed the Polish–Lithuanian Union in an intractable position.

The decline of the union also can be credited to the domestic instability of Poland, particularly in terms of the nobility's domination of the parliament, or Sejm, within which institution each member retained a "liberum veto" (the right of even a single nobleman to block the will of a majority of this assembly) over domestic affairs, and its struggles with the elected monarchs, especially those kings who attempted to introduce reforms. Other European powers were content to leave it alone, so long as the union remained internally unstable. However, attempts to revive Polish and Lithuanian strength resulted in cooperative efforts to diminish that potential source of opposition. Therefore, when King Stanislaw II August Poniatowski struggled with both reformist nobles (who had opposed his ascension) and conservative nobles regarding an attempt to promote the stability and power of the union, the other European powers reacted strongly.[20]

The partitioning of the Polish–Lithuanian Union among Prussia, Austria, and Russia initially affected only Polish territory, with the exception of certain Slavic lands in the east, that were ceded to Russia.

Nonetheless, the first partition of 1772 and the second partition of 1793 that resulted from international agreements among the three powers further weakened Lithuania so effectively that attempts at resistance not only were futile, but actually prompted the final partition of the union in 1795. This partition ceded almost all of the ethnically defined territory of Lithuania to the Russian Empire, which reorganized this territory, as it had already done for the Estonian and Latvian territories, as part of its realm.[21]

Initially, Courland, Livonia, and Estland retained a degree of autonomy within the Russian imperial structure. Consequently, Estonians and Latvians enjoyed a considerable degree of cultural freedom, as well as retaining some economic and administrative control.[22] This autonomy generally was not extended to Russia's Lithuanian territory. Agitation for political reforms, and even independence, persisted among the Lithuanians as a result of this loss of freedom. This frustrating situation led many Lithuanians to participate actively in the Polish uprising of 1830–1831. After suppressing the uprising, the Russian government imposed increasingly repressive policies upon the Lithuanian population. These policies included the closing of Vilnius University, in 1832, and the repeal, in 1840, of local Lithuanian legal codes that had previously been permitted after the third partition and which had been maintained for centuries.[23]

Another Polish uprising, again supported widely by Lithuanians, from 1863 to 1864 also was suppressed by the Russians. An imperial policy of Russification was imposed upon the Lithuanian territories following this uprising, especially through control of publishing, book and journal distribution, and education. Nonetheless, Lithuanian language and culture persisted, particularly with the assistance of Lithuanian publishing interests abroad, including just across the border in East Prussia. This resilience would prove to be a significant characteristic of all Baltic peoples. The Estonian and Latvian territories initially did not suffer from such imperial policies; they even flourished culturally and economically during the period of liberal reforms that took place throughout Russia in the middle of the nineteenth century.[24]

However, in an attempt to exert greater control upon the whole Baltic region, a policy of russification was extended to the Estonian and Latvian territories, as well as the Lithuanian lands. This policy also was resisted, with relative success, by these ethnic groups, which had not lost their sense of national identity, despite having experienced such a long period of time without political independence. Therefore, attempts to impose the Cyrillic alphabet upon the populace, to teach the Russian language exclusively to Baltic schoolchildren, to impose Russian administrative policies and practices, and to limit the authority for publishing journals, books, and other items only to Russian editorial sources ultimately were not successful within this region.[25]

Throughout the remainder of the nineteenth century, the people of the Baltic region were affected by the social and economic changes which took place throughout the Russian Empire, including the emancipation of the serfs, the migration from rural to urban areas, and advances in transportation and manufacturing. The rise of a professional urban class within the Baltic region helped to keep nationalist aspirations alive while it gradually improved the socio-economic status of the people. However, Russian control of the region remained relatively firm throughout this period.[26]

In 1905, Russia suffered an unexpected defeat as a result of the Russo–Japanese War. The overwhelming victory of the forces of the Japanese Empire undermined Russia's stability at home, as well as abroad. The Revolution of 1905 precipitated by this defeat (although the conditions which prompted it had been building for a long time) not only prompted demands for liberal reforms (culminating in the creation of a limited parliament in the form of the Duma) but also provided an opportunity for various nationalist groups throughout the empire to agitate for cultural and political autonomy. These demands were pressed by Estonians and Latvians through varied participation in revolutionary disturbances, particularly within the rural areas. Lithuanians simultaneously convened a congress in Vilnius that passed a resolution demanding the creation of an autonomous Lithuanian state. The establishment of social democratic parties within all three areas (especially among Estonians and Latvians) and the growing presence of Marxist, and other, activists throughout the region helped to consolidate these nationalist desires and reinforced them during the following, turbulent decade.[27]

World War I provided the opportunity for independence that the various Baltic nationalists ultimately sought. Russia's pursuit of the war on the side of the Allies had been inept, and its forces eventually were defeated by the Central Powers, led by the German Empire. This defeat, coupled with the internal corruption of the imperial system, prompted a revolution in February 1917 that overthrew the czarist regime and replaced it with a provisional liberal government. This liberal government, headed, first, by Prince George Lvov and, later, reorganized under Alexander Kerensky, continued to prosecute the war, even though German armed forces had made impressive gains against the crumbling Russian armed forces, including an occupation of much of the Baltic region. As a result of these continuing military disasters and the chaotic economic and political situation throughout the country, this provisional government fell to the Bolsheviks during the revolution that took place in November 1917. The Bolshevik government, under Lenin and Leon Trotsky, agreed to capitulate to the Central Powers, and the Treaty of Brest-Litovsk was signed on March 3, 1918. Germany gained control over the Baltic region as a result of this treaty, and German authorities and forces subsequently took formal possession of it. By that time, the Germans already had possession of all of Lithuania and most of Latvia. This confusing series of occupations made the attempts to establish and maintain independent Baltic regimes particularly difficult for all three of these emerging sovereign countries.[28]

The provisional liberal government of Russia had already created an autonomous Estonian province on April 12, 1917, partly as an attempt to bolster that area against the German incursions to the south. The Estonian National Council, or Maapäev, was elected and convened in June. The Bolshevik Russian government attempted to establish its authority over the area, which it managed to do tentatively and temporarily. But the *Bolshevik* forces fled in the face of a new German advance, and the Maapäev formally declared independence on February 24, 1918, which was the day before the German Army occupied the Estonian capital of Tallinn, overthrew the newly created Estonian government, and established its control over the country.[29]

Latvian nationalists living within that part of Latvia that had not yet been occupied by the Germans established the Latvian Provisional National Council and, following the Bolshevik Revolution, declared that the area had become an autonomous province of Russia on November 30, 1917. However, the Germans soon occupied the remainder of Latvian territory, and the council lost its authority.[30] Meanwhile, in German occupied Lithuania nationalists actually were able to create a national government, although it remained under strict German control. The Lithuanian National Council, or Taryba, proclaimed the country's independence on February 16, 1918, just as the czarist regime was collapsing. It received the formal recognition of the German Empire during the following month, but the de facto control of affairs remained with the German Army.[31]

This uncertain situation remained essentially unchanged for the three Baltic countries until the final defeat of the Central Powers by the Allies in late 1918. Once the armistice ending the war was proclaimed on November 11, 1918, nationalists in all three countries began to reestablish independent governments and prepared to defend their new independence, particularly against the anticipated aggression of the Red Army. The Baltic states consequently became unwilling participants in the Russian civil war and found themselves, at various times, combating both Red and White forces.

Russian forces invaded the Baltic countries from the east following the end of World War I. Most of Estonia was occupied by Red Army forces by the end of November 1918, and a provisional pro-Russian government was established. Likewise, Red Army forces captured the Latvian seat of government at Riga on January 3, 1919, and the Lithuanian capital of Vilnius on January 5, 1919, where puppet governments also were established. However, all three nationalist governments managed to elude capture and escape, with their remaining forces, to areas occupied by the western Allies, who were opposed to the Bolshevik regime that had been established in Petrograd. In some places, these Allied havens were protected by forces of the defeated German Empire, whose services had been retained for the purpose of assisting Western countries in their attempt to support the efforts of White armies to defeat the Bolsheviks and return a government that would be regarded as less hostile toward Western interests. The Baltic governments were a significant part of that overall effort, from the perspective of the Western Allies. Therefore, Baltic sentiments towards the West clearly formed during this early period of renewed independence, since their struggle, and its success, became part of a much larger, and more complex, struggle.[32]

The Estonian government was aided by Great Britain's Royal Navy and a force of Finnish volunteers. Bolstered by this assistance, the Estonians counterattacked and drove the Red Army forces from Estonia by the end of February 1919. Meanwhile, the Latvian and Lithuanian governments and their armed forces also benefited from Allied protection, such as the Royal Navy squadron that protected the Latvian government when it fled to Liepāja. However, these two governments were assisted by German forces under the command of General Rüdiger von der Goltz, which forces had been retained by the Western Allies to assist them in containing the Bolsheviks and the political repercussions of their revolution.[33]

However, General von der Goltz was joined by White Army forces and others, and he hoped to use this combined force to reestablish a Baltic duchy under German control, which had been created briefly during the last days of World War I. Thus, the Baltic governments and their armed forces found themselves struggling against the German force that had been retained, ironically, to defend them. The Latvians and Lithuanians, in particular, found themselves caught between two opposing threats of Red Army forces attacking from the east and a combined German and White

Army force attacking from the south, with friendly (though not always effective) Western Allied forces to the west. This initial pattern of conflict would be repeated (militarily, politically, and diplomatically) throughout the twentieth–century history of the region.[34]

The army that was led by von der Goltz attacked Riga and captured it from the Red Army on May 22, 1919. It continued its offensive northward, where it was opposed by a combined force of Latvians and Estonians. The Latvian–Estonian force defeated von der Goltz at the Battle of Cēsis, and his force retreated south. Meanwhile, a Lithuanian force that had been created under German protection began attacking Red Army forces and driving them eastward. The defeated German Empire had agreed to withdraw its Baltic forces into East Prussia during the summer of 1919, but von der Goltz organized another force of German monarchists and White Army volunteers under the White Army military leader Colonel Pavel Bermondt-Avalov. This force launched a simultaneous attack against Riga and western Lithuania on October 8, 1919.

Despite initial strategic success, Colonel Bermondt-Avalov's troops were counterattacked by both a Lithuanian force and a Latvian force that was supported by a combined British and French naval squadron, so that, by the middle of December, Bermondt-Avalov's White Army contingent had been forced from the region. This campaign provided the last serious military challenge that the Estonians and Latvians were forced to face during this initial period. By the fall of 1919, the territories of Estonia and Latvia had been largely cleared of foreign invaders, including German, White Army, and Red Army forces, although some of the Western Allies continued to maintain an armed presence, particularly a naval one.[35]

The Lithuanians, however, continued to struggle for control of Vilnius against both the Red Army and the armed forces of the newly independent Polish Republic under the political and military leadership of Marshal Józef Piłsudski, who was of combined Polish and Lithuanian descent and who sought to annex Vilnius to Poland on the basis of ethnic and historical claims. The Red Army continued to occupy Vilnius until April 1919, when Polish forces drove them eastward. The Red Army counterattacked early next year and drove the Poles westward. Lithuanian forces took advantage of the situation. They reoccupied the city in July 1920 and signed an armistice with Poland. However, in September, Polish forces launched an attack which retook Vilnius. The Poles retained their control of that area and formally incorporated Vilnius into Poland in 1922.[36]

This episode proved to be a significantly enduring one. Lithuanian resentment over the loss of Vilnius to Poland prevented the two countries from establishing effective diplomatic relations. This diplomatic conflict undermined the possible creation of an effective coalition against German and Soviet aggression during the late 1930s.[37] However, despite this continuing problem, the Baltic states had effectively established their respective independent status by the end of 1920. The Bolshevik government of Russia, which was still engaged in a desperate civil war, abandoned plans to recapture the region. It concluded negotiations and signed separate peace treaties with Estonia on February 2, 1920, with Lithuania on July 12, 1920, and with Latvia on August 11, 1920. Finnish forces withdrew from Estonia to the newly independent Finland, which also had won recognition from Russia, while the Western Allied presence also eventually withdrew from the region.[38]

The struggle for independence left a deep impression upon all three Baltic states. Certainly, the struggle with Russia appeared to indicate a continuation of the conflicts that Estonians, Latvians and Lithuanians had experienced throughout their respective histories, going back as early as the ancient and medieval encounters with eastern Slavic tribes. The contradictory experience of Germans as liberators, protectors, invaders, and conquerors reminded many people within that region of the historic relationship with the Prussians, the Livonian Order, and the Teutonic Knights. This experience would reinforce the ambiguity with which the Baltic states would approach German relationships.

The Western Allies, as well as Finland (whose people were distantly related to the Estonians), also inspired contradictory attitudes among the Baltic people. In one sense, they had actively protected the fledgling governments of the Baltic states and their struggling armed forces against the Red Army. However, their support appeared to be qualified, for, at times, it seemed to depend upon the extent to which the presence of an independent Latvia, Lithuania, and Estonia was deemed to be beneficial to the larger struggle between the West and Bolshevik Russia, including the separate Russo–Finnish conflicts. Furthermore, the Allied use of German and White Army forces (both of them wished to recapture the Baltic region for their own respective purposes) as part of this complex struggle seemed to undermine the impression of sincerity with which the West claimed to approach its support for Baltic independence. An idealist foreign policy (such as that embraced by the administration of President Woodrow Wilson in the United States) could easily be supplanted by realist demands within the context of a more abstract and global conflict of which Estonia, Latvia, and Lithuania found themselves to be unwilling participants. Given previous historical experiences within the region, that perception was understandable.

Nevertheless, the Baltic states now faced the formidable task of building the political, social, and economic infrastructure for their newly independent regimes. This sort of responsibility usually proves to be daunting to all new nation-states. However, for Estonia, Latvia, and Lithuania, the challenge was made more difficult by the geographic, military, and financial conditions under which the transition to independence had occurred. Therefore, attempts at creating and maintaining these new political systems often proved to be inconsistent and uncertain.

Such a situation is not uncommon among new states, since the promise of freedom does not always correspond with its reality. That sense of frustration is especially common because of the very high and idealistic expectations that the struggle for freedom tends to inspire. Under such circumstances, attempts at liberal democratic reform can degenerate into internecine conflict and the threat of authoritarian dominance. Such a situation confronted the newly independent Baltic states.

Initially, all three Baltic states adopted constitutions that created parliamentary systems of government. The Latvian parliament, known as the Saeima, and the Lithuanian parliament, known as the Seimas, both divided the powers of government with a separately elected executive, while the Estonian parliament, known as the Riigikogu, delegated all executive responsibilities to the prime minister, who led the majority party within the legislature, of which institution that person was a member. Many political parties participated within the respective political systems, contributing to the diversity of democratic participation but contributing to political instability as it became difficult for dominant parties or stable coalitions to emerge from these systems to form and lead their respective governments.[39]

Latvia tended to be dominated by a coalition led by the progressively liberal Social Democratic Party. There were, initially, no restrictions upon the participation of political parties, including the Latvian Communist Party, until 1924. On December 1 of that year, an attempted coup by the Communists failed, and that party subsequently was banned in Latvia. However, despite the ease with which the government suppressed that coup, the political system did not prove to be particularly effective. The relative instability of the governmental process largely was the result of a polarization among the various political parties. The Social Democrats continued to play a leading role in forming government coalitions, yet struggles among right–wing and left–wing parties made it extremely difficult to hold these coalitions together and make them function.

As a result of this persistent tension, Latvian governments lasted, on average, less than nine months before the coalitions upon which they were based collapsed, and either a new government had to be formed or new elections had to be called by the president. This situation was similar to that which existed in Italy following the end of World War II (due largely to the Italian system of proportional representation in elections to parliament), but within Latvia the consequences of this sort of political uncertainty proved to be more damaging to its system than it ultimately proved to be in Italy several decades later.[40]

A similar situation existed within Estonia during its first years of independence. The Estonian Social Democratic Party also tended to dominate the government, although it needed to form coalitions among the various parties of the Riigikogu in order to secure the majority support necessary to govern. Unlike the situation in Latvia, the Communist Party of Estonia had been banned from any sort of political participation since the adoption of the constitution. The ability of any political party to form a stable government on its own was made particularly difficult because of the fact that the Estonian Constitution mandated the creation of an electoral system based upon the principle of proportional representation. The resulting instability within successive governments inspired popular agitation for fundamental reform originating outside the parliamentary system, which added to the pressures placed upon, and the difficulties experienced by, various Estonian governments.[41]

The political situation within Lithuania also suffered from uncertainty and instability. The more conservative Christian Democratic Party tended to dominate Lithuanian governments during the years following independence. The Communist Party of Lithuania also had been banned since the creation of the constitution, but its presence within that country was so small that the prohibition against it was practically redundant.[42]   Lithuania continued to face difficulties regarding the ambiguous status of its frontiers. Besides the controversy with Poland (regarding the possession of Vilnius and its environs), there also was uncertainty regarding the ownership of the port city of Memel (known in Lithuania as Klaipėda) and its surrounding territory.

Entitlement to this area (which historically had been part of the East Prussian region of the German Empire prior to the conclusion of World War I) had not been addressed by the Treaty of Versailles, which concluded peace between the Allied and Central Powers. While the city of Memel was populated predominantly by Germans, the surrounding area was dominated by Lithuanians. The government of Lithuania made the decision to occupy Memel, and the government of the Weimar Republic in Germany reluctantly acquiesced in that de facto annexation.[43] Nonetheless, disputes over the proper boundaries of Lithuania with Germany, Poland, and the Soviet Union added to the difficulties that successive Lithuanian governments experienced and contributed to the pressures placed upon that country prior to the start of World War II.

The political situation within Latvia had become so chaotic that the management of an effective government became almost impossible by the early 1930s. By that time, there were 24 political parties competing for power, making the task of building working coalitions extremely daunting. The effects of the global depression that began in 1929 exacerbated this sense of political crisis by undermining attempts to increase prosperity and improve industrial production.[44]

Prime Minister Kārlis Ulmanis, who had led previous Latvian governments, proposed constitutional reforms as a means for overcoming the political impasse. But his proposals were rejected (especially by the smaller parties and ethnic minorities, who would have lost political influence as the result of a meaningful constitutional reform effort) and political extremism, particularly among the German minority, threatened the political system, itself. Organizations such as the Latvian branch of the Baltischer Bruderschaft, which demanded the incorporation of Latvia into Germany, and the Latvian fascist party, or Perkonkrust, challenged the government directly. On May 15, 1934 Prime Minister Ulmanis declared a state of emergency, banned all political parties, and dissolved the *Saeima*. He subsequently formed a coalition government that included representatives of some of the former, less radical political parties. On April 11, 1936, Ulmanis succeeded President Alberts Kviesis, thus uniting the offices of prime minister and president. He then began to introduce both political and economic reforms that, he declared, would stabilize the government and increase prosperity.[45]

Lithuania's unstable political system reached a similar crisis by the middle of the 1920s. The Christian Democratic Party tended to be stronger than its opponents, yet changes of government still were frequent. The formation of a Populist–Social Democratic coalition government prompted military action against the political system. On December 16, 1926, a coup d'état, led by a group of army officers, overthrew the elected government. The next day, former president Antanas Smetona was installed in that office, and his fascist–influenced Nationalist Union Party was declared the only legitimate political organization within the country.

A new constitution was drafted in 1928 in order to confirm the existence of this authoritarian regime. Smetona used his authority to try to impose order upon Lithuania, especially in economic matters.[46]

By the latter part of the 1930s, the ruling Nationalist Union Party, under pressure from opposition groups, announced that the political situation had become stable enough for a gradual return to democracy to be initiated. The new constitution that was adopted on February 12, 1938 anticipated an eventual return to parliamentary government. Despite the fact that all political parties (except for the Nationalist Union) had been officially banned, the activities of these organizations had never stopped completely. Yet these formally banned parties continued to participate as part of an informal coalition government under the leadership of Smetona. Nonetheless, a real return to a liberal democratic political system remained absent.[47]

Within Estonia, frustration over unstable governments prompted the political activities of one organization, originally founded by veterans, to begin a movement directed against both communists and the parliamentary system. This League of Freedom Fighters, or Vabadussôjalaste Liit (generally known as the Vaps or Vabs),[48] initiated a referendum on constitutional reform that voters approved in October 1933 by over 70%. This constitution would have given the Estonian president wide powers to address the economic and political difficulties that the country faced (especially as a result of the global depression and the weakness of successive coalition governments) that could be addressed, decisively. However, the interim president, Konstantin Päts, regarded the situation as being too precarious and declared a state of emergency on March 12, 1934, thus setting aside the new constitution. The activities of all political organizations (including the Vaps) were prohibited, Vap leaders were arrested, and the Riigikogu was dissolved.[49]

Päts ruled as a dictator until he declared that the political and economic situation had become sufficiently stabilized to warrant the reintroduction of constitutional reform. A new constituent assembly was elected in late 1936, which drafted a constitution that restored democratic institutions. A new bicameral legislature was elected in February 1938, and it was dominated by the Patriotic League, which was the political party that supported Konstantin Päts. On April 23, 1938, Päts was elected president, thus further confirming his political popularity, despite his suspension of earlier constitutional reforms and his previous authoritarian rule.[50]

In general, much of the support for the imposition of authoritarian rule in all three Baltic states came from their respective armed forces, affluent peasants of the rural areas, and the business community of the urban areas. Despite the increasing size and growing political power of the urban working and middle classes throughout the region, the economic power of agricultural, industrial, and commercial leaders ultimately prevailed. A return to democracy occurred only when prosperity increased, and that goal often was frustrated by an initial lack of industrial infrastructure, the physical damage imposed by World War I and the struggle for independence, and the global depression that had begun during the late 1920s.[51]

However, some economic reform on behalf of workers and less affluent peasants did occur. In particular, the semi-feudal dominance of the established German nobility, especially within Estonia and Latvia, was broken, and much of the land they held was redistributed. Furthermore, some economic reforms were advanced with the intention of improving the working conditions found within urban industries, especially in terms of reorienting industrial production in favor of exports designated for sale throughout the West. Meanwhile, trade with the Soviet Union was kept to a minimum. Lithuania, on the other hand, remained largely rural and agrarian, although Antanas Smetona sponsored the creation of cooperatives in order to facilitate the production and marketing of agricultural products. Exports of these goods to the West were quite high, while trade with the Soviet Union also was kept small. Therefore, during the 1930s, the Baltic economies gradually recovered from the devastation of World War I and the global depression and became relatively more prosperous than they had been previously.[52]

Certain themes emerge from this history that are important in terms of gaining a greater appreciation of the strategy and development of the diplomatic behavior of Estonia, Latvia, and Lithuania, both before and after the World War II. The region has experienced a long history of dislocation, foreign pressure, and internal instability that has made it difficult to develop consistent foreign and diplomatic policies. Relations with the West (with the exception of Germany) had been relatively beneficial ever since the final defeat of the Teutonic Knights, but it also has been difficult for them to trust the sincerity of these nations.

The interests of the Baltic states have been most enthusiastically supported by Western powers when such support has conveniently served Western interests, as a whole. These interests have included Western Allied support for the Baltic struggle for independence against Bolshevik Russia. However, when they have not coincided with Western interests, Baltic interests have been ignored, such as the partitions of the Polish-Lithuanian Union. From a Baltic perspective, the needs of Estonia, Latvia, and Lithuania have been, at best, a secondary concern to friendly, as well as hostile, neighbors. Therefore, a high level of diplomatic cooperation has not been achieved easily.

The Western Allies were willing to use German and White Army forces in the Baltic region to further their struggle against the Red Army, even though it threatened Baltic independence. Finland sometimes seemed more interested in harming Russia than in assisting its Estonian neighbors and distant relatives who were similarly besieged—a suspicion that would become more apparent as a result of Finland's eventual support for German aggression against the Soviet Union. But the most obvious area of diplomatic concern was the fact that the Baltic region continued to be caught within the historical struggle between Germanic invaders from the west and Slavic invaders from the east. This overwhelming conflict has been a predominant concern to the peoples of this region since ancient and medieval times, which has been reflected within the twentieth–century diplomatic policies and activities of Estonia, Latvia, and Lithuania.

The lack of internal stability is an important theme that has affected the diplomatic history of this region. The uncertainty and inconsistency of democratic governments and the rigidity and suspicion of authoritarian regimes made it difficult to establish diplomatic policies and strategies that could be entirely coherent and effective. This theme also may have contributed to the ultimate inability (unlike other nations occupied by foreign invaders during World War II) of any of these Baltic states to create and maintain (with brief and ineffectual exceptions) governments-in-exile, either during, or following, the European conflict.

Every aspect of a society, including its diplomatic activity, is a product of the context within which that society was created. Although World War II drastically altered the fate of the Baltic states, that fate could not remove these states from the influence of that broader historical experience that was, in some ways, unique to each country and, in other ways, shared. These heterogeneous and distinct societies developed similar approaches toward their respective diplomatic activities because of that shared experience, even after these countries were occupied and their foreign and diplomatic communities were separated from them. The extremely unusual diplomatic experiences of Estonia, Latvia, and Lithuania are part of those unique historical experiences, and understanding that general connection plays a significant role in comprehending the nature of that specific diplomatic development.

Notes

1.   The arbitrary application of the term "Baltic" and its more meaningful geographical, cultural, and ethnic connotation are discussed in Georg von Rauch, *The Baltic States*, Gerald Onn, trans. (Berkeley: University of California Press, 1974), pp. 1–3; Royal Institute of International Affairs, *The Baltic States* (Westport, CT: Greenwood Press, 1970), pp. 3–5; V. Stanley Vardys and Romuald J. Misiunas, eds., *The Baltic States in Peace and War, 1917-1945* (University Park: Pennsylvania State University Press, 1978), pp. 1–2.

2.   Walter C. Clemens, Jr., *Baltic Independence and Russian Empire* (New York: St. Martin's Press, 1991), pp. 16–17; Alfreds Bilmanis, *A History of Latvia* (Westport, CT: Greenwood Press, 1951), pp. 4–10.

3.   John Hiden and Patrick Salmon, *The Baltic Nations and Europe* (New York: Longman, 1991), pp. 9–11.

4.   Toivo U. Raun, *Estonia and the Estonians* (Stanford, CA: Hoover Institution Press, 1991), pp. 3–13; Rein Taagepera, *Estonia: Return to Independence* (Boulder, CO: Westview Press, 1993), pp. 11–14.

5.   William Urban, *The Baltic Crusade* (De Kalb: Northern Illinois University Press, 1975), pp. 19–29.

6.   Urban, pp. 49–64.

7.   Rauch, pp. 2–3; Urban, pp. 33–45.

8.   Hiden and Salmon, pp. 11–12; Romuald J. Misiunas and Rein Taagepera, *The Baltic States: Years of Dependence* (Berkeley: University of California Press, 1983), pp. 1–3; Royal Institute, p. 13.

9.   Ernest J. Harrison, *Lithuania, Past and Present* (London: T. Fisher Unwin, 1922), pp. 40–41.

10.   Harry E. Dembkowski, *The Union of Lublin* (New York: Columbia University Press, 1982), pp. 14–18; Harrison, pp. 41–44.

11.   Dembkowski, pp. 19–23; Pawel Jasienica, *Jagiellonian Poland*, Alexander Jordan, trans. (Miami: American Institute of Polish Culture, 1978), pp. 41–52.

12.   Wenceslas J. Wagner, "Justice for All: Polish Democracy in the Renaissance Period in Historical Perspective," in *The Polish Renaissance in Its European Context*, Samuel Fiszman, ed. (Bloomington: Indiana University Press, 1988), pp. 131–132.

13.   Bilmanis, pp. 113–133;   John B. Leighly, "The Towns of Medieval Livonia," in *University of California Publications in Geography*, J. B. Leighly and C. O. Sauer, eds. (Berkeley: University of California Press, 1939), vol. 6, no. 7, pp. 235–299; Raun, pp. 17–18.

14.   Jasienica, pp. 53–70.

15.   Harrison, pp. 44–46.

16.   Dembkowski, pp. 25–26; Jasienica, pp. 97–113.

17.   Dembkowski, pp. 134–174.

18.   Bilmanis, pp. 170–180; J. Hampden Jackson, *Estonia* (Westport, CT: Greenwood Press, 1979), pp. 54–66.

19.   Ingvar Andersson, *A History of Sweden*, Carolyn Hannay, trans. (New York: Praeger, 1957), pp. 224–236; Robert I. Frost, *After the Deluge: Poland-Lithuania and the Second Northern War, 1655–1660* (Cambridge: Cambridge University Press, 1993), pp. 26–52.

20.   Dembkowski, pp. 213–221; Frost, pp. 168–179.

21.   George Eversley [Lord Eversley], *The Partition of Poland* (New York: Howard Fertig, 1973), pp. 35–65, 117–144, 227–256.

22.   Edward C. Thaden, "Reform and Russification in the Western Borderlands, 1796–1855," in *Russification in the Baltic Provinces and Finland, 1855–1914*, Edward C. Thaden, ed. (Princeton, NJ: Princeton University Press, 1981), pp. 15–24.

23.   Alfred Erich Senn, *The Emergence of Modern Lithuania* (New York: Columbia University Press, 1959), pp. 2–5; J. N. Westwood, *Endurance and Endeavor* (Oxford: Oxford University Press, 1993), pp. 66–67.

24.   Marc Raeff, *Comprendre l'Ancien Règime Russe* (Paris: Editions du Seuil, 1987), pp. 189–190.

25.   Andrejs Plakans, "Russification Policy in the 1880s," in Thaden, ed., pp. 227–247; Toivo U. Raun, "Russification and the Estonian National Movement," in Thaden, ed., pp. 327–341; Senn, pp. 5–16.

26.   Hugh Seton-Watson, *The Decline of Imperial Russia* (New York: Praeger, 1952), pp. 35–36, 161–162.

27.   Alfreds Bilmanis, *Latvia as an Independent State* (Washington: Latvian Legation, 1947), pp. 43–46; Westwood, pp. 125–126.

28.   Westwood, pp. 225–251.

29.   Taagepera, pp. 42–45.

30.   Bilmanis, *Latvia as an Independent State*, pp. 47–48.

31.   Senn, pp. 28–46.

32.   Clemens, pp. 24–34.

33.   Clemens, pp. 34–40; Albert N. Tarulis, *American-Baltic Relations, 1918-1922: The Struggle over Recognition* (Washington, DC: Catholic University of America Press, 1965), pp. 111–122.

34.   Richard Luckett, *The White Generals* (New York: Viking Press, 1971), pp. 314–321.

35.   Luckett, pp. 315–332.

36.   Senn, pp. 105–130.

37.   Senn, pp. 222–224.

38.   Clemens, pp. 40–44; Royal Institute, pp. 65–66.

39.   Royal Institute, pp. 41–62.

40.   Bilmanis, *A History of Latvia*, pp. 332–346.

41.   Raun, pp. 112–118.

42.   Leonas Sabaliūnas, *Lithuania in Crisis* (Bloomington: Indiana University Press, 1972), pp. 3–8.

43.   John Hiden, *The Baltic States and Weimar Ostpolitik* (Cambridge: Cambridge University Press, 1987), pp. 64–68.

44.   Bilmanis, *A History of Latvia*, pp. 342–356.

45.   Bilmanis, *A History of Latvia*, pp. 357–378.

46.   Sabaliūnas, pp. 8–9, 25–40.

47.   Sabaliūnas, pp. 113–121.

48.   The identity and nomenclature of this liberation movement is treated in Jackson, p. 188; Vincent E. McHale, ed., *Political Parties of Europe: Albania-Norway*, Sharon S. Skowronski, asst. ed. (Westport, CT: Greenwood Press, 1983), pp. 394–395; Taagepera, p. 267; Vardys and Misiunas, p. 73.

49.   Jackson, pp. 184–196.

50.   Jackson, pp. 197–211.

51.   A general assessment of this political and economic development can be found in Hiden and Salmon, pp. 76–87.

52.   Royal Institute, pp. 103–120.

Chapter 3

The Diplomacy of the Independent Baltic Countries

Estonia

Estonian diplomacy began during World War I with the departure of a delegation (sometimes called the Foreign Delegation) to Finland on February 1, 1918, and then to Sweden on March 13, 1918.[1] Its task was to secure recognition of Estonia by foreign governments in their respective capitals, including Christiania (this name was changed to Oslo in 1925), Copenhagen, London, Paris, Petrograd, Rome, and Stockholm, and, while in those capitals, to deal with the representatives of other governments[2] — for example, Brazilian diplomats in Paris[3] and Chinese diplomats in Rome.[4] An excerpt from Malbone W. Graham's work on the subject provides a small insight into the delegation's efforts.

> The Estonian diplomatic mission made its representations to Sweden on March 16, 1918; Martna, Tonisson, and Menning then proceeded to Copenhagen, arriving April 5, and presented their views to the Danish and American Governments; Tonisson and Menning then proceeded to Christiania with Piip, Pusta, and [Virgo]. . . . They laid their views before the Norwegian Government on or about April 17, whereupon Tonisson and Menning returned to Copenhagen while Piip,

>Pusta, and [Virgo] proceeded to London and
>Paris. The remaining delegates announced
>through Martna their intention of proceeding
>to Berlin, Vienna, and Budapest.[5]

The delegation included Jaan Tõnisson (who already was in Stockholm by January 1918), Ferdinand Kull, Mihkel Martna, Karl Menning, Ants Piip, Kaarel Robert Pusta, and Edward Virgo. They were joined later by Jaan Poska in Paris. Menning, Piip, Pusta, and Virgo, upon formal diplomatic recognition of their country, would serve as Estonian diplomats, all as chiefs of mission (ministers at the head of legations), and their diplomatic careers are detailed in the biographical sketches provided in the appendices of this book. As for the others, Kull (1884–1957) was a Tallinn businessman[6] and Mihkel Martna (1860–1934) was a house painter and newspaper deliverer who "by sheer hard work and determination [had] made for himself, as a pioneer of the Estonian Social Democrat Movement, a place in the social and political history of Estonia."[7] Jaan Poska (1866–1920) did not leave Estonia with the Foreign Delegation in February 1918, but he joined Piip and Pusta in Paris on January 3, 1919 as head of the Estonian delegation to the Paris Peace Conference. Earlier, he and Piip had engaged in contacting American, Belgian, British, and French diplomats in Petrograd, and he became Estonia's first minister of foreign affairs.[8] He was a mayor of Tallinn and had been appointed commissioner (commissar) of Estonia by the Russian Provisional Government in April 1917.[9] Jaan Tõnisson (1868–1941?) already was in Stockholm by January 1918.[10] He was a leader of the Estonian Progressive People's Party, as well as editor of *Postimees*,[11] and he was nominated to head the Estonian mission that sought recognition from the United States, but a change in plans ended his participation.[12] He was foreign minister during the early 1930s[13] and was Premier four times—twice during 1919 to 1920, again from 1927 to 1928, and during 1935.[14]

Piip became informal Estonian representative in London. Pusta and Virgo left London for Paris and met with the French foreign minister, Stephen Pichon.[15] Thereafter, the two Estonians traveled to Rome, dealing with the Italian government and with the Holy See. Virgo then returned to Copenhagen.[16] Back in London, Piip, in addition to treating with the British, was in contact with the Japanese.[17] Piip also dealt with the American Embassy in London, which was not a very easy chore, given the influence in Washington of the first post–czarist Russian ambassador, Boris A. Bakhmetev.[18] Generally, however, members of the Estonian delegation had been welcomed by governments of the Allies, principally because it was in their interest to prevent German domination of the Baltic lands.[19]   Permanent Estonian representatives (but not full diplomatic missions) had been established in cities such as Helsinki, Stockholm, London, and Paris.[20]

On January 3, 1919, Poska, who was the chairperson of the Estonian delegation to the Paris Peace Conference, arrived in Paris. The members of this delegation included Martna, Piip, Pusta, Tõnisson, Menning, Virgo, and a former Estonian minister of trade and industry, Nicolas Koestner (1889–1959).   Menning, who had remained in Copenhagen, went to Paris later, as did Virgo, who had been engaged in Rome.   The secretary of the Paris delegation was Rein Eliaser (1885–1941), the press attaché was Eduard Laaman (1888–1941), and the commercial and economic adviser was Joakim Puhk (born in 1888, deported to the Soviet Union during 1940–1941), who was a wealthy industrialist and honorary consul of Lithuania and Finland in Estonia.[21] Despite the able assistance of Piip, Pusta, and others, Poska never managed to receive a direct hearing before the Allies, and the Foreign Delegation's notes to the peace conference secretariat received little attention.   Poska returned to Estonia, resigned as minister of foreign affairs, and remained politically active until his death on March 9, 1920, at the age of 54.[22] Poska and the others were the pioneer diplomats of Estonia; their efforts in foreign chancelleries and embassy chanceries ultimately achieved the recognition of the new state. Indeed, it has been suggested that the things Eduard Beneš "did for Czechoslovakia, Poska, Pusta and Piip did for Estonia--and not only for Estonia but for the other Baltic States as well."[23]

By December 1920, Estonia had been recognized de jure by Finland, recognized *de jure* by Russia in the Treaty of Tartu of February 2, 1920, and recognized de facto by Belgium, Denmark, France, Germany, Great Britain, Italy, Japan, the Netherlands, Poland, and Sweden.[24] Estonia, Latvia, and Lithuania applied for admission to the League of Nations, but all three were rejected on December 16, 1920. The vote on Estonia was 5 in favor, 27 opposed, and 10 absent or abstaining. The vote on Latvia was 5 in favor, 24 opposed, and 13 abstaining. The vote on Lithuania was 5 in favor, 23 opposed, and 14 abstaining. The five votes for the Baltic states came from Colombia, Italy, Paraguay, Persia [Iran], and Portugal.[25] Estonia and its two Baltic neighbors sought membership, again, and all three were admitted on September 22, 1921. Estonia and Lithuania received 36 votes for admittance, none against admission, and 12 absent or abstaining, while Latvia's figures were 38–0–10.[26]

The United States did not grant de jure recognition to the three Baltic States until 1922. Lieutenant Commander John A. Gade (a former naval attaché in Copenhagen) was appointed American Commissioner to the Baltic provinces, resident in Riga, Latvia, on October 14, 1919.[27] Gade resigned on March 1, 1920, and was succeeded as commissioner by Evan E. Young (1878–1946), former minister to Ecuador, on May 1, 1920, serving until 1922.[28] The United States maintained consular offices in Riga and in Tallinn. Given the on-site roles of Gade, Young, and the American consuls, it was each Baltic state's desire to have similar access to American officials in the United States. Estonia had proposed Ferdinand Kull of the Foreign Delegation as an emissary to the United States as early as 1918, but he was denied a visa.[29] In 1920, Estonia requested that Eduard Virgo, who also was a member of the Foreign Delegation, be accepted by the United States with the title of commissioner, allowed to issue passports, use code, and enjoy diplomatic privileges as did Commissioner Young in Tallinn.[30]

In response to these overtures, Secretary of State Bainbridge Colby informed Young to tell the Estonian authorities that an American consul (Charles H. Albrecht) was stationed in Tallinn on the "assumption that such a move would be agreeable to the Estonian people in their effort to reestablish their commerce and industry," adding, "if this consular officer is not welcome, he can very easily be withdrawn." Colby continued that the United States "cannot, in any event, grant an exequatur to a Consul from a non-recognized Government." Regarding an Estonian commissioner in the United States, Colby advised Young that Estonia could not have a representative in the United States enjoying a status superior to that of the unofficial agents of Latvia and Lithuania. If Estonia persisted, Colby declared, such action "can only result in the withdrawal of any American representative in Estonia."[31] Eventually, Nicolas Koestner, also a Foreign Delegation member, was permitted to come to the United States in an unofficial capacity. On July 28, 1921, he called at the State Department and was told that he could *not* designate any office he might open as "consulate."[32]

Exactly one year later, on July 28, 1922, the United States gave de jure recognition to all three Baltic states. Secretary of State Charles Evans Hughes provided specific instructions to Young on July 25.

> Advise Foreign Offices of Esthonia [sic], Latvia and Lithuania as nearly at the same time as possible on the morning of July 28 that the United States extends to each full

recognition. The fact will be communicated to the press at Washington for publication in the morning press of July 28 and the following statement will be made: The Governments of Esthonia, Latvia and Lithuania have been recognized either *de jure* or *de facto* by the principal Governments of Europe and have entered into treaty relations with their neighbors.

In extending to them recognition on its part, the Government of the United States takes cognizance of the actual existence of these Governments during a considerable period of time and of the successful maintenance within their borders of political and economic stability.

The United States has consistently maintained that the disturbed conditions of Russian affairs may not be the occasion for the alienation of Russian territory, and this principle is not deemed to be infringed by the recognition at this time of the governments of Esthonia, Latvia, and Lithuania which have been set up and maintained by an indigenous population.[33]

Estonia first appears in a *U.S. Diplomatic List* in 1924, upon Piip's presentation of credentials as minister on December 31, 1923. Piip remained the only Estonian to hold a senior ranking (either as minister or as ambassador to the United States) until Ernst Jaakson, who had been assigned to the United States since 1929 and presented credentials as ambassador to the United States on November 25, 1991. Jaakson was succeeded by Toomas Hendrik Ilves, who presented credentials on September 3, 1993, and Ilves was followed by Grigoire Kalev Stoicescu, who presented credentials on May 14, 1997, departed on January 15, 2000, and was succeeded by Sven Jürgenson on June 14, 2000.[34]

The United States, on the other hand, had no fewer than five ministers accredited to Estonia (all resident in Riga, Latvia), from 1922 to 1940, beginning with Frederick W. B. Coleman's presentation of credentials on November 22, 1922, and continuing until John C. Wiley's withdrawal on July 25, 1940, following the Soviet occupation of Riga and Tallinn on June 17. All American diplomatic personnel were withdrawn from Tallinn on September 4, 1940, including the chargé d'affaires, Walter A. Leonard. The next day, Legation Tallinn, which had been established on June 30, 1930, subordinate to the American minister in Riga, was closed.[35] There would be no American diplomatic representation in Tallinn until October 2, 1991, when embassies opened in all three Baltic States. The first ambassador to Estonia from the United States was Robert C. Frasure, who, after serving initially as chargé d'affaires, presented credentials on April 9, 1992. He departed on July 8, 1994 and was followed by Lawrence P. Taylor, who presented credentials on August 3, 1995, departed on August 7, 1997, and was replaced by Melissa Wells, who was presented credentials on November 3, 1998.[36]

The fact that, after Piip's departure as minister on December 18, 1925, there was no replacement at the ministerial level and his successors served with consular titles in New York City as being "in charge of Legation" did not meet with the approval of the State Department. The absence of an Estonian minister was due to the fact that the Estonian parliament, in the fall of 1925, eliminated from the Estonian budget the funds needed for maintaining a legation at Washington. It was a matter that Piip, who was strongly opposed to the closing of the legation, had hoped to rectify upon his assumption of the foreign ministership after leaving Washington.[37] On February 8, 1927, the State Department's Chief of the Division of Eastern European Affairs, Robert F. Kelley, wrote to Assistant Secretary of State J. Butler Wright that the Department agreed to Piip's suggestion that Colonel Viktor Mutt of the Estonian Consulate at New York should be recognized as chargé d'affaires with residence in New York. However, he stressed that it was intended to be a *temporary* arrangement. Kelley wrote that more than a year had passed since Piip's departure, and there were no indications of any intention on the part of Estonia to name a new minister. Kelley recalled the analogous case of Latvia. After having closed its legation in Washington, Latvia then suggested that its consul general at New York should be accredited as chargé d'affaires. The State Department responded that a diplomatic representative should be stationed in the capital and not reside permanently in New York. Further, the State Department informed Latvia that the consul general in New York could serve as the channel to Washington and be received there, but he would have merely a consular, and not a diplomatic, status. Kelley and Wright concluded that Estonia should be subject to the same arrangement.[38]

In a letter of October 11, 1927, to the secretary of state, the Estonian foreign minister, Friedrich K. Akel, declared that Estonia was, "much to its regret, constrained provisionally to forego a continuation of its Legation" in the United States, that no minister would replace Piip, that Mutt's role as chargé "must also be considered to have come to an end," and that Mutt would resume "the title and duties of Consul General of Estonia at New York which he previously had." Akel added that "temporary circumstances" induced Estonia to close its legation "for a while."[39]

The issue was pursued, for example, in a 1935 document that observed that the consular representatives of Estonia and Latvia had been included in the *Diplomatic List* for the past eight years, and there seemed to be no early prospects that those countries would have diplomatic representation. The document recounted that Luxembourg had been removed from the *Diplomatic List* for the reason that the chargé d'affaires had been absent for "so long a time." It was noted that Luxembourg had consular representation in the United States—the implication being that no Luxembourg consul had become chargé d'affaires. Liberia was mentioned, as well; the document stated that, should the Liberian Consul General at Baltimore, Dr. Ernest Lyon, learn of the Estonian/Latvian cases, he "would have his country at once give him similar representative qualities."[40]

The following statement from the State Department's Division of Protocol and Conferences, dated September 30, 1936, would appear to have addressed the issue conclusively.

> In March, 1931, Colonel Victor Mutt, Consul
> General of Estonia in charge of the Legation,
> departed from his post and left Mr. Charles
> Kuusik, Acting Consul General of Estonia, in
> charge of the Legation. Now, Mr. Kuusik is
> going away and leaving in charge of Legation
> Mr. Ernst Jaakson, who is a Secretary of the
> Consulate General. This procedure has now
> been going on since November, 1927, and it
> seems to me that Estonia should send a
> Minister to this country or be taken from our
> Diplomatic List.[41]

On August 7, 1937, the American minister to the three Baltic states, Arthur Bliss Lane, paid his official farewell visit to the Estonian foreign minister, Akel, during which Akel stated that he had always favored a legation in Washington and, despite considerations of budget, he supported reestablishment of the legation. Akel added that Estonia had eight legations abroad but learned in a conversation with the Norwegian minister that Norway had 28 legations abroad—the Norwegian having commented that Norway was too small a country to have fewer legations. At the customary luncheon given by the president of Estonia to retiring ministers accredited to Estonia, President Konstantin Päts told Lane that he had hoped that funds could be found to establish a legation in Washington. In his report of these conversations,[42] Lane expressed the opinion that his own experience taught him that it was not possible for one minister to represent the United States in all three Baltic states from a base in Riga, Latvia. Therefore, he welcomed the 1937 appointment of an American minister to Lithuania, stating that American prestige in Estonia and Latvia would be enhanced further by a separate minister to each country—something that would not occur until 1991, when the reestablished Baltic States and the United States exchanged ambassadors.

American procedure for the Baltic states was to send one resident minister to all three countries, stationed at Legation Riga, Latvia, with, as of 1930, a chargé d'affaires at Legation Tallinn, Estonia and a chargé d'affaires at Kovno (later renamed Kaunas), Lithuania. Legation Tallinn was established June 30, 1930, with Harry E. Carlson as chargé d'affaires, while Legation Kovno was opened May 31, 1930, with Hugh S. Fullerton as chargé d'affaires. Subsequently, Owen J. C. Norem presented credentials as the first American minister resident in Lithuania on November 26, 1937. The United States never did have a resident minister in Estonia.[43]

An interesting commentary on Estonia's concern with diplomatic funding was the opinion of the Estonian Assistant Foreign Minister, August Rei, on April 22, 1937, that a joint legation with Latvia would be "the best solution to the problem." He contended that there were no conflicting political interests between the two countries regarding the United States and that both countries could be represented for half the cost. Rei also said that the two countries could alternate in appointing a minister (he suggested five–year periods of tenure); if a Latvian should be minister, then an Estonian could be counselor, and vice versa. Rei, however, did not feel that conditions were "ripe" for the Estonian/Latvian collaboration.[44]

Latvia

The most prominent pioneers of Latvian diplomacy were Jānis Čakste, Jānis Goldmanis, Jānis Kreicbergs, Zigfrīds Meierovics, and Jānis Seskis.[45] Jānis Čakste (1859–1927) would become the first president of Latvia, serving from

1922 to 1927. Goldmanis (1875–1955) was a Latvian delegate in the Russian Duma at Petrograd and became head of the Latvian Commission for Foreign Affairs,[46]which seriously began the international activities that resulted in Latvian independence and diplomatic recognition.[47] Kreicbergs was one of the three members of the Latvian National Council selected to seek recognition abroad.[48] Meierovics (1887–1925) was in a class by himself; he was surely the preeminent Latvian engaged in foreign affairs. He served as Latvia's first foreign minister from November 18, 1918, to January 26, 1924, and, for part of that tenure (June 28, 1923, to January 26, 1924), also as premier.[49] He met a tragically early death at age 38 in an auto accident on August 22, 1925.[50] Seskis would have a diplomatic career as minister to Estonia and to the Soviet Union, as stated in his biographical sketch within Appendix B.

Given their preoccupation with internal concerns, the Latvians were delayed in addressing international matters. Certainly, Goldmanis, Meierovics, and Seskis were operating actively in Petrograd by January 1918, but Meierovics would not get to London until August of that year, and Čakste arrived in Paris even later. The Latvians also had been less active in Scandinavia than the Estonians. In fact, not until July 1918 did the Latvians select Čakste, Kreicbergs, and Meierovics to begin diplomatic missions to the Allied countries.[51] Latvian independence was not declared until November 18, 1918, while the other two Baltic states declared independence in February. The Latvian delegation to the Paris Peace Conference included Čakste, Meierovics, Seskis, Fēlikss Cielēns, Arveds Bergs, and Margers Skujenieks.[52] Cielēns remained a diplomat and became vice-minister for foreign affairs, foreign minister, and minister to France, Spain, and Portugal. Bergs (born in 1875 and deported to the Soviet Union during 1940–1941) was a conservative politician, newspaper editor, and interior minister from 1919 to 1921.[53] Skujenieks (born in 1886 and deported to the Soviet Union during 1940–1941) was a politician of the political "Left" who would serve as Premier from December 19, 1926 to January 23, 1928 and, again, from December 6, 1931 to March 23, 1933.[54] Čakste was head of the delegation at the Paris Peace Conference from January until May 20, 1919, when Meierovics succeeded him and served until June 30. Thereafter, Seskis headed the delegation.[55]

A lesser member of the Paris delegation who would rise to eminence in Latvian diplomacy deserves special mention. Kārlis Zariņš (also known as Charles Zarine) would have a brilliant diplomatic career. He became minister to Britain, in 1933, and would face the tremendous challenges of World War II and the Sovietization of his country. No Baltic diplomat fought the subjugation of his country and struggled to maintain its international status as diligently as Zariņš. Likewise, he courageously battled the British Foreign Office for the status of his legation, the Latvian diplomatic service, and a consular network. He certainly lived up to the title given him in 1940 (upon his nation's absorption by the Soviets) as the "Bearer of the Special Emergency Power of the Latvian Government." Many of Zariņš' missives are preserved at the Public Record Office in London, and one can read among them passages that render a sense of extraordinary indomitability. These records offer quiet testimony to a "diplomat without a country" who refused to accept that fate.

The efforts of these Latvians achieved some of the desired recognition by December 1920. Latvia had received de jure recognition from Russia in the Treaty of Riga, signed on August 1, 1920. Recognition de jure came from Germany in 1920 and, then, was suspended, pending the de jure recognition of Latvia by one of the "Great Powers" that were signatory to the Treaty of Versailles. Formal German recognition was reinstated in 1921. Meanwhile, de facto recognition came form Belgium, Denmark, Finland, France, Great Britain, Japan, and Poland.[56] All three Baltic States had been denied admission to the League of Nations in 1920, but they all were admitted in 1921.

On May 26, 1920, Kārlis Ozols notified the State Department that he had taken residence in the United States as the authorized commercial representative of Latvia. Previously, Jānis Kalnins had acted unofficially as a Latvian consular agent—remarkably, at his own expense.[57] Ozols originally had come to the United States in 1915 as a member of a czarist commission, and he remained in America until he went to Europe in January 1919 as a representative of Latvians in the United States. He conferred in London with Jānis Goldmanis of the Latvian National Council.[58] He requested, upon his return to the United States, a visa for his secretary, Alfred Nagel, who came to the United States but was declared persona non grata. Nagel was an interesting personality who had professed friendship with Lenin, had served in the Russian Embassy in Stockholm, and would turn up in Moscow, later.[59]

Ozols kept busy in New York City[60] but, while regarded by Latvia as a consul, was never accepted as such by the United States government. Ozols was allowed to function simply as an unofficial Latvian agent—a matter that the United States had brought to the attention of Estonia when rejecting Estonia's request for a representative who would have the title of "commissioner," issue passports, use codes, and enjoy diplomatic privileges.[61] When Latvia sent Ludvigs Sēja (also known as C. Louis Seya, Charles L. Seya, and Charles Louis Seya) to seek recognition from the

United States in April 1921, Ozols continued his activities on behalf of Latvia by working with Sēja.[62] The latter diplomat would become Latvia's first accredited chief of mission in the United States as chargé d'affaires. In 1923, Ozols was assigned as Latvia's minister to Moscow.

Latvia made its first appearance in the *U.S. Diplomatic List* in the October 1922 issue, with Sēja serving as chargé d'affaires from September 28 of that year. By June 1923, he would be replaced by a consul in New York City named Arturs Lūle,[63] but he would reappear as Latvia's first minister to the United States, presenting credentials on June 17, 1925.[64] When Sēja was recalled in 1927, Latvia returned to the "Consul General in New York City in charge of Legation" style of representation with Lūle.[65] Inasmuch as this practice by Estonia disturbed the State Department, Latvia would be treated the same way.

On June 26, 1933, Undersecretary of State William Phillips (who was serving as Acting Secretary of State) wrote to Felix Cole, American chargé d'affaires in Riga, that the department had replied to the request of the Latvian consul general in New York City to be chargé d'affaires by saying that it could not accredit him as such "since it did not recognize diplomatic representatives residing outside the national capital" and adding that his name in the *Diplomatic List* was there only as an act of courtesy. Phillips declared that the arrangement that provided that the Latvian Consul General in New York City should be treated as that country's principal representative was meant to have been temporary, but more than six years had passed without a minister. Therefore, Phillips wrote, Cole should inform the Latvian foreign minister of the American desire to "regularize the anomalous situation with regard to the status" of the consul general. He explained that, as in the past, the United States would discuss with the consul general any matters he wished, but, once the incumbent, Arturs Lūle, retired, it was to be made clear to the Latvian government that, if no Latvian legation with a minister was reestablished in Washington, a Lūle successor as consul general would not be entered in the *Diplomatic List*, nor addressed as "in charge of legation." Finally, Phillips told Cole that he may inform the Latvians that the department was taking the same action regarding Estonia.[66]

However, Estonian diplomats were not subjected to that same action. Of the previously mentioned Estonian consuls general (Mutt, Kusik, and Jaakson), only Mutt ever held the title of chargé d'affaires, during the period from 1925 to 1927. Johannes Kaiv (previously unmentioned as an Estonian consul general) served without having been titled as chargé d'affaires. Nevertheless, all four of these Estonians were cited as being "in charge of Legation," and they appeared as such in the

Diplomatic List.   Jaakson served in that capacity until 1991, when he became Estonian ambassador to the United States.

Consul General Lūle was succeeded as principal Latvian diplomat in the United States when Dr. Alfreds Bīlmanis presented credentials as minister on November 20, 1935, and assumed residence at the Latvian Legation in Washington at 2448 Massachusetts Avenue, NW.[67] Bīlmanis served until he died in 1948, when Dr. Anatol Dinbergs became chargé d'affaires.[68] In 1949, Julijs Feldmanis was named chargé d'affaires, with the personal rank of minister plenipotentiary.[69] Upon his death, in 1953, Dinbergs again assumed the duties of chargé d'affaires.[70] Dr. Arnolds Spekke was the next chargé d'affaires, serving from 1954[71] to 1970, also with the personal rank of minister plenipotentiary. Thereafter, Dinbergs would enter upon 21 more years of service as chargé d'affaires,[72] until his appointment as ambassador in 1991 and presentation of credentials as such on March 11, 1992.[73] Ojars Eriks Kalnins succeeded Dinbergs, presenting credentials on April 4, 1993. In 2000, Kalnins was followed by Aivis Ronis as ambassador.[74]

American diplomatic representation in Latvia began officially with the aforementioned Frederick William Backus Coleman. He initiated American representation in the Baltic States by presenting credentials in Riga on November 13, 1922. The system, it will be recalled, was "three–for–one": an American minister, resident in Riga, was accredited to all three Baltic States.[75] When Coleman left Riga on October 20, 1931, he was succeeded by Robert Peel Skinner, who had presented credentials on January 28, 1932. Skinner left his post on April 29, 1933, and he was followed by John Van Antwerp MacMurray, who presented his credentials on December 13, 1933. When MacMurray exited Latvia on February 2, 1936, Arthur Bliss Lane became the next minister, presenting his credentials on July 2, 1936, and staying until September 16, 1937. Frederick Augustine Sterling initially was appointed to replace Lane, but (in State Department parlance) he "did not proceed to post."

By 1937, there was a change in this "three–for–one" system when the United States appointed a separate minister to Lithuania. Thus, the last American minister to Latvia and Estonia was John Cooper Wiley, who assumed command of the Riga legation (which had been devoid of a minister since Lane's departure in 1936) upon his presentation of credentials on October 6, 1938. Soviet forces occupied Riga on June 17, 1940, and Wiley bade farewell to the city on July 25, 1940. Earl L. Packer was serving as chargé d'affaires when the Legation in Riga closed on September 5, 1940.[76] The United States would not be represented there again until 1991, when it opened embassies in all three of the Baltic states on October 2. The first American ambassador to Latvia was Ints M. Silins, who presented credentials on April 10, 1992, having originally arrived in Tallinn as chargé d'affaires. Silins left in July 1994 and was succeeded by Larry C. Napper, who presented credentials on August 1, 1995 and was succeeded, in turn, by James Howard Holmes, who presented credentials on August 28, 1997.[77]

Of the American ministers previously cited, Coleman would become minister to Denmark, Skinner would become minister to Greece, and MacMurray (who had been minister to China before going to Riga) would become ambassador to Turkey. Furthermore, Sterling (who did not take up the Riga post) had served previously as minister to Ireland and Bulgaria and, later, as minister to Sweden. Lane had gone to Riga after having been minister to Nicaragua and, upon conclusion of his Latvian duty, was minister to Yugoslavia and Costa Rica and ambassador to Colombia and Poland. Wiley, after serving in Riga, became ambassador to Colombia, Portugal, Iran, and Panama. Packer would serve later as chargé d'affaires in Burma.[78]

Among the American diplomats who served at Riga, George F. Kennan and Loy W. Henderson were distinguished representatives who are particularly worthy of mention.[79] Gade and Young, who served as American commissioners to the Baltic provinces from 1919 to 1922, were not ministers. There is absolutely no mention of them among the listings for Estonia, Latvia, and Lithuania in the State Department's *Principal Officers of the Department of State and United States Chiefs of Mission 1778–1990* . They do appear, however, in the Latvian Foreign Ministry's *Le Corps Diplomatique en Lettonie 1918–1938* (along with the ministers cited above), but they are clearly presented as commissioners, not ministers, within that text.[80]   In the statement to the press announcing the recognition of the Baltic States by the United States, one finds the announcement that "pending legislation by Congress to establish regular diplomatic representation Mr. Young will continue as Commissioner of the United States and will have the rank of Minister."[81] This declaration should be understood as Congress' granting Young the *personal* rank of minister; it should *not* be interpreted as confirmation of Young's appointment as minister to the Baltic States in the manner of Coleman, Skinner, and the other designated American ministers to those countries.

Lithuania

Among those persons taking Lithuania into the realm of diplomacy, one can begin with the first three foreign ministers of the country: Augustinas Voldemaras (1883–1944? – deported to the Soviet Union 1940–1941), Mykolas Sleževičius (1882–1939), and Juozas Puryckis

(1883–1934). Voldemaras held the foreign ministership simultaneously while serving as Lithuania's first premier in 1918, and he was foreign minister in the next four cabinets, sharing the position with Sleževičius when the latter statesman was premier in the fourth cabinet in 1919. Puryckis was foreign minister in the sixth cabinet, which commenced on June 20, 1920. Voldemaras was premier twice (1918 and 1926–1929), and Sleževičius held the premiership three times — twice during 1918–1919 and in 1926.[82]

Antanas Smetona (1874–1944), the republic's first and last president, joined with Voldemaras in traveling about Scandinavia in 1919, seeking recognition for their state. Voldemaras then traveled to London and Paris. Smetona was a virtual ambassador-at-large, as missions were established in Copenhagen, Helsinki, and Stockholm.[83] After receiving recognition from Germany on March 23, 1918, Voldermaras launched the Lithuanian foreign service by sending Dr. Jurgis Šaulys as minister to Berlin in November of that year. All other Lithuanian representatives abroad held an informal status until the latter half of 1919.[84] This informal status continued for some of them into 1920 and beyond.

Vincas Čepinskis (1871–1940) became an informal representative of Lithuania in London in March 1919, and he would serve as his country's minister of education in 1926.[85] He was succeeded by Count Alfred Tyskiewicz (1882–1930) as informal representative to Britain in December 1919. Tyskiewicz (also spelled Tyskevicius) was a member of Polish nobility resident in Lithuania. He had served previously with the czarist embassy in London.[86] Lithuania would not appear in the *British Foreign Office List and Diplomatic and Consular Year Book* until the 1925 issue, which shows Ernestas Galvanauskas as having presented credentials as minister on December 10, 1924. Among those diplomats who served in informal missions abroad and continued diplomatic careers were Jurgis Savickis, Ignas Šeinius (whose actual surname was Jurkunas, and he also was known as Ignas Jurkunas-Šeinius), and Vaclovas Sidzikauskas.[87]

The Lithuanian delegation to the Paris Peace Conference (which officially opened on January 18, 1919) included Voldemaras as its chairperson. This delegation also included persons who would continue to serve as Lithuanian diplomats: Tomas Naruševičius (his name also was spelled as Norus-Naruševičius), Bronius Kazys Balutis, Galvanauskas (the previously–mentioned first Lithuanian minister to London), and Petras Klimas. Naruševičius served as an acting chairperson of the delegation, which went through several reorganizations. Other members of the Lithuanian delegation to the Paris Peace Conference were Pijus Bielskus, the Reverend Juozas Dabuzis, Oscar V. Lubicz-Milosz, Balys Mastauskas, Dominikas Siemaska (Domonik Semashko), Simanas Rozenbaumas (Simon Rosenbaum), Martynas Yčas, and Jonas Žilius.[88]

Bielskus (1880–1958) was a Roman Catholic priest who later would be involved in Lithuanian negotiations with the Vatican.[89] Dabuzis (1878–1934) was in Europe as a member of a delegation which had been sent by the American–Lithuanian National Council to Switzerland in 1918 for discussions with Lithuanian representatives from neutral countries and from German-occupied Lithuania.[90] Lubicz-Milosz (1877–1939) was a French poet of noble Lithuanian background with contacts in Paris who served as Lithuania's first informal representative to France and declined the post of minister there in 1925, though he remained of service to the Paris legation.[91] Mastauskas (1889–1961) was with the same American-Lithuanian delegation as Dabuzis.   He was the leader of the American–Lithuanians at Paris—the Americans having had a large role in the formation and operation of the delegation as well as financing it, almost totally. He later called himself Frank Mast, moved to Chicago in 1928, and taught law there at Loyola University.[92]   Rozenbaumas (1859–1935) was the Jewish representative. He served as minister for Jewish affairs and left for Palestine in 1929, where he was Lithuanian consul general at Tel Aviv until his death.[93] Siemaška (1878–1932) was the Byelorussian representative, with responsibility for Byelorussian affairs.[94] Yčas (1885–1941) was minister of finance in the first three cabinets (1918–1919), a banker, and a political leader.[95]   Žilius (1870–1932) was a Roman Catholic priest who emigrated to the United States in 1892, returned to Europe, left the priesthood, and returned to the United States with Jonas Vileišis (about whom more will be related, later) on a Lithuanian government mission.[96]

Two other Lithuanians in Paris at the time deserve special mention: Juozas Gabrys (1880–1944) and Father Konstantinas Olšauskis (1867–1933). Gabrys had lived in Paris (which provided French government connections),[97] ran a Lithuanian Information Bureau (first in Paris, then in Geneva), and was said to have been the first Lithuanian known internationally as a leader of the national movement.[98]   Father Olšauskis headed a Lithuanian government delegation to the Allies gathered at Spa, Belgium, in November 1918. He sought aid against the Bolsheviks; then his delegation went to Paris and formed a special Peace

Conference delegation (including the American–Lithuanians), chaired by Olšauskis. The official Lithuanian delegation was established under Voldermaras in Paris during mid-February 1919.[99]

Lithuania's early diplomats had managed to secure recognition from 13 countries by December, 1920. De jure recognition was granted by Germany and Russia—the latter country through the Treaty of Moscow on July 12, 1920. De facto recognition came from Great Britain, Denmark, Finland, France, Italy, Latvia, Norway, The Netherlands, Poland, Switzerland, and Sweden.[100] As already stated, Lithuania was denied admission to the League of Nations in 1920, but it was admitted, with the other two Baltic states in 1921. Lithuania had only seven de jure recognitions, and 10 de facto recognitions (compared with 20 de jure recognitions for Estonia and 21 de jure recognitions for Latvia) at the time of its admission to the league.[101]

Upon the recognition of the Baltic States on July 28, 1922 by the United States, its representation followed the aforementioned three–for–one system, whereby the American minister was resident at Riga but was accredited to all three states. The United States established legations in Tallinn and Kovno (later named Kaunas), with Harry E. Carlson assigned as chargé d'affaires in Tallinn on June 30, 1930, and Hugh S. Fullerton as chargé d'affaires in Kovno on May 31, 1930. Unlike Estonia, to which the United States never appointed a minister, Lithuania received an American minister when Owen Joseph Christoffer Norem presented credentials on November 26, 1937. Norem would be the only American minister to Lithuania. Soviet forces occupied Kaunas on June 15, 1940, and Norem departed on July 30, 1940. Bernard A. Gufler was serving as chargé d'affaires when the American Legation in Kaunas was closed on September 5, 1940.[102] All American ministers to the Baltic states were career diplomats except for two: the first minister to serve, Frederick W. B. Coleman, and Norem.

Lithuanian activity in securing the accreditation of its diplomats by the United States was noteworthy. On April 18, 1918, the American–Lithuanian National Council informed the State Department that Dr. Jonas Šliupas (also known as John Szlupas),[103] who was a leading figure in early emigration to the United States, had been "detailed to act as the envoy to the United States."[104] Šliupas never made it onto the Diplomatic List.[105] On December 18, 1919, an official mission from Lithuania seeking recognition, as well as financial and commercial relations, from the United States arrived in New York.[106] Jonas Vileišis (1872–1942), a signatory of the Lithuanian Declaration of Independence[107] and a former cabinet minister (internal affairs 1918, finance 1919),[108] led the mission. The two other members were Povilas Zadeikis (later minister in Washington) and the previously mentioned Žilius of the delegation to the Paris Peace Conference. All three members of the mission were in Washington by January 5, 1920.[109]

Vileišis submitted two memorandums to Secretary of State Robert Lansing, which were not acknowledged. On March 24, he dispatched another memorandum to the brand–new successor of Lansing, Secretary of State Bainbridge Colby, but he signed it "Representative of Lithuania in America." Several more missives to Colby followed that one. Finally, on April 3, he met with Colby, but his goal remained unrealized. Lithuania remained unrecognized, and he was regarded by the State Department simply as "Mr. John Vileišis."[110]   Therefore, Vileišis, like Šliupas, never entered the Washington *Diplomatic List*. However, his efforts were not a total loss. On June 22, 1921, Vileišis bade farewell to Secretary of State Charles Evans Hughes and introduced his successor, Voldemaras Čarneckis, who also was received as an informal representative.[111]

Finally, following recognition of Lithuania by the United States on July 28, 1921, Čarneckis became chargé d'affaires on October 11, 1922 and the first Lithuanian to appear on a *U. S. Diplomatic List*. The counselor of legation was listed as the aforementioned Balys Mastauskas.[112]   By October 1923, Matas J. Vinikas was chargé d'affaires[113] and, on December 11, Kazys Bizauskas became chargé d'affaires.[114] On August 6, 1924, he presented credentials as the first Lithuanian minister to the United States[115] He left his post on May 21, 1927,[116] and Dr. Mikas Bagdonas began service as chargé d'affaires on that date.[117] Next, Bronius Kazys Balutis presented credentials as minister on November 2, 1928.[118] Upon the departure of Balutis, Bagdonas resumed his service as chargé d'affaires until the arrival of Povilas Žadeikis, who presented credentials on August 21, 1935[119] and continued as minister throughout World War II and into the Cold War, until his death on May 11, 1957. On that date, Juozas Kajeckas assumed the duties of chargé d'affaires,[120] serving until he was succeeded by Dr. Stasys A. Backis on January 1, 1977.[121]   Backis would be followed by Stasys Lozoraitis, Jr. as chargé d'affaires on November 15, 1987.[122]   On December 20, 1991,[123] Lozoraitis (who was the son of a famous Lithuanian diplomat and the brother of an ambassador) was appointed Lithuania's first ambassador to the United States and presented credentials on March 11, 1992.[124] Upon his appointment as ambassador to Italy, he was succeeded by Alfonsas Eidintas, who presented credentials as ambassador on December 9, 1993.[125] Eidintas, in turn, was followed by Stasys Sakalauskas, who presented credentials on November 12, 1997.[126]

The United States opened embassies in all three Baltic countries on October 2, 1991, following the restoration of their independence. The first American ambassador to Lithuania was Darryl N. Johnson, who presented credentials on April 14, 1992, having previously served in Vilnius as chargé d'affaires. Johnson left on May 23, 1994, and was succeeded by James W. Swihart, Jr., who presented credentials on September 26, 1994, and was followed by Keith C. Smith, who presented credentials on September 9, 1997.[127] These appointments brought to a successful culmination the American policies of maintaining recognition of Lithuanian diplomats within the United States and refusing to accept the Lithuanian loss of sovereignty that resulted from Soviet annexation in 1940.

These policies relating to Baltic diplomacy may have seemed unusual or eccentric to the casual observer during the Cold War era, but their ultimate validation proved to be a victory for the Baltic states, American diplomatic policy and, indirectly, for foreign relations specialists who seek to employ creative approaches toward international relations, generally. It is unfortunate that this episode of American diplomacy has been so neglected, for it is one of the most noble efforts in the history of American foreign policy and offers an inspirational contrast with the often unscrupulous dealings that can be found throughout the Cold War era. It is a unique story, but its success should continue to serve as an example of the real possibilities that a creative and optimistic approach to international law and foreign relations, in general, and diplomacy, in particular, can offer to the modern, post–Cold War world.

Notes

1.   Eric A. Sibul, "The Origins of Estonian Diplomacy, 1917–1922: The Roles of Kaarel Robert Pusta, Antonius Piip, and Jaan Poska" (master's thesis, San Jose State University, 1989), pp.36–38.

2.   Malbone W. Graham, *The Diplomatic Recognition of the Border States. Part II: Estonia* (Publications of the University of California at Los Angeles in Social Sciences) vol. 3, no. 3, (Berkeley: University of California Press, 1942), pp. 231–238.

3.   Graham, p. 296, 372 n. 44.

4.   Graham, p. 375 n. 57.

5.   Graham, p. 340 n. 11.

6.   Sibul, p. 29.

7.   [Tallinn], June 4, 1931, [No name], FO371/15538-N3925/273/59, "List of Leading Personalities in Estonia."

8.   Sibul, pp. 29–31, 197.

9.   Malbone W. Graham, *New Governments of Eastern Europe* (New York: Henry Holt, 1927), p. 283; Toivo U. Raun, *Estonia and the Estonians*, 2d ed. (Stanford, CA: Hoover Institution Press, 1991), p. 100; Some sources (such as Graham) refer to Poska as "Commissioner," while other sources (such as Raun) refer to him as "commissar."

10.   Sibul, p. 29.

11.   Rein Taagepera, *Estonia's Return to Independence* (Boulder, CO: Westview Press, 1993), pp. 35, 37; Raun, pp. 120 and 297.

12.   Albert N. Tarulis, *American-Baltic Relations, 1918–1922: The Struggle over Recognition* (Washington, DC: Catholic University Press, 1965), p. 321.

13.   [Tallinn], June 4, 1931, [No name], FO371/15538-N3925/273/59, "List of Leading Personalities in Estonia."

14.   Artur Mägi, *Das Staatsleben Estlands während seiner Selbständigkeit*, vol. I, *Das Regierungssystem* (Stockholm: Almqvist and Wiksell, 1962), pp. 322–323.

15.   Sibul, pp. 45, 47.

16.   Graham, *Diplomatic Recognition: Estonia*, p. 245; Sibul, pp. 51–53.

17.   Sibul, p. 17.

18.   Graham, *Diplomatic Recognition: Estonia*, pp. 245–285; Tarulis, passim.

19.   Graham, *Diplomatic Recognition: Estonia*, pp. 237–238, 337 n. 9.

20.   Sibul, pp. 68–69.

21.   Sibul, pp. 80–81.
          [Tallinn], June 4, 1931, [author unknown], FO371/15538-N3925/273/59, "List of Leading Personalities in Estonia."
          A detailed treatment of Koestner is provided in different dispatches:
          Tallinn, February 13, 1923, Harold B. Quarton to F.W.B. Coleman; Reval [Tallinn], September 30, 1921, Charles H. Albrecht to Evan E. Young; Reval, February 19, 1923, Harold B. Quarton to F.W.B. Coleman, USNA 701.60i 11/7.
          Riga, March 1, 1923, F.W.B. Coleman to D.C. Poole, USNA701.60i 11/7.
          Washington, March 28, 1923, D.C. Poole repeating report of Evan E. Young

to Robert Woods Bliss, USNA701.60i 11/6.

22.   Graham, *New Governments*, pp. 383–384. The date of Poska's untimely death is taken from RHA.

23.   J. Hampden Jackson, *Estonia* (Westport, CT: Greenwood Press, 1979, reprint of 1948 edition published by George Allen and Unwin), p. 151. The book is dedicated to August Torma, the late Estonian minister to Great Britain.

24.   League of Nations, *Official Journal*, Records of the First Assembly, Plenary Sessions, Twenty-seventh Meeting, December 16, 1920 (Research Publications, microfilm pt. 29, reel 37, part I), p. 628.

25.   League of Nations, *Official Journal*, Records of the First Assembly, Estonia, p. 627, Latvia, p. 630, and Lithuania, p. 630.

26.   League of Nations, *Official Journal*, Records of the Second Assembly, Plenary Sessions, Sixteenth Meeting, September 22, 1921 (Research Publications, microfilm, pt. 29, reel 39, part I), Estonia, p. 318, Latvia, p. 319, and Lithuania, p. 320; By the time of its admission to the League, Estonia had been recognized de jure by 20 countries, League of Nations, *Official Journal*, Second Assembly, p. 334.

27.   U.S. Department of State, *Papers Relating to the Foreign Relations of the United States: Russia, 1919* (Washington, DC: U.S. Government Printing Office, 1937), p. 722.

28.   John A. Gade, *All My Born Days: Experiences of a Naval Intelligence Officer in Europe* (New York: Charles Scribner's Sons, 1942), pp. 149–188; Tarulis, passim; Young served as minister to Ecuador, 1911–1912, and minister to the Dominican Republic, 1925–1929. He was named minister to Bolivia in 1929, but he did not proceed to that post, U.S. Department of State, Office of the Historian, *Principal Officers of the Department of State and United States Chiefs of Mission, 1778–1990* (Washington, DC: U.S. Government Printing Office, January 1991), pp. 57, 77, 79, 219.

29.   Graham, *Diplomatic Recognition: Estonia*, pp. 343–344 nn. 22–25; Tarulis, p. 86.

30.   U.S. Department of State, *Papers Relating to the Foreign Relations of the United States, 1920* (Washington, DC: U.S. Government Printing Office, 1936), 3: 662–663.

31.   Department of State, *Papers Relating to the Foreign Relations of the Unied States, 1920*, 3: 661–664.

32.   Tarulis, p.341; The consideration of appointing Koestner as a possible Estonian minister to the United States is addressed in USNA701.60i 11/7 and 11/6.

33.   U.S. Department of State, *Papers Relating to the Foreign Relations of the United States 1922* (Washington, DC: U.S. Government Printing Office, 1938), 2: 873–874; The effort had been made in the third paragraph of the recognition announcement to state that recognition of the Baltic states did not infringe upon Russia's territorial integrity. Earlier, however, in a note to Baron Camillo Avezzana (the Italian ambassador in Washington) on August 10, 1920, Secretary of State Colby suggested that independence for the Baltic states *would* infringe upon Russian territorial integrity (U.S. Department of State, *Papers Relating to the Foreign Relations of the United States, 1920*, 3: 463–468).

Adding insult to injury, the Russian minister to Switzerland, Ivan Efremov, in what amounted to a thank-you note, informed the American minister there, Hampson Gary, that he believed the rejection of the Baltic states by the League of Nations on December 16, 1920, was "decisively influenced by the sound and powerful arguments of" Colby's note to the Italian, word of which Efrimov spread amid delegations to the league *prior* to the voting. He expressed his gratitude and that of "all patriotic Russians" for the "enduring" service provided by Colby's note (U.S. Department of State, *Papers Relating to the Foreign Relations of the United States, 1920*, p. 480); Boris A. Bakhmetev, Russia's ambassador in Washington, also responded to the Colby note with gratifaction (U.S. Department of State, *Papers Relating to the Foreign Relations of the United States, 1920*, pp. 471–472).

34.   Ernst Jaakson, "A Short Biography of Ernst Jaakson," personal to the authors, June 6, 1996; USDL, November 1993 and Summer 1997. Mr. Lauri Lepik served as chargé from December 2, 1996, until Ambassador Stoicescu's assumption of office, USDL, Winter/Spring 1997.

35.   U.S. Department of State, *Principal Officers*, 1778–1990, pp. 83–84.

36.   This information was provided by Andrew Silski, Office of Nordic and Baltic Affairs, Department of State, Washington, DC, August 16, 1996. and U.S. State Department, U.S. Mission to Estonia, http://www.estnet.ee/usislib/wells.html.

37.   Tallinn, October 11, 1927, Estonian Minister of Foreign Affairs Friedrich K. Akel to Secretary of State [Frank B. Kellogg], USNA 701.60i 11/26.

38.   Washington, February 8, 1927, Robert F. Kelley to J. Butler Wright, USNA701.60i 11/24 1/2.

39.   Tallinn, October 11, 1927, Estonian Minister of Foreign Affairs Friedrich K. Akel to Secretary of State [Frank B. Kellogg], USNA 701.60i 11/26.

40.   Washington, July 11, 1935, Department of State, Division of International Conferences [no names], USNA F.W.401.60P 11/43.

41.   Washington, September 30, 1936, Richard Southgate to Robert F. Kelley USNA 701.60i 11/39.

42.   Riga, August 19, 1937, Arthur Bliss Lane to Secretary of State [Cordell Hull], USNA 701.60i 11/46.

43.   U.S. Department of State, *Principal Officers, 1778–1990*, Estonia, pp.83–84, Latvia, p.110, and Lithuania, p. 113.

44.   Tallinn, May 3, 1937, Walter A. Leonard, Chargé d'Affaires to Secretary of State [Cordell Hull], Conversation of Rei with Third Secretary Walter C. Trimble, USNA 701.60i 11/44.

45.   Jānis A. Samts, "The Origins of Latvian Diplomacy, 1917–1925: The Role of Zigfrīds Anna Meierovics in the Formulation of Latvian Foreign Policy" (master's thesis, San Jose State University, 1975), p. 29 et seq.; Malbone W. Graham, *The Diplomatic Recognition of the Border States, part III: Latvia* [Publications of the University of California at Los Angeles in Social Sciences, vol. 3, no. 4, 1941] (Berkeley: University of California Press, 1942), pp. 404–409.

46.   Georg von Rauch, The *Baltic States, The Years of Independence: Estonia, Latvia, Lithuania 1917–1940* (Berkeley: University of California Press, 1974), pp. 15, 24, 26, and 48; Graham, *Diplomatic Recognition, Latvia*, p. 555; Tarulis, p. 89.

47.   Graham, *Diplomatic Recognition, Latvia*, p. 402.

48.   Graham, *Diplomatic Recognition, Latvia*, p. 405.

49.   LAM, p. 102.

50.   LKV, 13, pp. 26, 343.

51.   Graham, *Diplomatic Recognition, Latvia*, pp. 404–406, 500 n. 13.

52.   Graham, *Diplomatic Recognition, Latvia*, p. 409; Samts, p. 62.

53.   Riga, July 7, 1939, C. W. Orde, Records of Leading Personalities in Latvia, F0371/23609-N3444/3444/59; William J. H. Hough, III, "The Annexation of the Baltic States and Its Effect on the Development of Law Prohibiting Forcible Seizure of Territory," *New York Law School Journal of International and Comparative Law*, 6 (Winter 1985), p. 486.
        Additional information on Cielēns is located in his biographical sketch, which can be found within the Appendix B.

54.   Hough, 486; The dates that Skujenieks served as premier are reported in Andrejs Plakans, *The Latvians: A Short History* (Stanford, CA: Stanford Hoover Institute Press, 1995), p. 200.

55.   Samts, pp. 67–68.

56.   League of Nations, *Official Journal*, Records of the First Assembly, Plenary Sessions, Twenty-seventh Meeting, December 16, 1920 (Research Publications, Inc., microfilm, pt. 29, reel 37, part I), p. 637; By the time of its admission to the League, Latvia had been recognized *de jure* by 21 countries (League of Nations, *Official Journal*, Records of the Second Assembly, Plenary Sessions, Sixteenth Meeting, September 22, 1921 [Research Publications, Inc., microfilm, pt. 29, reel 39, part I], p. 336).

57.   Tarulis, pp. 300–301.

58.   Tarulis, pp. 166–167.

59.   Tarulis, pp. 300–301.

60.   Tarulis, p. 301.

61.   Tarulis, pp. 320–321.

62.   Tarulis, p. 341; Additional information on Ozols and Sēja is provided by their biographical sketches in Appendix B.

63.   USDL, June 1923.

64.   USDL, July 1925.

65.   USRD, January 1, 1928, p. 275.

66.   Washington, June 26, 1933, William Phillips to Felix Cole, USNA701.60P 11/34A.

67.   USDL, November 1935.

68.   USDL, September 1948.

69.   USDL, July 1949.

70.   USDL, September 1953.

71.   USDL, June 1954.

72.   USDL, November 1970.

73.   USDL, May 1992.

74.   USDL, May 1993.

75.   The British used the same "three-for-one" system, basing a minister for all three Baltic countries in Riga. There is a poem about this system composed by the British minister to the Baltic states from 1930 to 1934, Sir Hugh Knatchbull-Hugessen, in his book, *Diplomat in Peace and War* (London: John Murray, 1949), pp. 248–249.

By 1938, 25 countries had accredited diplomats to Latvia. Nineteen of those missions were in Riga, three were in Helsinki, two were in Warsaw, one was in Tallinn, and one, the Spanish mission, was listed without any place of residence cited (LAM, pp. 7-51).

76.   U.S. Department of State, *Principal Officers, 1778–1990*, Latvia, p. 110.

77.   Information provided by Andrew Silski, Office of Nordic and Baltic Affairs, Department of State, Washington, August 16, 1996, and it also is found within U.S. State Department, Biographies of U.S. Chiefs of Mission, www.state.gov/www/about_state/biography/holmes_james.html.

78.   U.S. Department of State, *Principal Officers, 1778–1990*, passim.

79.   George F. Kennan, *Memoirs 1925–1950* (New York: Pantheon Books, 1967), pp. 29–31, 47–48, 61.

80.   LAM, p . 55.

81.   *Papers Relating to the Foreign Relations of the United States, 1922*, 2: 874.

82.   Alfred Erich Senn, "The Formation of the Lithuanian Foreign Office, 1918-1921," 21 *Slavic Review* (September 1962), 501, 503; Alfred Erich Senn, *The Emergence of Modern Lithuania* (New York: Columbia University Press, 1959), pp. 237-238; Rauch, p. 258.

83.   Senn, *The Emergence*, p. 86; Senn, "The Formation," pp.500–502.

84.   Senn, "The Formation," pp. 501, 503.

85.   Senn, *The Emergence*, pp. 85, 160, 178 n, 239; Alfred Erich Senn, *The Great Powers, Lithuania, and the Vilna Question 1920–1928* (Leiden: E. J. Brill, 1966), pp. 7, 177; Tarulis, pp. 130, 235, 249; ELI, 1, pp. 484–485.

86.   Senn, *The Emergence*, p.178; Senn, "The Formation," p. 505; ELI, 5, pp. 517-518; Kovno, February 9, 1921, Ernest C. Wilton [British Commissioner in Lithuania], F0371/6724/N2251/N2252/N2314/359/59.

87.   Senn, *The Emergence*, p. 239. All three of these diplomats have biographical sketches within Appendix C.

88.   Senn, p. 239.   Balutis, Galvanauskas, Klimas, and Naruševičius have biographical sketches included within Appendix C.

89.   ELI, 1, p. 353.

90.   Tarulis, p. 81.

91.   Senn, *The Emergence*, pp. 90, 178, 239; ELI, 3, 533-535; Senn, *The Great Powers*, pp. 73, 75, 80; When the Conference of Ambassadors (Britain, France, Italy, Japan) granted de jure recognition on July 13, 1922 to Lithuania, the conference addressed the note to Lubicz-Milosz, as reported in Senn, *The Great Powers*, p. 97.

92.   Senn, *The Emergence*, pp. 89-90; Tarulis, p. 81; ELI, 3, p. 484.

93.   Senn, *The Emergence*, pp. 91, 214, 239; Senn, *The Great Powers*, pp. 42, 55, 81-82; ELI, 4, p.531; Bronis J. Kaslas, *The USSR-German Aggression Against Lithuania* (New York: Robert Speller and Sons, 1973), p. 534.
        Rozenbaumas was a member of the delegation that negotiated the Treaty of Moscow, which granted de jure recognition by Russia on July 12, 1920. Naruševičius was the delegation chairperson, and Kilmas was a member, as well (Kaslas, pp. 68–81). These participants, and the result of their work, also are mentioned in Graham, *New Governments*, pp. 378–381.

94.   Senn, *The Emergence*, pp. 91, 214, 239; Kaslas, p. 535.

95.   Senn, *The Emergence*, passim; Senn, *The Great Powers*, pp. 7, 8, 16, 132 n, 153 n; Rauch, pp.23-26, 41, 43; Tarulis, pp. 4, 12 n.; Albertas Gerutis, ed., *Lithuania: 700 Years* (New York: Manyland Books, 1969), pp. 141, 147, 149; Riga, July 12, 1939, C.W. Orde, transmitting dispatch of Thomas H. Preston, Kovno, June 28, 1939, F0371/23609-N3452/3452/59, Records of Leading Personalities in Lithuania.

96.   ELI, 6, pp. 333–334; Tarulis, p. 292.
        Kaslas, p. 537.

97.   Senn, "The Formation," p. 503.

98.   Senn, *The Emergence*, pp. 22-23, passim; Senn, *The Great Powers*, pp.8–11; Tarulis, pp. 10, 128.
        Gabrys was a fascinating personality who can be described as a political adventurer. He assumed the pen name of "Marie Camille Rivas" and published anti-German propaganda. Simultaneously, he worked for the German Foreign Ministry under the pseudonym "Garlawa," reported in Senn, *The Great Powers*, p. 8.

99.   Senn, *The Emergence*, pp. 88–89, 55, 61 n, 92–93.

100.   League of Nations, *Official Journal*, Records of the First Assembly, Plenary Sessions, Twenty-seventh Meeting, December 16, 1920 (Research Publications, microfilm, pt. 29 reel 39, part I), p. 639.

101.   League of Nations, *Official Journal*, Records of the Second Assembly, Plenary Sessions, Sixteenth Meeting, September 22, 1921 (Research Publications, microfilm, pt. 29 reel 39, part I), Lithuania, p. 338, Estonia, p. 334, Latvia, p. 336.

102.   U.S. Department of State, *Principal Officers, 1778–1990*, Estonia, p. 83, Lithuania, p. 113.

103.   Tarulis, pp. 85–86.

104.   Senn, *The Emergence*, p. 16.

105.   Tarulis, pp. 85–86.

106.   Tarulis, p. 292.

107.   Kaslas, pp. 65–66, 536.

108.   Senn, *The Emergence*, pp. 237–238.

109.   Tarulis, p. 292.

110.   Tarulis, pp. 300, 310.

111.   Tarulis, p. 342.

112.   USDL, November 1922.

113.   USDL, October 1923.

114.   USDL, December 1923.

115.   USRD, January 1, 1926, p. 271.

116.   Washington, May 21, 1927, Kazys Bizauskas to Secretary of State Frank B. Kellogg, USNA701.60m 11/42.

117.   USRD, January 1, 1928, p. 275.

118.   Washington, November 1, 1928, Bronius K. Balutis to Secretary of State Frank B. Kellogg, USNA701.60m 11/57.

119.   Washington, January 1, 1936, Sir R. Lindsay, F0371/19832-A309/309/45; Washington, August 20, 1935, Robert F. Kelley, USNA701.60M 11/77.

120.   ELI, 6, pp. 285-286; USDL, June 1957; Gerutis, pp. 397-426, passim; Kaslas, pp. 229-401, passim, 537.

121.   USDL, February 1977.

122.   USDL, February 1988.

123.   USDL, February 1992.

124.   USDL, May 1992.

125.   USDL, February 1994.

126.   USDL, Winter 1998.

127.   Information provided by Andrew Silski, Office of Nordic and Baltic Affairs, Department of State, Washington, August 16, 1996, and U.S. State Department, U.S. Mission to Lithuania, http://www.usis.lt/Embassy.html.

Chapter 4

Baltic Diplomacy and International Law

The most unusual aspect of the diplomatic representations of Estonia, Latvia, and Lithuania between 1940 and 1991 is the manner in which they defied and, perhaps, redefined international law and legal theory. There were no conventional instruments, institutions, or points of reference that could provide adequate guidance regarding the legal interpretation of these activities. On the one hand, this state of affairs led to confusion and controversy among the governments that were forced to address it. On the other hand, it offered opportunities for reevaluating, as well as shaping the direction of, the international legal standards of diplomacy.

A conventional international relations analysis of Baltic diplomacy as a political phenomenon might offer the possibility of varying interpretations. The recognition of Estonian, Latvian, and Lithuanian diplomats and their diplomatic missions during the post–World War II Soviet era arguably could be interpreted as an idealist response. This argument could be based upon a largely symbolic reading of this gesture as a reaffirmation of certain principles of self-determination and human rights, as well as an expression of general sentiments against Soviet repression that are consistent with the goals of a peaceful international order.

But an idealist motivation also could be regarded as an unlikely interpretation, since that approach could have been criticized as a naive response that accomplished little and may have impeded relations between the West and the Soviet bloc unnecessarily, as well as created certain practical difficulties regarding the promotion of true Western and Baltic interests.   Therefore, this unusual diplomatic recognition more appropriately might be interpreted as a realist response; it reflected long-range Western goals, it could be useful for the bargaining purposes during international conferences (such as the one that produced the Helsinki Accord), and it provided an excuse for Western interference within the Soviet sphere of influence, thus disrupting the balance of power in a small but annoying manner, nonetheless.

Furthermore, a particular government's policy toward the Baltic states and their diplomatic representatives could be explained in terms of a nation's political culture and the rhetoric and concerns of domestic politics. For example, within the United Kingdom, a general resentment among the population and within certain governing circles toward the overbearing dominance of American foreign policy and a related desire to treat Soviet fears of invasion (as confirmed by that country's history) and other objectives with a certain sympathy may have influenced British interpretations of international law as they related to the unusual subject of Baltic diplomats.[1]

Likewise, the appeal to traditional American "values" and ideals regarding freedom and a single-minded fear of communism may have made it difficult for the American Government to abandon the representatives of small European countries that were struggling against oppression, since election campaign rhetoric during this period of history especially emphasized and exploited these sorts of highly emotional sentiments.[2] International law is, arguably, the most subjective area found within the vast realm of law, and, since no single international standard or theory that could impose a standard and universal interpretation of its norms, national variations are inevitable.[3]   The unusual circumstances surrounding the diplomatic representatives and missions of Estonia, Latvia, and Lithuania made such variations of interpretation a near certainty.

The unanticipated nature of the Baltic missions during the period of Soviet occupation resulted in an absence of specific guidance regarding these issues within the text of the Vienna Conventions, the Charter of the United Nations, additional treaties or conventions of the United Nations, and any other conventional source of public international law. Official and unofficial political and legal reactions to these missions varied from country to country, where their "validity" ultimately was determined and established. Consequently, a consistent explanation and examination of this issue, even among relatively disinterested scholars, becomes confusing and difficult.

However, despite this diversity of interpretation, it is possible to facilitate this examination by classifying the responses of the international community under three headings: nonrecognition, recognition, and qualified extension of diplomatic privileges. These three approaches were adopted, in different ways, by various countries, but they are best represented by the policies of, respectively, the Soviet Union, the United States, and the United Kingdom. By examining each approach separately (especially from the perspective of the country that most prominently embraced it), it is possible to assess these conflicting interpretations of international law regarding these Baltic diplomatic missions. It may be possible to use this approach to assess the larger and historical implications that these missions have posed for diplomatic policy and international relations.

The Soviet response, predictably, was a rejection of the validity of the Baltic diplomatic missions, regardless of the place where they were established. However, it is entirely possible that other countries, while not sharing the obvious Soviet motivation that guided its approach toward these missions, agreed with the basic arguments posed in support of this rejection of any diplomatic recognition. These arguments essentially emphasize the logical absurdity of a diplomatic mission that, in effect, represents "nothing." This emphasis is reinforced by an interpretation of conventions and treaties governing diplomacy that strongly implies, it is claimed, the necessary relationship between diplomatic missions and a tangible government or international organization.[4]

However, despite any such implications, there have never existed any *formal* requirements regarding the status, or even existence, of a sending state relative to its diplomatic mission. This absence of a positive point of reference regarding the unusual position of the Baltic missions and their diplomatic representatives made it both difficult and frustrating for anyone who wished to make a formal protest against such recognition, as the Soviet ambassador to the Court of St. James's, Ivan Maisky, did during World War II. In fact, this situation is so unusual that even descriptions of prevailing customary legal traditions regarding diplomatic relations within international law generally fail to address or anticipate it.

The closest customary consideration in this area probably would relate to the generally accepted political conditions regarding the "tests" governments are expected to employ for recognizing new governments and, consequently, their diplomatic missions. The United Nations has, in its capacity as an international and diplomatic organization, habitually employed these same tests and, in doing so, has provided a model for their theoretical interpretation and practical application.

The most important test, which has been adopted in the practice of states in the matter of recognition of governments, is the principle of effectiveness of governmental power of the authority which claims to be recognised. There are certain other considerations which have also been taken into account from time to time. . . . Some of these tests have, however, been largely abandoned in modern state practice, and it is primarily the test of effectiveness which has emerged as the predominant and governing principle. This can be judged with particular reference to the absence or otherwise of any other authority which claims to be the government, the obedience which it is able to command from the people and the governmental agencies including the armed forces, and its ability to perform international obligations. The test of 'consent of the people governed' has sometimes been treated as one of the criteria of the effectiveness of the government, but it is clear that the absence of such consent could not be a conclusive factor against the government on the issue of effectiveness.[5]

This practice appears to be implied by the language of the Vienna Convention, despite the lack of direct reference within that document (or, for that matter, any other example of positive international law) to this issue of the continuing status of the sending state. Certainly, Articles 2 and 3 of the Vienna Convention would be rendered moot without the logical presence of both clearly recognized receiving *and* sending states.

Article 2
The establishment of diplomatic relations between States, and of permanent diplomatic missions, takes place by mutual consent.

Article 3
1. The functions of a diplomatic mission consist, inter alia, in:
(a) Representing the sending State in the receiving State;
(b) Protecting in the receiving State the interests of the sending State and of its

nationals, within the limits permitted by
international law;

(c) Negotiating with the Government of the
receiving State;

(d)   Ascertaining by all lawful means
conditions and developments in the receiving
State, and reporting thereon to the
Government of the sending State;

(e) Promoting friendly relations between the
sending State and the receiving State, and
developing their economic, cultural and
scientific relations.[6]

Perhaps another significant, indirect reference can be drawn from
Article 19 of the Vienna Convention. This article deals specifically with
the replacement of a head of mission, yet it appears to be predicated upon
the assumption that a legitimate and recognizable sending state is
necessary for the maintenance, as well as the creation, of a valid
diplomatic mission. This dilemma confronted those countries (primarily
the United States) that considered accepting the credentials of new
Estonian, Latvian, and Lithuanian heads of mission as those Baltic
diplomats who had continued in their posts since 1940 and now
approached retirement or death. The reemergence of the independent
Baltic republics made the entire issue moot, so the potentially difficult
dilemma regarding the appointment of new diplomatic representatives for
these missions never needed to be tested. Otherwise, the legations (which
were *not* recognized as governments-in-exile) would have attempted to
perform a function that, under international law, could be performed only
by a sending state. Under those circumstances, the American Government
would have been required to address the responsibility of accepting the
credentials of diplomatic representatives whom it, in effect, had helped to
select—contrary to the clear spirit, if not the unambiguous letter, of
Articles 5, 7, 8, and 9 of the Vienna Convention.

The British approach to the diplomatic representatives of the
Baltic states was prompted, in part, by the anticipated reaction of the
British courts, which, it was assumed, might apply a traditionally "monist"
approach to the international law of diplomacy in the absence of firm
guidance from Parliament.[7] Since English or Scottish courts never were
required to rule in such matters, the reaction of the British judicial systems
can be, for the most part, only speculated.[8] However, the American
judicial system has provided precedents which reveal jurisprudential

support for the reverse monist approach to this issue that was embraced by the State Department.

In order to appreciate the American response to this issue, and to understand its interpretation of international law as it related to this unusual diplomatic situation, it is important to appreciate, as well, the traditional approach to international law, in general, as adopted by the American political and constitutional systems. The American legal tradition has adopted the theoretical perspective of a "reverse monist" approach for the purpose of reconciling domestic, or "municipal," law (particularly its own constitutional law) with international law, as opposed to embracing either a conventional "monist" approach or a "dualist" approach.

A "dualist" approach conceptualizes municipal (domestic) law and international law as being two distinct and separate realms of legal ideas, principles, and practices that neither relate to, or affect, each other. A "monist" approach considers all law as part of a theoretical hierarchy of legal and moral values, with the universal values of international law taking precedence over municipal law in situations where a particular domestic law and the principles of international law are found to be in conflict—a claim often made in the area of human rights and liberties. On the other hand, a "reverse monist" approach also regards law as having a single hierarchy, but it regards the municipal law of a particular sovereign state (especially constitutional law) as taking precedence over international law when the two legal realms are found to be in conflict. This perspective is reinforced by the weakness of international law, in relation to its lack of force and authority, as compared to the sovereignty of the state, which provides municipal law its recognizable "command" and practical effect.[9]

Both the American political and judicial systems have traditionally embraced this "reverse monist" approach as necessary for maintaining the independence, prestige, and effectiveness of the constitution and legal system of the United States. Strong American sympathy and support for the principles of international law have long existed, especially in the area of human rights and liberties. However, an even stronger tradition has existed of upholding the jurisdiction of American constitutional interpretation over conflicting interpretations of international law, especially when important domestic and foreign policy objectives are at stake.[10]

The American interpretation of the Vienna Convention and other rules and conventions of international law in the area of diplomacy have posed no exception to this tradition, especially in terms of American policy toward the diplomatic representatives of Estonia, Latvia, and Lithuania.

The fact that this interpretation tended to support American political opposition toward perceived human rights violations in the former Baltic states, as well as foreign policy objectives of isolating and, when appropriate, embarrassing the Soviet Union (within an overall, though constantly shifting, Cold War strategy) also strongly aided this particular policy.[11]

The most important American case that addresses the legal status of diplomats in the United States is the 1821 Supreme Court appeal of the civil case, *The Bello Corrunes*. This case was appealed from the Circuit Court of Rhode Island, where a Spanish vessel, named the *Bello Corrunes*, and its stranded cargo were claimed by both the original Spanish owners and the owners of an Argentinean vessel that had captured it off the Cuban coast. This Argentinean vessel had been seized by American authorities for violation of revenue laws. It also allegedly was equipped in American ports, in violation of the American Neutrality Act of 1797.[12] One of the arguments made by the United States Attorney General, William Wirt, against the Spanish claim was that it was not made by the original owners but by the Spanish vice–consul on their behalf.

> The consul of Spain has no authority to claim, in his own name, and in his official character, the property of persons to him unknown, and by whom he cannot therefore have been invested with a special procuration. He is not invested with a general authority for that purpose, *virtute officii*, nor is there evidence in this particular case that the consul is the agent, consignee, or correspondent of the owners, who are sometimes permitted to claim for their principal, when the latter is absent from the country. Great public inconveniences and mischief might follow from allowing foreign consuls, not specially authorized by their own government, or by this, nor by the parties to receive restitution of property, for which they may interpose a claim as belonging to their fellow subjects.[13]

Attorney General Wirt referred to a decision rendered by a French judge, Monsieur Portalis, regarding a similar claim that had been made by a Danish consul in Paris who wanted to represent citizens of Denmark in a civil case. In that 1800 case, French jurists ruled that diplomatic officials were not, under the law, qualified or authorized to represent the interests of their private nationals who could not be present to make their own claims before judicial bodies—in this instance, *le Conseil des prises*.[14] The authority of diplomatic representatives was interpreted narrowly as valid only when it reflects the direct relationship between the diplomat and the sending, sovereign government or when it reflects the terms of treaties between the sending and host governments that specifically define these diplomatic functions.[15] Admittedly, they were regarded as not being limited to the sole authority of representing their respective states, but those additional responsibilities should involve *only* those matters directly relating to their nationals who are *actually present* within the physical scope of their diplomatic jurisdiction and, then, primarily in matters concerning administrative and legal requirements associated with their consular duties.

> Leur jurisdiction ne se borne pas alors aux affaires contentienses des nationaux. Ils ont aussi la jurisdiction volontaire, c'est à dire la faculté de recevoir les declarations des capitaines des vaisseaux, et tous les actes que leur nationaux veulent passer dans leur chancellerie, de les légaliser, de recevoir leur testaments, de régler leurs successions et leur tutelles, de faire l'inventaire de leur biens délaissés et naufrages, etc.[*sic*][16]

However, in the United States, the Supreme Court rejected the government's arguments on this point, by accepting, instead, the idea that the French interpretation of international law, as it related to the authority of diplomats, rested upon a particular regulation of French civil law (which provided that the *procureur-général* would represent all foreign nationals who were neither present, nor represented by special counsel), rather than upon the common–law influences that have guided the American legal tradition.[17] Furthermore, this court issued its own interpretation regarding diplomats, their authority, and the relationship between American and international law on such an issue.

> On the first point made by the Attorney General, this Court feels no difficulty in deciding, that a Vice Consul duly recognised by our Government, is a competent party to assert or defend the rights of property of the individuals of his nation, in any Court having jurisdiction of causes affected by the

application of international law. To watch over the rights and interests of their subjects, wherever the pursuits of commerce may draw them, or the vicissitudes of human affairs may draw them, is the great object for which Consuls are deputed by their sovereigns; and in a country where laws govern, and from the only avenue through which their course lies to the end of their mission. The long and universal usage of the Courts of the United States, has sanctioned the exercise of this right, and it is impossible that any evil or inconvenience can flow from it. Whether the powers of the Vice Consul shall in any instance extend to the right to receive in his national character, the proceeds of property labelled and transfered into the registry of a Court, is a question resting on other principles. In the absence of specific powers given him by competent authority, such a right would certainly not be recognised. Much, in this respect, must ever depend upon the laws of the country from which, and to which, he is deputed. And this view of the subject will be found to reconcile the difficulties supposed to have been presented by the authorities quoted on this point.[18]

This position was reaffirmed by the 1916 New York Court of Appeals case of *Walter G. Hamilton vs. Erie Railroad Company*. In this case, the Russian consul general in New York attempted to settle a claim in an action brought for wrongful death involving Russian nationals. The court ruled that this specific act, according to treaties between the United States and the Russian Empire, was not authorized. But it also held that diplomatic officials were, in general, legally entitled to act on behalf of their nationals before the courts.[19] The principle largely was upheld, yet not out of deference to international law or the laws of Russia, although the court did allow that these considerations were relevant to this judicial question.[20] It was upheld primarily in deference to the constitutional provision whereby the United States bound itself to foreign treaties. It is from this municipal source that the legal authority of diplomatic officials was, ultimately, held to be valid.

It is clear, I think, that the general law of nations does not sustain as valid the settlement with the appellant of the consul-general, and this conclusion is assured by the fact that the counsel for the appellant does not invoke here that law. Nor has he brought to our attention any law of Russia or of this country supplementing, in this respect, international law. The treaty between the United States and Russia, in conjunction with that between the United States and Spain, of which we have already spoken, is the foundation of his claim and argument.

The Federal Constitution declares a valid treaty the supreme law of the land. (Article VI.) Where a treaty affects the rights of litigants, it binds those rights and is as much to be regarded by the court as an act of Congress. It is paramount to the Constitution and statutes of the state [of New York], but not to acts of Congress. Its application to any case and its construction, if construction is needed, are, as with any other law, questions for the court.[21]

The emphasis here is not upon international law, but upon American municipal law. The laws of the United States ultimately recognize the legal authority of a diplomatic mission and its representatives. International law and the laws of other countries need to be considered regarding matters of diplomatic recognition and authority. But the final American authority on these matters is the Constitution and the laws and treaties that it authorizes. Since the treaty was confirmed by Congress (as stipulated in Articles 1 and 6 of that constitution) the treaty between the United States and the Russian Empire became the proper focus for the court in determining the legal status of this diplomat—a ruling which the Supreme Court upheld, upon appeal.[22]

This case established the basis for the New York Supreme Court's ruling in the 1943 case of *Anatole Buxhoeveden vs. Estonian State Bank*. This case became the definitive precedent regarding the status of Baltic diplomats and their missions during the Cold War era. In this case, the plaintiff sought to recover an inheritance (specified in an Estonian will that was written in 1837) that, he claimed, was held by the Estonian State

Bank. He levied a warrant of attachment on funds of the Estonian State Bank that were held by the City Bank of New York. The consul general for Estonia, Johannes Kaiv, sought to block this attachment on behalf of the Republic of Estonia, which had been replaced (through the Soviet government) with the Estonian Soviet Socialist Republic and which, at that time, still was occupied by the invading forces of Nazi Germany. Buxhoeveden contested Kaiv's legal standing and authority to challenge his warrant, and the New York Supreme Court made its awareness of the political implications of this private case clear.

> The basic question of law presented by this application is the extent of the right of a Consul General of a foreign nation, at peace with this country, but completely occupied by an enemy, to protect and guard in our courts the rights and property of one of his own nationals, an Estonian corporation in which the said Republic owns a majority share interest, and which, if indeed it has knowledge of this action, is itself manifestly unable, because of present unprecedented world conditions, to defend the same or to take any steps specifically to authorize such defense.[23]

Buxhoeveden's counsel clearly felt that this question should be answered against Consul General Kaiv, who now represented a defunct government and, therefore, could not exercise authority in defending interests in the Estonian State Bank.

> The plaintiff disputes the Consul's contentions throughout, and maintains that he has no authority to appear for the said bank either under international law, Estonian law, or by virtue of the treaty between the United States and the Republic of Estonia, notwithstanding that the plaintiff's counsel on the application by the Consul to vacate the purported service of process herein, took the position that said Consul was properly served and had authority to appear for the defendant bank. Plaintiff, through his counsel, further urges that the Consul fails to show any meritorious defense to the action,

and that while 'plaintiff is a man of means and substance', and his claim is fully protected by the warrant of attachment, 'two years have passed since Estonia was invaded', and plaintiff now desires to recover the amount claimed; that if restitution is necessary he is in a position to make the same.[24]

Naturally, Kaiv disagreed with the plaintiff's assertions. He must have realized that the future of all Baltic diplomats and missions in the United States was at stake, since he was careful to emphasize the general treaty obligations between Estonia and the United States (which the latter government continued to recognize) and appealed to the American commitment of continuing to recognize his legitimacy, despite the loss of Estonia's independence and any sort of sovereign government.

The Consul General contends that he has the right and it is his duty under international law, under the Civil Code of Estonia by virtue of the right of *negotiorum gestio*', and under the treaty between the United States and the Republic of Estonia, to protect and preserve the rights and property of the defendant bank by the instant application, notwithstanding the fact that jurisdiction of the defendant bank could not be obtained in the first instance by service of process upon the Consul General. In that connection he claims that while he does not come within the provisions of Section 229, Civil Practice Act, relating to service of process on foreign corporations, he is 'representative' as that expression is used under Section 217, Civil Practice Act, the statute under which this application is made. He further urges that inasmuch as prior to the time a copy of the summons and complaint was mailed to the defendant bank, the Republic of Estonia was, in the first instance, occupied by the military forces of the Union of Soviet Socialist Republics and, later, by the armed forces of the German Reich, it is quite improbably that the summons and complaint herein were ever received by the defendant bank; that said

> bank, which is the Central Bank of the
> Republic of Estonia, has no representative in
> this country other than the Consul; that the
> officers and other persons who would
> normally act in its behalf are all in enemy
> occupied territory; and that no one can
> communicate with the defendant bank to
> ascertain the truth or falsity of the plaintiff's
> claim.[25]

Obviously, there was more at stake in this case than the disposition of this particular estate. The consul general primarily appealed to an American understanding of international law, American jurisprudential tradition, and American political sympathies in making his claim for standing and authority in this case. This strategy apparently was successful, at least in terms of the court's ruling on this awkward legal question.

> In my opinion, the position of the Consul
> General should be sustained, both on
> principles of international law as well as
> under the provisions between this country
> and Estonia. In the leading case upon this
> subject, *The Bello Corrunes*, the Supreme Court
> of the United States, whose Chief Justice was
> then John Marshall, stated the rule applicable
> here[26]

The court further supported the authority of this precedent by citing authoritative interpretations on the applicable rules of international law.

> Text book and digest writers support this rule.
> In Bouchard's *Fiore's International Law Codified*,
> at Paragraph 508, he states the rule thus:
> 'Consuls must always be considered as
> authorized to protect the interests of absent
> or incompetent citizens of the state which
> sent them; they may do whatever may be
> required by circumstances to safeguard and
> protect the rights and interests of these
> citizens, observing, however, the provisions
> both of the territorial law and of the consular
> convention.'

And in *Corpus Jurus Secondum* (3 C.J.S. Ambassadors and Consuls, @ 15, subd. b), we find this language: 'Under international law consuls are clothed with authority to protect the rights and property interests of their nationals, although in the absence of specific authorization they are not recognized as the latter's personal agents. It has been broadly stated that a foreign consular officer needs no special authorization to represent his fellow countrymen in the courts, and it is clear that under treaty he is often authorized to do so.'[27]

Another legal question in this area involves the international legal principle of "comity," through which concept the judicial system of one country extends recognition and, in some instances, enforcement of the legal acts of another country as a matter of custom, international legal duty, and political courtesy. It is, in fact, a common principle and practice throughout the international community.[28] Although raised as an issue within court cases such as this one, the Supreme Court ruled, in the case of *Hilton vs. Guyot*, that American courts need not feel necessarily restrained by claims of comity.[29] Therefore, as in this case, the issue of comity has been raised within, but it has not been necessarily decisive to the outcome of, these particular legal challenges.[30]

Of course, the one issue not explicitly addressed here is that of the legitimacy of Johannes Kaiv *as a consul general*, since he no longer had a government to represent. Implicitly, however, it can be deduced from the Supreme Court's opinion that such a question is regarded as one that resides properly with the elected branches of American government. This emphasis upon the treaty between the United States and Estonia (which the American Administration still regarded as valid) and its greater emphasis upon scholarly works of American jurisprudence than upon scholarly works in international law, strongly suggests the dominance of such an interpretation of the validity of the recognition of Baltic representatives (such as Consul General Kaiv) as both de jure and de facto diplomatic representatives of their respective countries and citizens.[31]

This interpretation was reinforced by the State Department's chief legal adviser, Ernest A. Gross, in a letter dated March 26, 1948, to all of the state governors. This letter (which was cited in a debate before the American Senate) contains a succinct summary of the American administration's policy on the Baltic states and their respective diplomatic missions—a policy that remained unchallenged by Congress and unaltered by successive presidencies.

> There have recently come to the Department's attention several cases in which a person acting as attorney for the Consul General of the Union of Soviet Socialist Republics in New York City, claimed the right, in behalf of nonresident Latvians, Estonians, and Lithuanians to receipt for their distributive shares derived from estates in process of probate.
>
> The Department has never recognized the incorporation of Latvia, Estonia, and Lithuania into the Soviet Union, and consequently does not regard Soviet consular officers or their attorneys as having any right to act on behalf of nonresident Latvian, Estonian or Lithuanian nationals with respect to distributive shares owing to them from estates of persons dying in the United States. . . . Moreover, even in the absence of applicable treaty provisions, the Department does not consider that Soviet consular officers in the United States have any right to represent nationals of a third country, whether residing in the United States or elsewhere, without the country's consent. It is respectfully requested that you advise the courts of your State having to do with probate proceedings of the position of the Department with respect to the incorporation of the Baltic States.[32]

The State Department further justified its position on the basis of the traditional American interpretation of international law in this area. Therefore, this letter confirmed the legal authority of those diplomatic representatives.

> As you doubtless know, it has been generally recognized by American writers on international law as well as by the courts that the questions as to what regime in a foreign country is to be recognized as the government

> thereof and what persons are to be recognized
> as representing such regime are matters for
> determination by the executive branch of our
> Government, although there have been some
> instances in which the legislative branch has
> had a part in the recognition of new states.
> Needless to say, where the conclusion of a
> treaty or the sending of an ambassador or
> minister is involved, the Senate has a part.[33]

Despite the precedent established by these varied opinions, the legal response to the legitimacy of Baltic diplomats in American courts continued to face uncertain interpretations. The primary legal difficulty that was addressed involved the subject of "notarial acts." These legal acts involve routine administrative functions that generally are associated with matters of identification, such as producing, and confirming the validity of, birth certificates. Although the United States refused to recognize the incorporation of the Baltic states into the Soviet Union, Baltic diplomatic missions were practically helpless in assisting their citizens in the United States with the routine performance of these notarial acts, since the Soviet Baltic governments controlled all access to such information and documentation.

The American legal system dealt with this problem in different ways. For example, if an Estonian national needed a copy of a marriage certificate, that person might seek legal counsel for assistance. That lawyer frequently would obtain the necessary documentation from Soviet officials of the Estonian Soviet Socialist Republic, who would notarize it. Once that act had occurred, an American consular official also would notarize the document, but this official would add a declaration to the document proclaiming that "[t]his authentication is not to be interpreted as implying recognition of Soviet sovereignty over Estonia."[34] This compromise often was regarded as unsatisfactory by the parties concerned, including Baltic diplomatic representatives.

A compromise position adopted by state courts would make a distinction between "notarial acts" and "political acts." The former acts generally involved civil cases, and courts would often defer to the authentication of Soviet officials as a matter of administrative pragmatism. The latter acts involved issues that seemed to touch upon the diplomatic status of Baltic missions and representatives, as well as deferring to official administration foreign policy. Since cases involving "political acts" include those controversies involving the defense of the interests (including the property interests[35]) of Baltic nationals, this distinction still offered a significant role for these representatives, as well as a legal confirmation of the American policy of diplomatic recognition of Baltic missions and representatives by American courts at both the state and federal levels.[36] This fact was articulated within the opinion of the 1978 case of *Daniunas vs. Simutis*.

> Even though the present government of Lithuania is not recognized by this country, since the powers of attorney relate to what has been determined to be solely a private, local and domestic matter, the inheritance rights of Lithuanian citizens, they will be given effect by the courts of this country.[37]

One problem that remained was the dilemma of sustaining the Baltic diplomatic missions once those representatives, who had been appointed prior to the 1940 annexation, died.[38]   British officials anticipated the deaths of these representatives as heralding an end to an awkward situation; American officials wished to maintain the viability of these missions through succeeding generations of Baltic nationals. By the 1970s, the United States began to contemplate the possibility of extending diplomatic recognition to persons who could not be appointed by independent governments of Estonia, Latvia, or Lithuania. It seems to have been primarily the Carter administration that most actively pursued this possible strategy, although it would be reasonable to assume that the Reagan Administration offered, at least, sympathetic attention to the idea as it continued to be promoted by existing Baltic diplomats and their respective missions.

The proposed plan entailed the recognition of the children of Baltic diplomats within the United States as the legal successors to their parents' diplomatic positions. This transfer would include a succession to the diplomatic powers and privileges their parents had continued to enjoy after the 1940 annexation of their respective countries. This idea became more appealing to some officials within the State Department following the Soviet invasion of Afghanistan in 1978. Such a policy would have complemented the Carter Administration's overall attempts to promote human rights throughout the world and, simultaneously, isolate the Soviet Union through political, economic, and diplomatic means.[39]

These children, for the most part, were still recognized as nationals of their parents' respective homeland, including those children who had been born, and reached the age of majority, within the United States. Yet the extension of diplomatic credentials solely by authority of a diplomatic mission, with no government available to authorize it, was a clear departure from the conventions and letter of international law.[40] The Vienna Convention is unequivocal on this point regarding the legal authority and legitimacy of diplomatic representatives and their missions.

> Article 19
> 1. If the post of head of the mission is vacant, or if the head of the mission is unable to perform his functions, a charge d'affaires ad interim shall be notified, either by the head of the mission or, in case he is unable to do so, by the Ministry for Foreign Affairs of the sending State to the Ministry for Foreign Affairs of the receiving State or such other ministry as may be agreed.
> 2. In cases where no member of the diplomatic staff of the mission is present in the receiving State, a member of the administrative and technical staff may, with the consent of the receiving State, be designated by the sending State to be in charge of the current administrative affairs of the mission.[41]

It was possible to assert the legality of the replacement of deceased diplomatic officials (such as the head of a mission) by diplomatic representatives who already had been assigned to these Baltic missions by their respective governments, prior to the demise of these governments.[42] These diplomats, though, were appointed only as chargés d'affaires (with the exception of the Estonian "acting" consuls general in New York City), in accordance with Article 19 of the Vienna Convention. It is implausible to assert that any new diplomatic representatives could present credentials to the receiving state without the benefit of a sending government to designate them. Nonetheless, State Department officials appeared to indicate to Congress that the recognition of successor diplomats for the Baltic states (who would be appointed, in the absence of recognized governments, by their own missions) was a possible option for the United States to adopt.[43] Robert L. Barry, deputy assistant secretary of state for European affairs, alluded to this issue in his carefully prepared statement that he made before a hearing of the House of Representatives Subcommittee on International Organizations in 1979.

The Baltic Legations in the United States remain important symbols to the Baltic peoples, and our continued recognition and accreditation of the diplomatic representatives of the last independent governments of Estonia, Latvia, and Lithuania serve to give tangible expression to our nonrecognition policy. It should be understood that we do not regard the Baltic Legations as government-in-exile. The Baltic Charges d'Affaires are persons who were commissioned diplomatic officers of the last three independent governments in 1940. Their role is to uphold the ideal of a free Estonia, Latvia, and Lithuania. . . .

As the corps of diplomats commissioned by the last independent governments of Estonia, Latvia, and Lithuania dwindles with the passage of time, the prospect of continued Baltic representation will have to be addressed. Baltic financial resources are also finite and dwindling, especially in the case of Lithuania. The Baltic Chargés d'Affaires and interested private citizens have discussed the questions of continued representation and finances with us in recent months. Aspects of these questions will require decisions by the U.S. Government which have not yet been made.[44]

The political and legal difficulties involved in formulating any reasonable plan for replenishing the "dwindling" diplomatic presence of the Baltic states probably dissuaded the Carter administration from implementing specific proposals in this area. The Reagan and Bush administrations offered no indication that they intended to address this issue, either, although their respective foreign policy records suggest that they were more confrontational toward the Soviet Union and less concerned about questions of international law and its interpretation than the Carter administration had been.[45] Nonetheless, the United States remained committed to the general principle of preserving an independent Baltic diplomatic presence throughout the period of Soviet incorporation. The reemergence of these independent republics made all previous legal questions regarding the Baltic missions moot, while their continued presence facilitated the transition to full and effective diplomatic representation, within the United States, on the part of the Baltic states.

Contrasting interpretations of international law between the United States and the United Kingdom reflect their different approaches to diplomatic issues, in general, as well as their different attitudes toward the Soviet Union, the Warsaw Pact, and the Cold War. Great Britain felt that it was placed within a difficult situation. Although it was a North Atlantic Treaty Organization [NATO] ally of the United States, the British government resisted the tendency to alienate the Soviet Union, completely. The military and political prominence of the Soviets was, in some respects, a more real concern to Britain and the European members of NATO than it was to Americans and Canadians. The ungainly diplomatic compromise between the Foreign Office and the Baltic diplomatic representatives reflected that concern. It was a policy that reflected the precarious position between hostile superpowers that many members of British society perceived to be the reality of the post–war world, and one that often motivated diplomatic responses from Whitehall.[46]

The aggressive American response toward supporting a Baltic diplomatic presence reflected its approach to the Soviet Union and the Cold War. Domestic attitudes regarding democratic ideals and the perceived threat posed by "world communism" prompted foreign policies that often were uncompromising in their methods and goals. It should not be surprising that the State Department officials appeared to be less concerned than their British counterparts with the implications of international law in this respect, including the disposition of Baltic assets frozen by the American Treasury Department.[47] American policy regarding the Baltic states and their diplomatic representatives reveals an overriding determination that reflected its general approach toward the Cold War. It was reaffirmed, despite the acceptance of the Helsinki Accord, which appeared to acknowledge the existence of a Soviet sphere of influence throughout Eastern Europe.[48]

Gerald Ford and his administration issued an official statement that reiterated American nonrecognition of the Soviet annexation of the Baltic states in order to counter speculation to the contrary following the signing of the Helsinki Accord.[49] Congress affirmed that policy by directing the president to declare February 16, 1983, as "Lithuanian Independence Day."[50] Therefore, a strong American policy on this issue continued until the restoration of Estonian, Latvian, and Lithuanian independence was assured. That support was reflected by the uninterrupted support for the diplomatic missions of those countries by successive American administrations.

International law and the legal theories through which it is interpreted lack a united, defining authority. It is, in practical terms, an unenforceable branch of law; many critics charge that it ought not to qualify at all as "law" in the proper sense. Even the creation of international covenants that include most of the planet's sovereign states does not guarantee either adherence or conformity, since a single concept (such as the source of diplomatic recognition) can be subject to radically different perspectives, based upon differences of culture, economics, politics, religion, and other considerations.[51]

Therefore, the variations of interpretation regarding this issue not only are understandable, but they should be anticipated. It would be highly surprising if there did not exist differences in interpretation and (since there is no effective agency of declarative justice and enforcement of international law) differences in implementation. The reemergence of independent Estonian, Latvian, and Lithuanian governments ultimately decided this specific issue, but the precedents established regarding this sort of diplomatic representation remain unclear and inconsistent. Nonetheless, the experiment did, in fact, occur, and it produced a body of evidence and experience. It is uncertain that a similar situation ever will arise again, but the possibility that it could occur now can be addressed with a greater degree of understanding, although probably not with a greater degree of confidence and clarity.

Notes

1.   An overview of British responses to American dominance in international affairs that addresses this theme is offered in Geoffrey Smith, *British Government and Its Discontents* (New York: Basic Books, 1981), pp. 78–83.

2.   The attacks of Senator Joseph McCarthy upon the patriotism of Secretary of State George C. Marshall (whom the senator accused of being "soft on Communism") provides a good example of the emotional context of American domestic politics during this era. This episode is evaluated in Stephen E. Ambrose, *Eisenhower* (New York: Simon and Schuster, 1983), vol. 1, pp. 562–567.

3.   One response to this problem is the recommendation that the international community practice broad tolerance of different human rights standards, as noted in Adamantia Pollis and Peter Schwab, eds., *Human Rights: Cultural and Ideological Perspectives* (New York: Praeger, 1980), vol. 1, pp. 14–17.

4.   For example, such an arrangement is considered logically necessary for the immunity of a diplomatic representative, acting in the capacity of a "personal" representative of a recognizable head of state, to be acknowledged and protected, as explained in Grant V. McClanahan, *Diplomatic Immunity* (New York: St. Martin's Press, 1989), pp. 18–43.

5.   Biswanath Sen, *A Diplomat's Handbook of International Law and Practice* (Dordrecht: Martinus Nijhoff, 1988), pp. 519–520.

6.   *Vienna Convention on Diplomatic Relations* [A/CONF.20/13 and Corr.1], 1961, art. 2, art. 3, sec. 1.

7.   An allusion to this monist approach of British jurisprudence can be found in Clive Parry and Sir Gerald Fitzmaurice, eds., *A British Digest of International Law* (London: Stevens and Sons, 1965, part VII, pp. 642–651.

8.   One exception is a series of decisions by English courts regarding the continued legitimacy of the promise of severance pay from the defunct Polish government-in-exile that these courts recognized, over the objections of the current Polish government, as noted in *Boguslawski vs. Gdynia-Ameryka Linie*, (1950) 1 K.B. 157 (1949), affirmed (1951) 1 K.B. 162 (C.A.), and *Gdynia Ameryka Linie Zeglugowe Spolka Akcyjna vs. Boguslawski*, (1953) A.C. 11 (1952).   Still, these decisions did not address the specific diplomatic issues that Baltic representatives within the United Kingdom posed.

9.   Horace B. Jacobini, *International Law: A Text* (Homewood, IL: Dorsey Press, 1968), pp. 39–43; Werner Levi, *Contemporary International Law* (Boulder, CO: Westview Press, 1991), pp. 22–29.

10.   The United States may bind itself to international law only through observance of specific treaty obligations. The continued effectiveness of this observance is left (especially in cases such as the pre-World War II treaties between the United States and the respective Baltic states) to the interpretation of the executive branch or the active intervention of the legislative branch. This issue is raised in Bernard Schwartz, *American Constitutional Law* (New York: Greenwood Press, 1969), pp. 314–332, and Laurence Tribe, *American Constitutional Law* (Mineola, NY: Foundation Press, 1988), pp. 226–228.

11.   Schwartz, pp. 326–328.

12.   19 U.S. 152 (6 Wheat.) at 152–153.

13.   19 U.S. 152 (6 Wheat.) at 153.

14.   Attorney General Wirt (who served in President James Monroe's administration) conveniently avoided any reference to possible problems of applying this decision by judges of a civil law system to the rulings of American judges operating within the principles of the common-law tradition, as expressed in Mary Ann Glendon, Michael W. Gordon, and Christopher Osakwe, *Comparative Legal Traditions in a Nutshell* (St. Paul, MN: West, 1982), pp. 1–12.

15.   De Steck, *des Consuls* (Paris, 1800), 64.

16.   De Steck, *des Consuls*, 64, at 64, cited in 19 U.S. 152 (6 Wheat.) at 154. "Their jurisdiction is not confined to disputes among nations. They also have voluntary jurisdiction, [but] so to speak, [only] the capacity to receive declarations from the captains of the vessels, and all actions involving their nationals that would occur in their chancellory, of notorizing the receipt of their testimony, of ruling upon their legal duties and trusteeships, of conducting inventory of their forsaken goods and shipwrecks, etc." (translation provided by McHugh).

17.   French legal scholars have interpreted international law regarding diplomacy, since that time, from a perspective that has become increasingly similar to the British perspective, despite the obvious differences between civil and common-law approaches. This influence can be noted within the French translation of the British text by T. J. Lawrence, *Les Principes de droit international*, Jacques Dumas and A. DeLapradelle, trans. (Oxford: Imprimerie de l'Université d'Oxford, 1920), pp. iii–ix, 314–334.

18.   19 U.S. 152 (6 Wheat.) at 168–169.

19.   219 N.Y. 343 at 350–351.

20.   219 N.Y. 343 at 351.

21.   219 N.Y. 343 at 351–352.

22.   248 U.S. 369.

23.   41 N.Y.S.2d 752 at 753.

24.   41 N.Y.S.2d 752 at 755.

25.   41 N.Y.S.2d 752 at 754.

26.   41 N.Y.S.2d 752 at 755.

27.   41 N.Y.S.2d 752 at 755–756.

28.   A brief description of the principle and practice of comity can be found in Charles G. Fenwick, *International Law*, 4th ed. (New York: Appleton-Century-Crofts, 1965), pp. 399–400.

29.   158 U.S. (1895) 113.

30.   Jacobini, p. 82 n.; Levi, pp. 35–38.

31.   An example can be found in 41 N.Y.S.2d 752 at 756–758.

32.   *United States Congressional Records—Senate*, vol. 94, pt. 5, June 1, 1948, p. 6795.

33.   *United States Congressional Records—Senate*, vol. 94, pt. 5, June 1, 1948, p. 6795.

34.   The court made note of this very declaration, as found within the relevant documents, in *Buxhoeveden vs. Estonian State Bank*, 41 N.Y.S.2d 752 at 754.

35.   Since the end of World War II, the political and civil nature of property rights has become one of the most important issues in international law, as explained in Jack Donnelly, *Universal Human rights in Theory and Practice* (Ithaca, NY: Cornell University Press, 1989), pp. 29–31.

36.   This issue is addressed in Robert A. Vitas, "U.S. Nonrecognition of the Soviet Occupation of Lithuania" (doctoral dissertation, Loyola University of Chicago, 1989), pp. 109–115.

37.   481 Fed.Supp. at 134.

38.   It was rare for a Baltic diplomat to retire during this period (even when faced with failing health) because of the desire to avoid losing any members of a dwindling staff. This sentiment was expressed by the Lithuanian chargé d'affaires in London, Vincas Balickas (who also commented about his own advanced age and ill health), in his letter to McHugh, March 6, 1986.

39.   McHugh interview with Dr. Anatol Dinbergs, Latvian chargé d'affaires in Washington, November 1982.

40.   An example is provided in Eileen Denza, *Diplomatic Law* (New York: Oceana Publications, 1976), pp. 68–71.

41.   *Vienna Convention on Diplomatic Relations* [A/CONF.20/13 and Corr.1], 1961, art. 19, sec. 1 and 2.

42.   The actions of prior governments, including governments-in-exile or other representatives of those governments, have been recognized as binding, even upon succeeding governments that have achieved de jure recognition, provided that those actions "do not interfere with the legitimate rule of the occupying power," *State of The Netherlands vs. Federal Reserve Bank of New York*, 201 F.2d 455 (1953) at 455.

43.   One interpretation of international law regarding the subject of governments-in-exile stresses the symbolic function of these institutions as a focus of political, legal, and cultural activities of the people (including *expatriate* nationals), organizations, and states that refuse to recognize the legitimacy of the current government and wish to return a former regime to power, provided in W. Michael Reisman and Edward Suzuki, "Recognition and Social Change in International Law," in *Toward World Order and Human Dignity*, W. Michael Reisman and Burns H. Weston, eds. (New York: The Free Press, 1976), p. 430. According to this interpretation, Baltic diplomatic missions might have qualified as "governments-in-exile" under international law that could, arguably, appoint additional diplomats that the government of the United States could recognize.

44.   "Human Rights and the Baltic States," Hearing Before the Subcommittee on International Organizations of the Committee on Foreign Affairs, House of Representatives [Y4.F76/1: H88/8], June 26, 1979, pp. 14–15.

45.   Daniel Madar, *The End of Containment?* (Toronto: Canadian Institute of International Affairs, 1989), pp. 6–9.

46.   A discussion of this general British strategy toward foreign policy is offered in Geoffrey McDermott, *The Eden Legacy* (London: Leslie Frewin, 1969), pp. 95–104, and Keith Robbins, *The Eclipse of a Great Power* (London: Longman, 1983), pp. 172–181.

47.   An example of this American approach to foreign policy is provided in William G. Hyland, *The Cold War* (New York: Random House, 1991), pp. 42–56, and George F. Kennan, *Measures Short of War*, Giles D. Harlow and George C. Maerz, eds. (Washington, DC: National Defense University Press, 1991), pp. 295–318.

48.   Walter C. Clemens, Jr., *Baltic Independence and Russian Empire* (New York: St. Martin's Press, 1991), pp. 298–299.

49.   Bill Anderson, "Ford Assures Baltics: No U.S. Sellout," *Chicago Tribune*, July 29, 1975, Sec. 2, 2:3; James McNaughton, "Ford Sees 35-Nation Charter as Gauge on Rights in East Europe," *New York Times*, July 26, 1997, 2:3.

50.   "Joint Resolution of the Senate and the House of Representatives to Direct the President to Issue a Proclamation Designating February 16, 1983 as 'Lithuanian Independence Day'" (Washington, DC: U. S. Government Printing Office, 1983), H.J. Res. 60.

51.   Attempts to discover a universal source for international law, especially through the development of a consistently accepted theory of natural law, have been imperfect, as acknolwedged in James T. McHugh, "I the Person: Natural Law, Judicial Decision Making, and Individual Rights" (doctoral dissertation, Queen's University, 1991), pp. 74-113.

Chapter 5

The Birth of a Separate Diplomacy

While the individual Baltic states are not homogeneous, their approaches to the growing world crisis of the late 1930s were remarkably similar. That same geography which made these three countries neighbors also placed them in a precarious historical position between hostile forces, particularly the Germanic and Slavic peoples. This historical position resulted, in the late 1930s, in Estonians, Latvians, and Lithuanians finding themselves caught between the expansionist designs of Nazi Germany to the west and the Soviet Union to the east and the mutual hatred of those two states for each other. It is, therefore, hardly surprising that the Baltic states followed similar policies (including diplomatic policies) as they each attempted to deal with this growing crisis, even though they may not have cooperated with each other formally.

Estonia, Latvia, and Lithuania each attempted to pursue a policy of neutrality during the late 1930s. Each country signed nonaggression pacts with the Soviet Union (Lithuania in 1926, Estonia and Latvia in 1932) and Germany (Lithuania in March 1939, and Estonia and Latvia in June 1939) in futile pursuit of that goal. These supposed assurances effectively were nullified as a result of the secret Nazi–Soviet nonaggression pact of August 1939, made between the respective dictators (and supposed bitter enemies) Adolf Hitler and Josef Stalin. This pact assigned certain Eastern European territories to these two states as part of their respective spheres of influence and lands targeted for future conquest. Although the division of Poland was the most infamous result of this pact, the Baltic states also were included within its parameters. The pact recognized Estonia and Latvia as part of a Soviet sphere of influence, while Lithuania was designated as part of the Nazi sphere. The opposition of Western nations, especially Great Britain and France, to this sort of expansion also extended to the Baltic states. Thus Anglo-French opposition to potential Soviet designs upon these states were made simultaneously with their guarantee to protect Polish sovereignty against Nazi demands regarding the Danzig corridor.[1]

On September 1, 1939, Germany invaded Poland. During the course of this invasion, the Nazi Government extended an offer to Lithuania to participate in this invasion, with a promise to return to it Lithuanian territory seized by Poland and formally annexed by that country in 1922. Nazi leaders believed that the regime of Antanas Smetona (who appeared to be sympathetic to fascist ideas) and his Nationalist Union Party would welcome the opportunity to join with their German neighbors in this endeavor. However, the Lithuanian government refused the offer, which may have motivated the Nazis, in part, to amend their nonaggression pact with the Soviets on September 28, 1939. The German government consequently agreed to reassign most of Lithuania to the Soviet sphere of influence, with the exception of lands located near the border with East Prussia.[2]

Stalin's government began to plan for the annexation of that region following this expanded recognition of Soviet interests in the Baltic states by the Nazis. In early October, the Soviet Union demanded of the Estonian, Latvian, and Lithuanian governments that they accede to pacts of mutual assistance drafted by the Soviet government. These pacts included requirements that each country accept the establishment of Soviet army, navy, and air force facilities upon its respective territory. All three Baltic countries reluctantly accepted these mutual assistance pacts and allowed those facilities to be established, given their relatively weak position in relation to the Soviet forces poised near their frontiers. The Soviet forces that were placed within Estonian and Latvian territory outnumbered each country's respective armed forces. In the case of Lithuania, the Soviet government attempted to win its active support by placating that country by returning control of Vilnius and the surrounding area (which the Red Army seized from Poland in mid-September 1939 as a result of its invasion of that country, in accordance with the Nazi-Soviet Nonaggression Pact) to the Lithuanian government.[3]

Meanwhile, to the north of the Baltic states, the Finns rejected Soviet demands that they accede to a mutual assistance pact. The Russo–Finnish War that followed this refusal resulted in a loss of Finnish territory but a guarantee of that country's independence—a fact that would have later implications for Estonia.[4] The Battle of France was launched by German forces on the western front with astounding success. When France capitulated to the Nazis on June 21, 1940, it signaled a change in Soviet policy that reflected its concern over this successful German expansion. The Soviet government feared German duplicity and the possibility of renewed Finnish resistance, so it demanded that the Lithuanian government admit additional Red Army units into the country and that it replace the present government with a pro-Soviet one. On July 17, 1940, similar demands were made of Latvia and Estonia, as Red Army units invaded all three Baltic nations.[5]

Perhaps the most dramatic developments took place in Lithuania. President Smetona fled the country as the Red Army invaded. He sought refuge in Germany, where he was welcomed as a leader in exile who was sympathetic to the Nazi cause. Prime Minister Antanas Merkys assumed the position of acting president and appointed Justas Paleckis as prime minister in his place. Once that move was accomplished, Merkys resigned as acting president so that Paleckis could assume both executive positions. Paleckis then agreed to cooperate with Soviet demands that new, pro-Soviet governments be created.[6]

Similar governments also were demanded by the Soviet occupiers of Estonia and Latvia. Elections were staged in which only the revived Communist Party of each country was allowed to nominate candidates for the newly created "people's assemblies." These assemblies were convened on July 21, 1940, and their first order of business was to request (as the Kremlin had demanded) formal incorporation into the Union of Soviet Socialist Republics, to which "request" the Supreme Soviet rendered quick confirmation for each Baltic country between August 3 and 6. A policy of economic nationalization was introduced. Meanwhile, mass deportations of Baltic people (including business leaders, landowners, and intellectuals, in addition to politicians and diplomats) to Siberia and the Soviet Arctic regions were begun officially on June 13, 1941. Western reaction to the Soviet occupation of 1940 was ambiguous, although it was officially protested by a number of countries. It was not solely the fact that these countries were preoccupied with the aggression of the Axis Powers that was the cause of this ambiguity. Western hostility toward the Soviet Union had been muted by an expectation that an alliance between Western powers and the Soviets potentially was possible.[7]

Nonetheless, none of the Western Allies nor any other countries appear to have recognized the Soviet incorporation of the Baltic states, so the Estonian, Latvian, and Lithuanian diplomatic missions abroad continued to function and represent their respective, and recently abolished, governments. This first period of Soviet annexation proved to be too brief for any meaningful action to be taken regarding these missions. Baltic diplomats apparently continued to function as they had prior to August 1940, although they operated, obviously, with no instructions from their respective former governments.

The Germans' surprise offensive against the Soviet Union on June 22, 1941, provided an opportunity for Estonian, Latvian, and Lithuanian nationalists to replace their Soviet–controlled puppet governments and restore a degree of political autonomy. While Nazi forces invaded the Baltic regions, provisional governments were established, particularly in Lithuania. It is unlikely that these provisional governments were able to engage in much, if any, contact with their respective diplomats or their missions abroad, since the situation was too fluid, and communications were too restricted, to allow these provisional governments to function effectively. The Germans initially were welcomed as liberators of the Baltic states (a reaction that occurred also in the Ukraine and Belarus), and there existed an expectation that the Nazis might allow autonomous governments to remain in place. However, Belarus and the Baltic region were reorganized into the German province of Ostland, although local and national level administrative units were maintained within these occupied countries. Therefore, the Baltic missions abroad continued to function without guidance from their respective homes.[8]

Nonetheless, the Soviet government continued to insist upon the legality of the previous acts of incorporation, thus claiming that the occupied Baltic states constituted occupied Soviet territory. It is not surprising, therefore, that many Estonians, Latvians, and Lithuanians were inclined to fight against the Soviets in much the same way that the Finnish government had allied itself with Germany and committed troops in support of Operation Barbarossa. The general population was opposed to German occupations, and many Baltic people actively resisted the Nazis. However, some Baltic nationals agreed to fight against the Soviets. Anti-Nazi guerrilla groups were formed throughout the region, and some of their efforts were successful in disrupting the German war effort. However, two Latvian and one Estonian Waffen-SS units also were formed, while thousands of Estonians joined their neighbors and fought the Soviets as part of the Finnish armed forces. Likewise, Baltic missions abroad strongly resisted Soviet claims made against them. It is understandable, therefore, that most of this diplomatic activity was directed against the Soviets rather than against the Germans. In fact, much of the attention of these missions would be occupied with a resistance to Soviet claims of both representation and the foreign assets that continued to be controlled by, or on behalf of, the three Baltic diplomatic services.[9]

No effective governments-in-exile appear to have been created during the war by any Baltic nationals, unlike many other occupied countries. Few political leaders escaped the invading forces of either the Soviet Union or Germany, which is understandable when the precarious geographical position of their countries is considered. Antanas Smetona, who had fled successfully to Germany, obviously was in no position to create an organized Lithuanian political structure. Therefore, Baltic missions abroad lacked guidance, as well as an official justification for existence. However, given the chaotic global situation that the World War II created, that fact assumed little significance in most capitals, especially among the Allied nations. Nonetheless, maintaining good relations between the Western Allies and the Soviet Union was a high priority among those countries that fought against the Axis Powers, and the conflicting claims of Baltic and Soviet diplomats often proved to be politically difficult.[10]

Resistance groups within the Baltic territories did manage to form provisional governments as the tide of the war turned against the Axis Powers. The Central Council of Latvia was formed on August 13, 1943. The creation of this institution was followed by the formation of the Supreme Committee for the Liberation of Lithuania on November 25, 1943, and the National Committee of the Estonian Republic on March 23, 1944. This last provisional government managed to establish contact with the outside world through Finnish sources and the government of Sweden, which remained neutral throughout the war. There is a lack of evidence that this provisional government communicated with Estonian diplomatic missions abroad. Nonetheless, it did represent, along with its Latvian and Lithuanian counterparts, a recognizable (especially among the Western Allies) political entity that could provide these missions with increased legitimacy.[11]

However, these provisional governments lacked time with which to establish themselves effectively. The Red Army managed to occupy much of the region by the fall of 1944, as the Nazis retreated, and their ultimate defeat became increasingly certain. As a member of the winning Allied coalition, the Soviet Union found itself in a position to maintain its dominance over the territory that it had liberated, especially since the region had been devastated by deportations, Nazi repressions, and prior Soviet deportations so effectively that it lost over a quarter of its population by the end of World War II. Therefore, the policies of incorporation and economic nationalization that had commenced prior to

Operation Barbarossa were renewed as soon as the last Nazi presence was destroyed, Baltic resistance was crushed, and Soviet political and administrative control was firmly reestablished.[12]

Josef Stalin's policy of establishing satellite states in Eastern Europe met with ineffective protests and political opposition from the Western Allies. In the case of the Baltic states, even the veneer of political independence was denied, since they had been reorganized as "republics" of the Soviet Union and controlled, almost directly, from Moscow. The economies of Estonia, Latvia, and Lithuania were centralized and urbanized, which resulted in a dramatic transformation that included the industrialization of this agrarian region by the late 1950s. Additional deportations occurred (especially between 1946 and 1953), while guerilla resistance was revived, especially in Lithuania, where it continued to fight Soviet rule until the early 1950s. A policy of "Russification" was instituted, which included the immigration of Russian workers, administrators, and professionals.[13]

The uneasy alliance between the Western Allies and the Soviet Union that had existed, by necessity, during World War II fell apart quickly following the cessation of hostilities in 1945. The creation of a Soviet sphere of control in Eastern Europe alarmed its suspicious former allies, and Western opposition to Soviet policies marked the beginning of the Cold War, which would divide the world, both politically and militarily, for over 45 years. Part of this Western opposition included the nonrecognition of the legitimacy of Soviet puppet states, as well as of the forced incorporation of the Baltic states.

This de facto incorporation was never effectively recognized by major Western powers and, in fact, the de jure independence of the Baltic states continued to be asserted (even if only as a legal fiction) by many of these countries.[14] This sort of opposition appeared to be largely symbolic, but it remained a component of Western Cold War strategy for the next four and a half decades. The most unusual manner in which this legal fiction was expressed was in terms of the continued recognition of the diplomatic missions of Estonia, Latvia, and Lithuania to several of these Western countries—especially the United States. This arrangement had not been unusual during World War II, since the diplomatic missions of many occupied countries (including countries as prominent as France) continued to function around the world throughout the conflict. However, these missions represented, for the most part, governments-in-exile; in any event, such an arrangement did not last beyond the end of the global conflict.

In the case of the Baltic states there were, after the war, neither independent countries nor governments (underground or in exile) for diplomatic missions to represent—just as they had been lacking during the war years, with the exception of the brief presence of the small resistance governments.[15] Therefore, diplomats serving the missions of Estonia, Latvia, and Lithuania continued to receive no instructions, were not subject to recall or new appointments, and represented no governments. Such an arrangement would appear to be, at the very least, a logical non sequitur—much like the concept of a political campaign with no party, candidate, ideas, or cause to present to an electorate. Certainly, the connection between a diplomatic mission and a represented government would appear to be, prima facie, so obvious that it is not surprising that international law, in general, or the Vienna Conventions, in particular, would neglect to address the legal and political implications of such an unlikely scenario. Yet, for over 40 years after the end of World War II, such a scenario was played out in the capitals and major cities of many Western countries, particularly the United States.

This unique situation raised interesting and difficult issues relating to international law, in general, and the laws governing diplomacy, in particular. Because of the unanticipated nature of the Baltic missions during the period of Soviet occupation, there is no specific guidance regarding these issues within the text of the Vienna Conventions, the Charter of the United Nations, or any other conventional source of public international law. Official and unofficial political and legal reactions to these missions varied from country to country, where their "validity" ultimately was determined and established. A consistent explanation and examination of this issue thus become confusing and difficult.

However, despite this diversity of interpretation, it is possible to facilitate this examination by classifying the responses of the international community under three headings: nonrecognition, recognition, and qualified extension of diplomatic privileges. These three approaches were adopted, in different ways, by various countries, but they are best represented by the policies of, respectively, the Soviet Union, the United States, and the United Kingdom. By examining each approach separately (especially from the perspective of the country that most prominently embraced it) it is possible to assess these conflicting interpretations of international law regarding these Baltic diplomatic missions. By doing so, it may be possible to assess the larger and historical implications that these missions have posed for diplomatic policy and international relations.

The Soviet Union, predictably, rejected the validity of the Baltic diplomatic missions, regardless of the place that they were established.

Soviet arguments upon the subject essentially emphasized the logical absurdity of a diplomatic mission that, in effect, represents "nothing." This emphasis is reinforced by an interpretation of conventions and treaties governing diplomacy that strongly implies, it is claimed, the necessary relationship between diplomatic missions and a tangible government or international organization.[16] However, despite any such implications, there have never existed any *formal* requirements regarding the status or existence of a sending state relative to its diplomatic mission.

This absence of a positive point of reference regarding this unique diplomatic situation made it difficult and seemingly bizarre to make a formal protest against such recognition. Nonetheless, objections obviously must have been raised frequently by the Soviet ambassador to the Court of St. James's, Ivan Maisky, during World War II—even if he did so, for the most part, informally. In fact, this situation is so unusual that descriptions of customary legal traditions regarding diplomatic relations within international law generally fail to address or anticipate it. Therefore, it is somewhat understandable that there is relatively little record of formal Soviet protests over the continued recognition of independent Baltic diplomatic missions, with the exception of attempts to acquire Estonian, Latvian, and Lithuanian funds held in foreign banks.

Two possible explanations are available regarding the apparent lack of formal interest in this issue by the Soviet government. The first reason may have related to a lack of importance placed by the Soviet government upon this issue. The second reason may have simply been an understandable lack of formal reaction to a situation that, by the standards of international law, was, prima facie, so absurd that it may well have seemed unnecessary (and perhaps even, from the Soviet perspective, counterproductive) to articulate formal objections toward it. The Cold War policies of all of the nations involved were so complex and, frequently, so surreal that this specific issue may have appeared to be, to many politicians, jurists, and foreign policy analysts, simply consistent with the post-war world of international relations.

Nonetheless, the Soviet position on this matter was made clear as early as 1942, when Ambassador Maisky addressed his concerns to the foreign secretary, Anthony Eden. In particular, he noted that the continued existence of diplomats and diplomatic missions representing the "former" independent Baltic states was clearly inconsistent with the widely accepted conventions of international law in that area.

> In the early part of 1942 the Soviet Ambassador (Monsieur Jean [Ivan] Maisky)

> drew the personal attention of the Foreign
> Secretary (Mr. Eden) to the continued
> inclusion of the names of the three Baltic
> Ministers in the Diplomatic List, and
> suggested that their retention was anomalous
> since the three countries which they
> purported to represent were in fact part of the
> Soviet Union and were not therefore capable
> of being separately represented at the Court
> of St. James's.[17]

It seems that particular emphasis was placed by the Soviet government upon the principle of "governmental effectiveness" in opposing the continued presence of the Baltic missions and their representatives, despite the policy of His Majesty's Government (as well as other Western governments) of refusing to recognize de jure the incorporation of Estonia, Latvia, and Lithuania into the Soviet Union. While the Soviet approach to this issue was both simple and unequivocal, the British approach was, obviously, more complicated and, therefore, more difficult to formulate, especially within the accepted rules and conventions of international law.[18]

This simple approach, as exemplified by the Soviet position on the issue, involved complete nonrecognition, so there are no interpretive difficulties regarding the extremely unusual (or, as the Soviet government regarded it, "anomalous") position of extending diplomatic privileges to representatives of governments that do not exist, even as governments-in-exile. Those countries that *did* extend such recognition offer two different approaches that can be broadly identified. These approaches generally were embraced because of foreign policy concerns and, in fact, reflect varying strategies regarding the Cold War. The first of these alternative approaches was, in this respect, the more circumspect of the two and can be best exemplified by the somewhat convoluted official policy of the British government toward the Baltic states and their "diplomatic representatives," as well as the frequently uncertain foreign policy of that government throughout the post-war era.

Great Britain was a member of the North Atlantic Treaty Organization and a Cold War ally of the United States, but the British Foreign Office often tried to position itself diplomatically between the "superpowers." Therefore, while the British government was willing to support policies that served to oppose the aggrandizement and expansion of Soviet power (especially within Europe), it also tried not to antagonize the Soviet Government, as it perceived the situation, unnecessarily.[19] Her

Majesty's Government went on record as opposing and officially refusing to recognize the annexation of the Baltic states by the Soviet Union, yet it also appeared to accept as reasonable a de facto recognition of the situation. The Foreign Office also seemed to address questions of diplomatic rules and protocol (and, arguably, international law, as a whole) from a rather parochial perspective. British officials appeared to be most comfortable when applying narrowly traditional constructions upon widely held conventions, as well as narrow interpretations of the letter of positive law guidelines, such as those rules found within the Vienna Convention.

On the other hand, British politicians also were sensitive to the political repercussions of a policy that might appear to contradict, or even undermine, the American response to this issue. Anthony Eden articulated this concern for his cabinet colleagues as early as 1942, while recommending the compromise that would form the basis of official British policy towards diplomats of the formerly independent Baltic republics.

> Since, however, the question of the recognition of the Soviet claims to the Baltic States in the proposed Treaty was at that time under discussion with President Roosevelt, and I did not wish to do anything that would complicate that discussion, I directed that the further issue of the Diplomatic List should be temporarily suspended. Its continued suspension is now beginning to cause considerable practical inconvenience. Since the conclusion of the Anglo-Soviet Treaty the matter has been mentioned again to M. Maisky, and he has made it clear that his Government still attach importance to the exclusion of the names of the three Baltic Ministers from the Diplomatic List.

> On the other hand, if their names and those of their staffs were to disappear entirely from the List at this moment, it would no doubt attract attention and might give rise to a suspicion in the United States and elsewhere that His Majesty's Government had, after all, reached some arrangement with the Soviet Government in regard to the Baltic States in connexion with the treaty negotiations.

> It is proposed therefore that the names of the three Ministers <u>and of their staffs</u> should no longer be included in the Diplomatic List itself but should be shown in an annex with the following heading:—
>> List of Persons no longer included in the foregoing List but still accepted by His Majesty's Government as possessing a diplomatic character.[20]

This approach would constitute the official British policy on this issue, but it was still subject to serious reconsideration well after the end of World War II. The British concern for technical conformity with international law, as well as consistency with diplomatic precedents, are evident in a Foreign Office note on the subject. G. G. Fitzmaurice advised prudence regarding any affirmation or reformulation of British foreign policy toward Baltic diplomats and missions.

> I think a little further research into the precedents should be attempted before we make up our minds what to do about this. It occurs to me for instance, that a somewhat similar situation must have existed during the period before the war when we had recognized <u>de facto</u> Italian sovereignty over Ethiopia but still recognized the Emperor as the <u>de jure</u> sovereign and still continued to have relations with him. How did we treat the Ethiopian Minister in London during that time?[21]

Fitzmaurice also raised the precedent of the British-recognized diplomatic representatives of the Republican Government of Spain following the fascist victory during the Spanish Civil War, which the British Government recognized de facto. Both of these precedents, however, provide examples of a recognition of diplomatic missions that represented governments-in-exile—a fact that Fitzmaurice acknowledged might leave the Foreign Office with no precedents to offer guidance.[22] This suspicion was confirmed by the requested research note on the subject,[23] and it led to Charles H. Bateman's formulation of a recommendation that would become the British Foreign Office policy regarding the Baltic diplomats, the diplomatic list, and the general problem of the recognition of the Soviet annexation of Estonia, Latvia, and Lithuania.

> It is a choice of evils. It is untidy to have a Sheriff's List consisting only of the 1942 list as subsequently amended; it is illogical, and apparently of doubtful legality, to retain on the Sheriff's List men who no longer represent any authority recognised by us and who therefore cannot be said to have any genuine diplomatic function. But this has been going on for 8 years without causing us more than a little mild inconvenience.
>
> If we strike the Balts off either the Sheriff's List or the Diplomatic List, there will certainly be questions about it in the House of Commons and we shall be accused, here and in the United States, of appeasing the Russians.
>
> I therefore recommend that we should let sleeping dogs lie. The problem will solve itself in the course of time and we can reconsider the position if it leads to serious embarrassment.
>
> The moral is, of course, always recognise de jure at once; anything else only leads to more and more trouble.[24]

That continuing policy that Bateman mentioned provided that the Baltic missions would not be recognized, but the diplomatic privileges of those representatives who had been appointed by the Estonian, Latvian, and Lithuanian governments prior to 1940 would continue to be honored. It is significant to note, once again, the British preoccupation with the issue of legality according to the strict interpretation of treaty rules (even where such rules are vague or silent) and accepted conventions of international law in the area of diplomacy and diplomatic representation. The American State Department seemed to find that this problem posed much less of an obstacle to its policies regarding the Baltic states.

British interpretations of international law regarding diplomacy have not always been clear on such issues. One interpretation has concluded that the de facto recognition of the extinction of the sending government or of the entire sending state should be sufficient to warrant the receiving of new diplomatic representatives and the dismissal of the former ones. That interpretation guided the British response to the issue of recognizing the diplomatic missions of the constantly changing French governments during the various phases of the French Revolution, as well as to the issue of dismissing the diplomatic missions of the Kingdom of the Two Sicilies after that country was absorbed by the emerging Kingdom of Italy in 1860.[25] But it also has been asserted that "[u]ntil the recognition of a new Government by H. M. Government no representative of the former can be received as its official representative."[26] That interpretation guided the British government's policy regarding its initial refusal to receive the diplomatic representatives of the Empire of Brazil in 1824, since Britain had not yet recognized the overthrow of Portuguese colonial rule. It also guided the Court of Chancery when it refused to allow the secretary of legation for the Kingdom of Spain to plead diplomatic privilege during Chancery proceedings in 1874, since the British government officially recognized the new Spanish Republic that had replaced the abdicated King Amadeus.[27]

Another issue motivating British policy in this area involved the presence of Estonian, Latvian, and Lithuanian funds deposited with the Bank of England. In 1940, the Latvian head of mission, Kārlis Zariņš, informed the Foreign Office of the source of Latvian funds present in the United Kingdom and inquired anxiously whether or not the legation would be free to dispose of them. This money included public funds provided by the former Latvian government and private funds invested in Latvian commercial enterprises, although these enterprises also had been largely government–owned.[28]

Foreign Office correspondence regarding Zariņš' request reveals uncertainty regarding the long-term disposition of these Latvian and other Baltic funds frozen within the United Kingdom, especially since it remained uncertain whether or not Britain ultimately would recognize the Soviet annexation of the Baltic states. It generally was felt that such controversies should be left to the courts, although it also was agreed that the Latvian (and, presumably, the Estonian and Lithuanian) Legation could continue to draw upon these funds in order to cover administrative costs and to settle outstanding debts of the Latvian government that remained owed to British companies.[29]

By 1950, this issue regarding frozen Baltic assets had still not been resolved. A tersely handwritten response to opinions, which had been previously expressed by Bateman and other persons regarding the Baltic missions and diplomats explained that the British Government literally could not *afford* to recognize the Soviet annexation de jure, and that this fact would continue to guide official British policy regarding both the Baltic diplomats and the frozen Baltic assets.

> The principal, but not by any means the only, reason [for the continued presence of Baltic diplomats in the diplomatic list] is that gold belonging to governments of the three [Baltic] states is deposited with the Bank of England. If HMG [His Majesty's Government] were to recognise the absorption de jure, this gold would be claimed by, and would have to be paid to, the Gov't [government] of the USSR. In point of fact, the Russians have claimed it.
>
> HMG has no intention of releasing the gold in question (it has been tentatively earmarked for the eventual compensation of BSS who lost property in the three countries owing to Russian action) & it follows that de jure recognition is not a possibility.
>
> Moreover, the Ministers of the three countries in London perform unpaid functions for us & relieve us of much trouble in connexion with ships & seamen of their various nationalities in so far as these still operate outside the Russian orbit. Indeed, the Ministers partly subsist on the fees derived from these services.
>
> One further point. When Mr. Eden directed that the names of the three Ministers & their staffs should be struck off the diplomatic list, he was anxious to please the Russians who were then our allies in war.[30]

These funds remained an important asset for both the British Government and the Baltic representatives because de jure recognition of the Soviet annexation of Estonia, Latvia, and Lithuania was not forthcoming. But many involved parties were concerned that this arrangement could be undermined by the courts, especially since Parliament did not provide any specific guidance in this area. All policies dealing with the Baltic states and their diplomatic representatives resulted from executive orders of the cabinet or were internally developed by the Foreign Office. There is evidence relating to the expenditures of Baltic diplomatic missions in Britain.[31] However, specific and tangible evidence relating to the source of these funds often, understandably, is lacking.

Successive British governments never entirely resolved this issue. They hoped, apparently, that the problem eventually would disappear. The fact that government policy on this issue never was laid before Parliament indicates also the concerns of British officials that British courts may overrule the informal policies that did exist; without legislative sanction, judges would be guided by their understanding of common and international law, rather than the commands of parliamentary supremacy.[32] In fact, nearly the only occasions when government policy on the Baltic states was raised at all in Parliament (even during the war) occurred during "question period" in the House of Commons. These evasive exchanges in the Commons reflected the British Government's avoidance of making any *official* commitment regarding the Baltic states (including the disposition and status of their diplomatic representatives), especially in comparison with the more definitive American position on these issues.[33]

These compromises continued to guide British policy toward the representatives of the former Baltic states in a seemingly ad hoc manner. Since this policy did not permit the replacement of these representatives, it was hoped that this awkward situation simply would disappear when these diplomats retired or died. By the time that independence was reestablished in Estonia, Latvia, and Lithuania, only one of these original diplomats remained. K. A. Neil of the Foreign and Commonwealth Office's Soviet Department noted that the eventual death of this final representative (Vincas Balickas) would have "solved" this difficulty for Her Majesty's Government.[34] The fact that Mr. Balickas remained to become Lithuanian ambassador to the Court of St. James's following the restoration of that country's independence was a result that nobody seriously anticipated.

This compromise position enabled the restored Lithuanian Government to reestablish full diplomatic relations with the United Kingdom with an easier transition than for the other two Baltic states. It also provided a politically favorable position for the British Government in its relationship with these newly independent states—not only of the Baltic region but, arguably, throughout Eastern Europe. Britain's refusal to recognize the annexation of the Baltic states de jure continued to have a tangible symbol in the person of Vincas Balickas and the diplomatic privileges that were still extended to him. This fact originally may have been an awkward and, for some members of the Foreign Office, annoying anomaly, but it probably proved to be a policy that enhanced Britain's image among former Soviet–dominated states with relatively little political or financial cost. It certainly seemed to be, with hindsight, a much simpler position than the one taken by the United States.

The American position on the Baltic states was much more rigidly anti-Soviet than the British position; it reflected the more polarized image of international relations that the United States adopted throughout the Cold War. The American Department of State not only refused to recognize the annexation of the Baltic states de jure, but it also refused to do it de facto. This approach resulted in an unusual interpretation of international law as it related to diplomatic rules and conventions—one that appeared to be vindicated through the unexpected collapse of the Soviet Union and the restoration of independent governments in Estonia, Latvia, and Lithuania. Officially, successive American administrations confirmed the tradition of embracing a "reverse monist" approach to international law and generally asserted that municipal (also known as "domestic") law, or domestic interpretations *of* international law, superseded attempts to impose "universal" interpretations of international law upon a particular society's municipal law and legal principles. Diplomatic status is determined, under a "reverse monist" approach, by the host government.

The American Government not only continued to extend diplomatic privileges to the representatives of the Baltic states but it also allowed their respective diplomatic missions to remain functioning. They functioned as "legations," as they had been called prior to World War II, rather than as "embassies" (in the case of Estonia, there was merely a "consul general in charge of legation"), so this designation placed them at the bottom of the formal order of precedence within the diplomatic corps in Washington.[35] The nature of this continued American diplomatic recognition of the Baltic missions aroused some concern among the United States' NATO allies, particularly the British. Western European governments remained opposed to the Warsaw Pact and to Soviet foreign policy, but they remained cautious about unnecessarily antagonizing the Soviet government.

Indeed, British foreign policy (especially on this issue) often seemed to attempt a mediation of the conflict between the two superpowers in order to appease the dangerous ambitions of both sides. This feeling of being "caught in the middle" possibly provided the strongest motivation for Britain's compromise policy toward the diplomatic representatives of the Baltic states. However, attempts by the

British, and other, governments to persuade the United States of the wisdom of this policy were unsuccessful. The American policy must have appeared to be especially frustrating to many other countries, since it endorsed the recognition of diplomatic missions that apparently represented "nothing."

This frustration was apparent when Latvian representatives attempted to replace one of their own colleagues. The Latvian government issued a directive on May 17, 1940, that conferred "emergency power" upon Kārlis Zariņš. The nature of this power was enumerated (it included responsibility for Latvian assets and nationals abroad), but its scope was vague. It is not explicitly clear whether or not diplomatic appointments were intended to be included within that scope, although it certainly could be inferred from that document.[36] Zariņš issued a 1954 communiqué that informed the diplomatic world of the death of Alfreds Bīlmanis, who had been minister in Washington and whom the directive of 1940 had designated as being Zariņš' deputy and successor. Zariņš' interpretation of that directive led him to assert his power to appoint additional diplomatic representatives abroad.   Therefore, he appointed, through the communiqué, Dr. Arnolds Spekke to succeed Alfreds Bīlmanis as Zariņš' deputy and the eventual successor to the position of having general responsibility for exercising the "emergency powers" conferred upon Zariņš by the Latvian Government that had been abolished by the invading Soviets in 1940.[37]

The American State Department apparently accepted these appointments without much notice, but the British Foreign Office was not so accommodating. A confidential telegram was sent to the British ambassador in Washington from the Foreign Office. This telegram made explicit the Foreign Office's position on this matter and the entire issue of diplomatic representation from the formerly independent Baltic states.

> You should not enter into 'official relations' with Dr. Spekke since he represents a country which we regard as having, for the time being, no independent existence as a Sovereign State and with which we are not therefore in Diplomatic Relations.
>
> You should therefore avoid any official diplomatic dealings with him and should not reply to his letter. It would be quite in order to explain [this] position to him informally

and there is naturally no objection to your
cultivating his acquaintance socially.[38]

This position was consistent with the British approach to Soviet
relations during, and after, World War II. The Foreign Office had feared
that the Soviets might negotiate a separate truce with the Nazis, despite
the latter country's violation of the nonaggression pact made between
Hitler and Stalin. British officials also were concerned regarding a
perceived insensitivity to the historic security concerns that preoccupied
the Soviet Government and society. This cautious approach continued to
guide British foreign policy during the years immediately following the
war, especially regarding European issues and relations between the United
Kingdom and the emerging "superpowers" of the post-war world.[39]

The American State Department assumed a different perspective
on these controversial issues. John Foster Dulles received a letter from
Kārlis Zariņš in response to Foggy Bottom's apparently favorable reaction
to the diplomatic replacement of the late Jūlijs Feldmans with Dr. Arnolds
Spekke as chargé d'affaires of the Latvian Legation in Washington (as
already noted, Spekke was also designated to replace Alfreds Bīlmanis as
Zariņš' deputy and successor for exercising "emergency powers"), contrary
to the position of Her Majesty's Foreign Office. The tone of the letter to
Secretary of State Dulles offers an insight into the very different approach
to the issue of Baltic diplomatic representation that was assumed by the
American Government. The American approach seems to have been
particularly audacious when compared with the more guarded, parochial,
and skeptical attitude adopted by the British government.

> The Latvians suffered a great loss in the death
> of Minister Julijs Feldmans, my appointment
> of whom as Chargé d'Affaires at Washington
> (by virtue of my Special Power from the
> Latvian National Government) the State
> Department were so good as to agree to, in
> March 1949.
>
> The State Department have expressed the
> wish that, to replace Mr. Feldmans, there
> should be a resident chief of mission of
> ministerial rank; and that besides being
> possessed of the necessary energy and
> initiative, he should be generally acceptable
> to the Latvian homeland, the Latvian
> diplomatic service, the Latvian emigration

> and to Americans of Latvian descent. The
> State Department's deep interest in this
> appointment has been very gratifying to me,
> and, after having given concentrated
> consideration to the choice, I have concluded
> that the most suitable man would be
> Professor Arnolds Spekke. It is known to me
> with exactitude that the homeland would
> learn of Professor Spekke's appointment with
> warm appreciation, and among Latvians
> abroad I anticipate that the reception would
> be generally most favorable. I already have
> proof of his acceptability from colleagues and
> other quarters.[40]

The United States also was accommodating in the area of financial support for the Baltic missions. For example, the American Government not only froze Latvian assets within the United States and prevented the Soviet government from seizing them, yet it made these assets easily available to the Latvian Legation in Washington. Latvian diplomatic representatives in the United States were able to draw funds from the interest that accrued upon $23 million in gold that was held by the Treasury of the United States and, unlike the arrangement with the Bank of England, there were no apparent restrictions upon the use of this money by the Latvian Legation, including support of social, cultural, and political activities of the larger American community of Latvian expatriates.[41]

A similar situation existed for the Lithuanian Legation, with frozen assets being used to fund diplomatic salaries, a Lithuanian Information Center, summer camps, language schools, and other cultural and political activities.[42] However, despite the existence of these relationships, no *formal* association between these groups and the Lithuanian Legation existed, especially regarding political organizations such as the Supreme Committee for the Liberation of Lithuania.[43] This lack of a formal connection was imposed, in part, in order to avoid the impression that these organizations represented an actual Lithuanian government-in-exile. This legation had received its credentials from the Lithuanian government that was illegally overthrown during World War II, so it was crucial to assert its continued legitimacy in order to support the theoretical legitimacy of these Lithuanian diplomats and their respective missions.[44] Should "new" Lithuanian governments emerge, they could undermine this unique diplomatic situation, which, arguably, was more effective in promoting the cause of Baltic freedom (since it invoked formal recognition among those Western powers that allowed these missions to be maintained) than the claims of a non-elected government-in-exile.[45] Furthermore, it probably was wise for these missions to avoid taking sides, should competing Lithuanian liberation organizations emerge.

On the other hand, no such funds seemed to be available for support of the mission of the Estonian consul general at New York in charge of legation. This diplomatic mission was funded, after 1940, through private donations and business interests in the New York area in which the consul general, Ernst Jaakson, had maintained an involvement.[46] Even after the restoration of independence, the Estonian Consulate General continued to fund itself through the sale of visas, donations, and other private means, since the newly reestablished Estonian Central Council lacked the financial resources to fund that mission or to establish immediately an embassy in Washington.[47] Estonia seemingly always has lacked substantial assets within the United States (although its mission in London reportedly was subsidized by the British government, at one point), and it has grown accustomed to functioning without them.[48]

The political and legal difficulties involved in formulating any reasonable plan for replenishing the "dwindling" diplomatic presence of the Baltic states probably dissuaded the Carter administration from implementing specific proposals in this area. The Reagan and George H. W. Bush administrations offered no indication that they intended to address this issue either, although their respective foreign policy records suggest that they were more confrontational toward the Soviet Union and less concerned about international law and its interpretation than the Carter administration had been.[49] Nonetheless, the United States remained committed to the general principle of preserving an independent Baltic diplomatic presence throughout the period of Soviet incorporation. The reemergence of these independent republics made all previous legal controversies regarding the Baltic missions moot, while their continued presence facilitated the transition to full and effective diplomatic representation on the part of the Baltic states within the United States.

The contrast between the American and British interpretations of international law reflect their different approaches to diplomatic issues and their different attitudes toward the Soviet Union, the Warsaw Pact, and the Cold War. The United Kingdom perceived itself as caught between two warring superpowers. While it sided with its American allies, the British government often sought "to carve its own niche" within the post-war world. While wishing to support the principle of self-determination, it also wished to promote better relations with the Soviet government, whose military and political position posed a much closer concern to

Britain and the rest of Europe than it could possibly pose to Americans. The awkward compromise position that the British Foreign Office assumed toward Baltic diplomatic representatives reflected that desire to pursue, whenever possible, a "middle path" between the "superpowers" while remaining true to its broad political obligations to its NATO allies. It was a typically cautious policy on the part of the British government.[50]

The aggressive response of the United States toward recognizing and maintaining the Baltic diplomatic presence reflected that country's confrontational approach to the Soviet Union and the Cold War. Domestic attitudes regarding democratic ideals and the perceived threat posed by "world communism" prompted foreign policies that often were uncompromising in their methods and goals. It should not be surprising that the State Department appeared to be less concerned with the international law implications of maintaining the presence of the Baltic missions and also less concerned about the disposition of Baltic assets frozen by the Treasury Department than were their British counterparts. It was a pattern that would differentiate the foreign policy behavior of these two NATO allies, even though their long-term goals essentially were the same.[51]

The American policy in this area certainly was audacious in its methods and clear in its purpose, and it reflected a single-mindedness that was indicative of the broader approach that it assumed toward the Soviet Union, the Warsaw Pact, and the Cold War. It was a policy that was reaffirmed, even within the context of the conclusion of the Helsinki Accord between the two superpowers that appeared to acknowledge the Soviet sphere of influence in Eastern Europe.[52] Gerald Ford and his administration issued an official statement, that reiterated American nonrecognition of the Soviet annexation of the Baltic states, in order to counter speculation to the contrary following the signing of the Helsinki Accord.[53] A few years later, Congress reinforced that sentiment by directing the President to declare February 16, 1983, as "Lithuanian Independence Day."[54] The relatively aggressive American policy on this issue remained in place until the time that the independence of the Baltic states was restored. That fact was most notably evident in terms of the continued support of successive American administrations for the diplomatic missions of those separate countries.

This support proved to be a cornerstone of arguably the most unusual episode of modern diplomatic history. The absence of staunch American support for Estonian, Latvian, and Lithuanian diplomats and their missions in the United States and, indirectly, in other countries probably would have made their respective claims meaningless. The mere fact of the inclusion of these representatives in the American *Diplomatic List* established a level of legitimacy that was nearly impossible to ignore, completely. The Soviet Union never could overcome entirely this obstacle in asserting its absolute claims to the Baltic states. Other former Soviet republics managed to assert their independence, despite the absence of such external symbols and working institutions that could promote their own claims to sovereignty. But their transitions to independence would lack the quick and smooth resurrection in the area of foreign relations which the Baltic missions offered their respective governments. The United States Government secured for itself an inestimable amount of good will in that region of Eastern Europe, which could prove to bring lasting benefits for its own foreign policy.

Perhaps the most important legacy of Baltic diplomacy during this period was its effect upon international law. Modern history has included numerous records of national movements that have attempted to find notable expression. It is possible that the diplomatic experience of Estonia, Latvia, and Lithuania from 1940 to 1991 offers a model that other former states, national groups, or aspiring peoples could emulate. However, in order to evaluate the significance of this development, it is necessary to appreciate the obstacles of international law and legal theory, as well as the power politics of international relations that these diplomats and the missions they maintained were forced to handle.

Notes

1.   The Nazi–Soviet Nonaggression Pact, which was reached by the senior German diplomat Joachim von Ribbentrop and Soviet Foreign Commissar Vyacheslav Molotov, had great significance for the rest of the world, as well as for the Baltic states. It is reproduced, with comments regarding its consequences for Baltic (particularly Lithuanian) history and politics, in Bronis J. Kaslas, ed., *The USSR–German Aggression against Lithuania* (New York: Robert Speller and Sons, 1973), pp. 343–370; A classic account of the general implications of this pact is provided in Sir Winston S. Churchill, *The Second World War* (Boston: Houghton Mifflin, 1948), vol. I, pp. 389–397.

2.   Romuald J. Misiunas and Rein Taagepera, *The Baltic States: Years of Dependence, 1940–1980* (Berkeley: University of California Press, 1983), pp. 13–17.

3.   Clarence A. Manning, *The Forgotten Republics* (Westport, CT: Greenwood Press, 1971), pp. 206–212. These events and their implications were noted in a report to the German Foreign Office, reproduced in Kaslas, ed., pp. 117–118.

4.   William R. Trotter, *A Frozen Hell* (Chapel Hill, NC: Algonquin Books, 1991), pp. 206–212, 263–270.

5.   Misiunas and Taagepera, pp. 18–20.

6.   Alfonsas Eidintas, "The Meeting of the Lithuanian Cabinet, 15 June 1940," in *The Baltic and the Outbreak of the Second World War*, John Hiden and Thomas Lane, eds. (Cambridge: Cambridge University Press, 1992), pp. 165–173; Leonas Sabaliūnas, *Lithuania in Crisis* (Bloomington: Indiana University Press, 1972), pp. 185–188.

7.   Misiunas and Taagepera, pp. 20–29.

8.   Documents relating to the German "liberation" and the activities of the respective provisional governments of the Baltic states are reproduced, with editorial comments and explanations, in Kaslas, pp. 343-370.

9.   Misiunas and Taagepera, pp. 47–68.

10.   Misiunas and Taagepera, pp. 121–123;   Izidors Vizulis, *The Molotov–Ribbentrop Pact of 1939: The Baltic Case* (Westport, CT: Praeger, 1990), pp. 51–61.

11.   August Rei, *The Drama of the Baltic Peoples* (Stockholm: Vaba Eesti, 1970), pp. 334–336; Vizulis, pp. 39–41.

12.   Manning, pp. 230–238.

13.   V. Stanley Vardys, "The Partisan Movement in Postwar Lithuania," in *Lithuania under the Soviets*, V. Stanley Vardys, ed. (New York: Praeger, 1965), pp. 85–108; Vizulis, pp. 63–77.

14.   Georg von Rauch, *The Baltic States: Years of Independence*, Gerald Onn, trans. (Berkeley: University of California Press, 1974), pp. 227–234.

15.   A request by Latvian officials to come to Great Britain and establish a government-in-exile there during the war was denied for fear of antagonizing the Soviet government, as reported in Conversation of Laurence Collier, British Foreign Office, with Kārlis Zariņš, Latvian Minister to London, London, September 12, 1940, FO371/24761-N6581/1224/59.

    A letter from a British diplomat in Oslo, W. Barker, reported the "recasting" of an Estonian government-in-exile, with headquarters in Stockholm, including a list of cabinet ministers representing various political parties of pre-war Estonia. This list presumably included members of the Estonian Cabinet in 1940, particularly the Estonian vice president, August Rei, who officially made these appointments, as recorded in Oslo, February 11, 1953, letter from W. Barker to H.A.F. Hohler, Northern Department, Foreign Office, FO371/106114-NB1821/4G, Secret. However, no other reference to a government-in-exile among Estonian diplomats, Baltic scholars, or British and American documents appears to exist, and any indication that Estonian diplomatic representatives received instructions from these officials also is not readily available.

16.   This sort of arrangement, for example, is regarded as logically necessary if the immunity of a diplomatic representative, acting in the capacity of a "personal" representative of a recognizable head of state, is acknowledged and protected, as noted in Grant V. McClanahan, *Diplomatic Immunity* (New York: St. Martin's Press, 1989), pp. 18–43.

17.   London, April 12, 1950, "Note on the Position of the Representatives of the Former Baltic States," Treaty Department, British Foreign Office, FO372/7063-T107/1903/1.

18.   However, it has been noted that the continued recognition of these diplomats by British authorities could have been interpreted as a tacit legal acceptance of Baltic "governments-in-exile" in spirit, if not in reality, by the British government, in "Phantom Governments Carry on in Britain, *Wall Street Journal*, December 9, 1970, 1:4.

19.   Sir David Kelley, "British Diplomacy," in *Diplomacy in a Changing World*, Stephen D. Kertesz and M. A. Fitzsimons, eds. (Westport, CT: Greenwood Press, 1974), pp. 195–203.

20.   London, June 27, 1942, memorandum by the Secretary of State for Foreign Affairs, "Representatives of the Baltic States," FO371/32735-N3447/G, Secret.

21.   London, May 3, 1950, minute by G. G. Fitzmaurice, Foreign Office, FO372/7063-T107/1903/1.

22.   London, May 3, 1950, minute by G. G. Fitzmaurice, Foreign Office, FO372/7063-T107/1903/1.

23.   London, May 31, 1950, minute by G. G. Fitzmaurice, Foreign Office, FO372/7063-T107/1903/1.

24.   London, June 1, 1950, minute by Charles H. Bateman, FO 372/7063-T107/1903/1.

25.   Clive Parry and Sir Gerald Fitzmaurice, eds., *A British Digest of International Law* (London: Stevens and Sons, 1965), part VII, pp. 642, 647–649.

26.   Parry and Fitzmaurice, part VII, p. 650.

27.   Parry and Fitzmaurice, part VII, pp. 650–651.

28.   London, September 12, 1940, Aide Memoire of September 11, 1940 from Kārlis Zariņš, Latvian minister to London, to Sir William Malkin, Foreign Office, FO371/24761-N6581/1224/59.

29.   London, September 21, 1940, letter of October 29, 1940 from Treasury Office to the undersecretary of state, Foreign Office, London, and letter of November 8, 1940, from Laurence Collier, Foreign Office, to Kārlis Zariņš, Latvian minister to London, FO371/24761-N6581/1224/59.

30.   London, June 1, 1950, Foreign Office minute FO372/7063-T107/1903/1.

31.   An example is provided in London, [1921], "Salaries Allotted to Lithuanian Representatives Abroad for Themselves and Their Staffs," FO371/6739-N13939/13939/59.

32.   However, leading precedents would seem to indicate strongly that English (and, most likely, Scottish) courts are guided by decisions of the cabinet regarding issues of diplomatic status, even if Parliament has not had the issue of the recognition of a particular state or government laid before it, Parry and Fitzmaurice, part VII, pp. 642–651.

33.   The brief exchange between Commander Sir Archibald Southby and Anthony Eden offers an example of the latter official refusing to give direct answers to the former official regarding the government's policy towards the Soviet annexation of the Baltic states, in *Debates of the House of Commons* [Hansard], January 17, 1945, ll. 136-137. Between 1940 and 1955, the question of the Baltic states was raised only a few times, and each occasion usually was the result of a brief and (from the government benches) noncommittal exchange during question period.

34.   Correspondence from K. A. Neil, Soviet Department, Foreign and Commonwealth Office, March 12, 1986.

35.   Estonia's diplomatic mission in the United States was headed by the consul general in New York, rather than from a legation in Washington. Estonia's diplomatic representatives reportedly chose to focus their efforts upon the lobbying of diplomats from various countries at the United Nations, rather than just focusing upon the American government, as reported in McHugh interview with Ernst Jaakson, Consul General of Estonia at New York City in charge of Legation, November 1982.

36.   This document is reproduced in Arturs Bērziņš, *Kārlis Zariņš: Dzīvē un Darbā* (London: Ruja, 1959), p. 226. An English translation of this document can be found in "Third Interim Report of the House of Representatives Select Committee on Communist Aggression, 83rd Congress, 2nd Session" (Washington, DC: U. S. Government Printing Office, 1954), p. 433.

37.   London, May, 1954, statement of Dr. Kārlis Zariņš, Latvian minister to London, FO371/111382-NB1901/9.

38.   London, June 10, 1954, British Foreign Office to British Embassy to the United States, FO371/111382-NB1901/5, No. 2688, confidential.

39.   Lawrence Juda, "United States' Nonrecognition of the Soviet Union's Annexation of the Baltic States: Politics and Law", *Journal of Baltic Studies*, 6, no. 4 (Winter 1975), pp. 274–276.

40.   London, February 16, 1954, letter from Dr.Kārlis Zariņš, Latvian minister in London, to John Foster Dulles, United States Secretary of State, FO371/111382-NB1901/1.

41.   McHugh interview with Ojars Kalnins, Political and Press Officer, Latvian Embassy, Washington, March 15, 1992. Kalnins was named Latvian ambassador to the United States on April 14, 1993.

42.   McHugh interview with Stasys Backis, Lithuanian chargé d'affaires in Washington, November 1982; McHugh interview with Victor Nakas, political and press officer, Lithuanian embassy, Washington, March 16, 1992. It is likely that this funding also was used in support of The Lithuanian American Community, which is an organization located in Glenside, Pennsylvania that published a scholarly annual report, entitled *The Violations of Human Rights in Soviet Occupied Lithuania*, from 1971 until the final collapse of the Soviet Union.

43.   This organization issued statements to, and corresponded with, other governments and political organizations, as did other Lithuanian officials and organizations in exile. However, they did it separately from the Lithuanian legation in Washington and other diplomatic representatives, so they remained independent from each other. Examples of these communications and activities (including appeals to the United Nations) can be found in Kaslas, pp. 394–416.

44.   McHugh interview with Stasys Backis, chargé d'affaires in Washington, November 1982; McHugh interview with Victor Nakas, political and press officer, Lithuanian embassy, Washington, March 16, 1992.

45.   An exchange between H. A. F. Hohler of the Foreign Office's Northern Department and the Latvian minister in London, Kārlis Zariņš, alluded to this possible consequence of the undermining of Baltic diplomatic missions in the event of the establishment of Baltic governments-in-exile, London, February 12, 1953, FO371/106114-NB1821/4.

46.   McHugh interview with Ernst Jaakson, consul general of Estonia at New York in charge of legation, New York, November 1982.

47.   McHugh interview with Okke Metsmaa, vice consul of Estonia at New York, March 16, 1992.

48.   H. A. F. Hohler of the British Foreign Office's Northern Department implied that Estonian representatives and activists throughout Britain and the rest of Europe needed to be similarly self-reliant, in London, February 12, 1953, FO371/106114-NB1821/4.

49.   Daniel Madar, *The End of Containment?* (Toronto: Canadian Institute of International Affairs, 1989), pp. 6–9.

50.   A discussion of this general British strategy towards foreign policy can be found in Geoffrey McDermott, *The Eden Legacy* (London: Leslie Frewin, 1969), pp. 95–104, and Keith Robbins, *The Eclipse of a Great Power* (London: Longman, 1983), pp. 172–181.

51.   An example of this American approach to foreign policy is offered in William G. Hyland, *The Cold War* (New York: Random House, 1991), pp. 42-56, and George F. Kennan, *Measures Short of War*, Giles D. Harlow and George C. Maerz, eds. (Washington, DC: National Defense University Press, 1991), pp. 295–318.

52.   Walter C. Clemens, Jr., *Baltic Independence and Russian Empire* (New York: St. Martin's Press, 1991), pp. 298–299.

53.   Bill Anderson, "Ford Assures Baltics: No U.S. Sellout," *Chicago Tribune*, July 29, 1975, sec. 2, 2:3; James McNaughton, "Ford Sees 35-Nation Charter as Gauge on Rights in East Europe," *New York Times*, July 26, 1975, 2:3.

54.   "Joint Resolution of the Senate and the House of Representatives to Direct the President to Issue a Proclamation Designating February 16, 1983 as 'Lithuanian Independence Day,'" (Washington, DC: U. S. Government Printing Office, 1983), H.J. Res. 60.

Chapter 6

The Canadian Response

The approach of most countries to the diplomatic anomaly posed by the continued presence of Estonian, Latvian, and Lithuanian missions was determined, in large part, by considerations raised within the broader context of international relations, particularly within the context of the Cold War. However, domestic political considerations (especially issues related to the values and principles formally embraced by these societies) also could present a decisive consideration regarding the recognition of Baltic diplomats following the end of World War II. Canada offers a good example of a country that was motivated by both influences, as well as by its own history as a former colonial possession, an immigrant nation, and an emerging industrial power.

Canada's initial recognition of the Baltic states occurred as a result of Britain's post–World War I foreign policy. Although it had made a significant contribution to the Allied victory in that war, Canada remained a formal part of the British Empire. However, it possessed "dominion" status within the imperial system, so Canada exercised sovereignty within its domestic affairs and policies. Meanwhile, the imperial government in Westminster continued to maintain its control over foreign affairs and policies on behalf of Canada and the other "dominions." Therefore, once the United Kingdom extended diplomatic recognition to Estonia, Latvia, and Lithuania, this recognition extended to Canada, automatically.[1] But Canada's progress as a nation-state and its emergence as a growing economic, political, and military power (especially in terms of its contribution to the war effort) indicated that this continued imperial relationship was not destined to last. By 1926, the British government recognized the equal status of the dominions as fellow independent countries; by 1931, the British Parliament's passage of the Statute of Westminster formalized this recognition.[2]

Canada continued to honor the diplomatic obligations that previously had been undertaken, on its behalf, through the British Empire, despite these relatively rapid changes in Canada's international status. Therefore, Canada continued to extend diplomatic recognition to the Baltic states. This recognition did not entail much activity on the part of the Canadian government, since there had been no Baltic diplomatic missions established in the capital of Ottawa (although Baltic consular officials occasionally had been sent, especially to Toronto), and no Canadian missions (independent of the British missions that formerly had overseen Canadian interests) had been established within Estonia, Latvia, or Lithuania.[3]

Baltic governments had conducted formal diplomatic activities toward Canada through their respective missions in London prior to the late 1920s. However, the establishment of a completely sovereign Canadian foreign policy shifted responsibility for Canadian issues from Baltic diplomats in London to the Baltic missions established within the United States. This change reflected both Canada's separation from its formal ties to the British Empire and a more profound alteration of its foreign policy perspective away from European concerns and toward more immediate North American ones.[4] Traditional and sentimental ties with Great Britain would remain important to Canada (especially in terms of its membership and participation within that association of Britain and its former colonies known as the Commonwealth of Nations), but, despite a history of antagonism and distrust regarding the United States (including a traditional fear of American military and economic expansion and domination), Canada was beginning to identify its broad foreign policy aims as increasingly tied to American perspectives and interests.[5]

Therefore, Canada's diplomatic relationship with the Baltic states, which was initiated by the British, began to resemble the American approach toward this region of the world. This fact became increasingly clear during World War II, when the United States, Great Britain, and Canada found themselves, once again, as allies engaged within a global struggle. The Canadian government continued its de jure recognition of the formerly independent states of Estonia, Latvia, and Lithuania, both during and after the conclusion of the Second World War. This fact was explained in a statement that had been provided in response to inquiries that had been made upon the subject at the end of 1952.

[W]hen these [Baltic] states came into existence, Canada did not conduct its own external affairs. At that time this was done by Great Britain. Shortly after the First World War, Great Britain extended *de jure* recognition to the states and governments of Estonia, Latvia and Lithuania. It can be assumed that this action on the part of Great Britain was binding on Canada. Consequently Canada can be considered as having recognised the sovereignty and independence of these states and their governments. Since the time when Canada assumed the responsibility for the conduct of its own external relations, there has been no occasion when the Government of Canada, in its own right, considered it necessary either to reaffirm or withdraw formally *de jure* recognition of these states. Moreover, it is not possible to point to any event or occasion which might imply that the Government of Canada has given *de jure* recognition to the absorption of these states into the U.S.S.R. There has never been any question of Canada acquiescing in or approving of the action taken by the U.S.S.R. To the best of my knowledge, the Governments of the United States and the United Kingdom have not withdrawn formal *de jure* recognition of these states and have not recognised *de jure* their entry into the Soviet Union.[6]

This statement appeared to represent a clear and categorical position upon the issue, but it did not indicate whether Canada would follow the British lead and extend only a nominal diplomatic recognition to Baltic representatives or whether it would follow the American example of embracing a more extensive, and even aggressive, policy of diplomatic recognition of functional Baltic missions and diplomats. In order to attempt to gain meaningful insight regarding this Canadian approach, it is useful to note that, while Canada did not engage in diplomatic relations at the ministerial or legation level with the Baltic countries prior to World War II, it did host consular officials who assumed responsibility for overseeing Estonian, Latvian, and Lithuanian interests within that country.

> I do not believe the question of diplomatic
> representatives in the strict sense of the term
> has arisen in that we never exchanged
> diplomatic representatives directly with those
> countries.   There   were   consular
> representatives and there are at the present
> four representatives of the three Baltic states
> performing consular functions in Canada.
> They are exercising these functions with the
> knowledge and consent of the government of
> Canada. They are acting on behalf of Latvia
> and one each on behalf of Estonia and
> Lithuania. With the difficulties prevailing in
> these countries the government [of Canada]
> has not certified the status of these consuls
> but this has not prevented them carrying out
> certain work on behalf of their nationals.[7]

This final statement signifies an ambiguity regarding Canadian policy on this issue during the post-war era. It may, in fact, signify a broader desire of Canada to pursue its foreign policy issues in concert with the United States, while maintaining an agenda based upon its own particular goals and values and asserting its own sovereignty as a legitimate power within the realm of global politics and international relations. It is reasonable to assume that many Canadians wanted to avoid the perception that their country meekly acquiesced in its role as an ally of the United States, particularly within the context of the Cold War.[8] Simultaneously, Canadians were becoming increasingly aware of the importance of their own multicultural heritage as a component of a struggling national identity, which included an emphasis upon prominent immigrant groups. These groups included (especially after World War II) émigrés from Eastern Europe, including immigrants from the Baltic region, particularly people and families from Lithuania.[9]

The "consular representatives" mentioned within the previous question specifically represent three categories of diplomats who have operated in Canada on behalf of Estonia, Latvia, and Lithuania. The first category includes Baltic consuls appointed by their respective governments prior to the World War II. The second category includes diplomatic officials who formally were attached to Baltic missions within the United States. These officials would oversee (consistent with the extended responsibilities of these missions) the interests of Baltic nationals in Canada. Although their diplomatic credentials had been received in Washington, the Canadian government routinely would allow them to perform diplomatic functions within Canada and extended recognition of their diplomatic privileges and immunities, accordingly. The third category includes "honorary consuls," as accepted both informally and, later, formally by the Canadian government in Ottawa.[10]

Honorary Consuls have been recognized under international law, specifically, within the Vienna Convention on Consular Relations. However, host nations are under no obligation to accept or recognize them, and these officials may, if it is applicable, continue to be treated as citizens of the host nation. Many privileges and immunities accorded to normal diplomatic representatives do not apply to honorary consuls. Nonetheless, the convention does provide for an extensive number of conditional protections.

Article 58

1. Articles 28, 29, 30, 34, 35, 36, 37, 38 and 39, paragraphs 3 of Article 54 and paragraphs 2 and 3 of Article 55 shall apply to consular posts headed by an honorary consular officer. In addition, the facilities, privileges and immunities of such consular posts shall be governed by Articles 59, 60, 61, and 62. . . .

Article 63

If criminal proceedings are instituted against an honorary consular officer, he must appear before the competent authorities. Nevertheless, the proceedings shall be conducted with the respect due to him by reason of his official position . . . .

Article 65

Honorary consular officers, with the exception of those who carry on for personal profit any professional or commercial activity in the receiving State, shall be exempt from all obligations under the laws and regulations of the receiving State in regard to the registration of aliens and residence permits. . . .

Article 68

Each state is free to decide whether it will appoint or receive honorary consular officers.[11]

The Canadian government took advantage of these provisions for the purpose of addressing this unusual and difficult problem of its response to the occupied Baltic states and Baltic nationals living within Canada. Normally, this type of consular representative provides a relatively inexpensive way for a sending nation to address its interests within other states.

> Honorary consuls may head a consular post and carry out most of the functions of career consuls. They are generally unpaid by the sending government and they can do much useful work, which in part explains their survival. . . .
>
> Consular posts headed by an honorary consul enjoy most of the facilities, privileges and immunities of those headed by career consuls . . . . The receiving state shall accord them full facilities for their functions, permit them to display the flag and coat of arms of the sending state, assist them in finding consular premises and accommodations, give members of the post freedom of movement and of communication, treat their official correspondence as inviolable, and permit their use of a consular bag. They are free to maintain contact with nationals of the sending state, address the authorities, and levy consular fees and charges. . . .
>
> Yet, at almost every turn, the privileges and immunities of honorary consular officers are trimmed down compared to those of career consuls. Although the receiving state is obliged to protect their premises against intrusions, damage, or impairment of dignity (article 59), there is no inviolability.[12]

In accordance with these guidelines, Ottawa extended honorary consular recognition to various persons throughout the post–World War II era. Consul General Gerald L. P. Grant–Suttie, who had been appointed by the Lithuanian Government in 1937, was succeeded in his post by Vytautus Gylys in 1949. Since this appointment had been an internal one (having been made with the approval of the Lithuanian chargé d'affaires in Washington), the Canadian government declined the opportunity to extend full recognition or diplomatic immunity to him. Instead, Gylys was recognized as an honorary consul general.[13]

The implications of this arrangement were very different from the conditions experienced by Lithuanian diplomats in the United States or Great Britain. Gylys was regarded as being subject to Canadian jurisdiction, so, although he became entitled to a certain degree of official respect and special treatment, he also retained the status of any other private citizen or landed immigrant residing within Canada. His position was, in this respect, consistent with the laws governing honorary consuls.

> The honorary consuls on the other hand are permitted to engage in gainful employment in addition to their consular duties and they are selected locally from persons resident in the receiving state. It is immaterial whether they are nationals of the receiving state or the sending state, or of a third state.[14]

Furthermore, Lithuanian officials did not enjoy access, through the intervention of the Canadian government, of frozen Lithuanian assets or other funds. Therefore, the activities of the honorary consulate general, located in Toronto, were funded entirely by the consul general's own "gainful employment" and resources or through contributions provided by the Canada's Lithuanian community through the Lithuanian Council of Canada.[15]

A similar arrangement was made regarding Estonian representatives who offered a diplomatic presence within Canada. Since Estonia never had a diplomatic mission within that country, unlike Lithuania, there was no pre-existing base for such activities. Such a presence was established through the arrival of Johannes Markus, who had served in a diplomatic capacity in Poland and Hungary prior to, and during, World War II. He emigrated to the United States after the war, where he worked with the Estonian community until the early 1950s. Markus then left the United States and, with the support of the Estonian consul general at New York in charge of legation, assumed the post of honorary consul general at Toronto. Again, the Canadian government did not respond officially to this move, but it informally acknowledged his presence and role. Markus chose to establish the consulate general in Toronto, rather than the federal capital of Ottawa, because of the high concentration of Estonian *expatriates* and Estonian-Canadian citizens. This post also was funded privately, with additional support provided through the Estonian Consulate General at New York, with which office Markus maintained contact.[16]

This situation was far less advantageous for Baltic representatives in Canada than it was for their counterparts within the United States, but it offered, arguably, a more beneficial arrangement than the one experienced by Baltic diplomats within the United Kingdom. It was the intention of successive British governments simply to allow those Baltic missions and diplomats who had been appointed by their respective governments, prior to the Soviet annexation, to continue to receive diplomatic recognition. Once these representatives either retired or died, that Baltic diplomatic presence also would end.[17] British officials never indicated any intent to allow the perpetuation of even a symbolic Baltic diplomatic presence once the original diplomats were gone, particularly since such a move almost certainly would antagonize the Soviet government. Britain, despite its firm commitment to the North Atlantic Treaty Organization [NATO] and its alliance with the United States in opposition to Soviet expansion, generally sought to avoid unnecessary antagonism of such a nature.[18]

Successive Canadian governments generally adopted a position upon this matter that fell between the American and British positions. Canada also was committed to NATO and supported the general opposition toward Soviet aggression that was led by its neighbor to the south. But it also sought to be somewhat more conciliatory towards the Soviets than did the United States, which it often regarded as being unnecessarily aggressive and provocative. On the other hand, Canadian society generally appeared to embrace certain principles and values that would discourage the suppression of the sort of activity represented by the continued presence of these Baltic representatives. Some of these principles revolved around the image of Canada as a society that supported and promoted (similar to the American self-perception) the cause of freedom and self-determination throughout the world, even if only through symbolic actions, such as the informal recognition of honorary Baltic consuls general.[19] But, perhaps, an even more compelling motivation than that one was the growing popular image of Canada as a "multicultural" society.

Much of the appeal of this image has been derived from its comparison with the "melting pot" image of American society and the effect of that comparison upon the larger desire to establish a distinctive definition of Canadian nationalism.[20] The controversy of whether or not Canada is a nation, and not merely a political state, has been a prominent one throughout Canadian history.[21] It has become an especially significant issue in relation to the persistence and growth of Québécois nationalism and accompanying desires for, and movements toward, political and cultural separation from the rest of Canada.[22] Simultaneously, a certain resentment has developed toward the perceived "special treatment" that French–Canadians have received in relation to other Canadian ethnic groups, especially among, but not limited to, Canadians living in the Prairie provinces.[23] This resentment was expressed formally during the 1960s by the Royal Commission on Bilingualism and Biculturalism.

> However, the idea of Canada having a dual nature aroused fears among members of the other ethnic groups. The question was posed in Winnipeg: 'Are we, west of the Ontario border, to be considered second-class citizens? We are a third of the population in this country . . . and should be considered equal citizens.' . . .
>
> We were reminded of the prominent role which men and women from Germany, the Ukraine, the Scandinavian countries, Holland, Poland and elsewhere had played in the settlement of the West. In many communities, we were told, a vigorous sense of cultural identity persists. . . .
>
> What image of Canada would do justice to the presence of these varied ethnic groups? This question preoccupied western participants especially, and the answer they often gave was 'multiculturalism', or, more elaborately, 'the Canadian mosaic'. They asked: If two cultures are accepted, why not many? Why should Canada not be a country in which a multitude of cultural groups live side by side yet distinct from one another, all contributing to a richly varied society? Certainly, it was stated, the mosaic idea was infinitely preferable to the 'melting pot.'[24]

The identification of a sense of Canadian nationalism has been so historically elusive, in part, because of the country's strong ties to, and similarities with, American society and culture. One strategy that has been adopted for overcoming that problem has been the claim that Canada, unlike the United States, remains a "mosaic" of distinctive ethnic, linguistic, and cultural groups whose collective participation within the larger Canadian context has shaped certain shared values of tolerance, cooperation, and diversity that have helped to make Canada an enlightened society.

> Reaching for and affirming in-group identity have long been objectives of English Canadian nationalism. Nearly a century ago, problems of foreign influence and especially US domination of Canadian cultural life were identified by the Canada Firsters. The sense of cultural threat has hardly receded in recent years . . . . In fact, with the perception that culture in a global sense has become more Americanized, more standardized, and less open to contributions that are not American in origin and sensibility has come a view that Canada's historic predicament is analogous to that of the rest of the contemporary world.[25]

The true nature and worth of multiculturalism have been debated, including the extent to which it truly differs from the ethnic and cultural heritage of the United States.[26] But it has remained such a compelling aspect of Canadian politics that it has been included within the Canadian Charter of Rights and Freedoms and is promoted through a federal Ministry of Multiculturalism.[27]

It becomes easier to understand Canada's response toward Baltic diplomatic representatives under such circumstances, particularly since the Estonian, Latvian, and, especially, Lithuanian communities are significant participants within that country's multicultural "mosaic." Successive Canadian governments have been reluctant to antagonize the Soviet Union unnecessarily, and they also have resisted taking actions that would lead to the perception that Canada is subordinately compliant to American foreign policy methods and objectives.[28] Yet it is reasonable to assume that they also have been reluctant to be perceived as nonsupportive of the reasonable aspirations and activities of a people who are represented by visible ethnic communities within Canada. However, some Canadian leaders have been more enthusiastic than others in supporting such efforts. This apparent enthusiasm was evident particularly during the premiership of John Diefenbaker.

The idealistic vision of a strong and united Canada that included and celebrated the multicultural diversity of that country was a central theme of Diefenbaker's political career, and it was expressed during his years in office in attempts to promote the cause of freedom and tolerance at home and abroad, as well as his own, specific political agenda.[29] During the difficult parliamentary electoral campaign of 1962, Diefenbaker extended this sense of idealism toward the Baltic communities of Canada and the struggle for Baltic independence from the Soviet Union. He lanned to make public a proposal to extend "official" diplomatic recognition to Baltic representatives (the term that government officials tended to use was "acting" consuls) who already were operating informally as honorary consuls. However, Diefenbaker's motives were not entirely idealistic; in a close election, the support of ethnic communities was regarded as potentially crucial, as reflected within the diary of one of his close advisers, H. Basil Robinson.

> A report from the Ambassador in Moscow reminded PM [Prime Minister Diefenbaker] of ethnic group vote. He phoned PC [Progressive Conservative] candidate in [electoral riding of] Spadina, John Bassett, who promptly put in a word re the need for a statement to attract the Baltic community vote. PM assured him he had a statement but couldn't be sure of making it because Ukrainians might feel they were being discriminated against.[30]

Diefenbaker did, indeed, issue such a statement during a campaign speech to a gathering of Baltic-Canadians in Toronto. His promises were, understandably, somewhat vague, but they did indicate a willingness on the part of his government to make the status of the honorary consuls general "official."[31] Diefenbaker complied with this promise, despite the fact that his Progressive Conservative Party was returned to power with only minority support in Parliament. That result may explain the fact that this subject was not raised officially by his minority government (in fact, it was not raised at all) within Parliament. It was, instead, handled administratively as an executive matter.[32]

Thereafter, while Canada followed a broad foreign policy that was less overtly hostile toward the Soviet Union than American policy, it also refused to suppress the honorary Baltic consuls general, as the Soviet government occasionally demanded that it do. However, despite the willingness of later governments to continue to recognize this status, the government of Pierre Trudeau often declined, reportedly, the opportunity to extend this commitment and recognize the appointments, generally through the auspices of the American government, of replacements for honorary consuls, once they died.[33] One exception to this policy was the Canadian government's recognition of the appointment, by the Estonian consul general at New York, Ernst Jaakson (despite the fact that Jaakson was recognized as being responsible only for Estonia's legation to the United States), of an Estonian-Canadian, Ilmar Heinsoo, as a replacement for honorary consul general Johannes Markus. In 1971, Jaakson sent a letter to the Trudeau Government, through Canada's diplomatic mission to the United Nations, informing him of this appointment. A year later, Canada's secretary of state for external affairs, Mitchell Sharp, responded to Jaakson with a letter that granted informal recognition to Heinsoo, which action was consistent with former Canadian policy in this area.[34]

Lithuanian diplomatic representation did not change until the late 1980s, during the premiership of Brian Mulroney. In 1989, a Lithuanian-Canadian, Haris Lappas, was appointed by Stasys Lozoraitis, Jr. (who was Lithuanian chargé d'affaires in Washington) to replace the recently deceased Dr. Jonas Zmuidzinas (who had replaced Gerald L. P. Grant-Suttie in 1959 and had received formal recognition in 1962) as Lithuania's honorary consul general to Canada. By that time, events occurring within the Soviet Union were altering the political situation for the Baltic states dramatically, as the Soviet government met its ultimate demise. Under those circumstances, continued Canadian recognition of honorary Baltic diplomats assumed an increased, though still largely symbolic, significance.[35]

The honorary Baltic consuls general within Canada continued to function, following the reestablishment of independent governments in Estonia, Latvia, and Lithuania. However, now the appointments of these officials were confirmed by the restored Baltic governments. The lack of financial and infrastructural resources that former Soviet republics have experienced caused the Baltic governments to assign a relatively low priority to the establishment of Baltic embassies in Ottawa. Therefore, the continuation of the honorary consuls general, with guidance from the respective Baltic embassies in Washington, provided a convenient alternative for the new governments. Furthermore, this situation represents an interesting continuity, since Baltic diplomatic activity within Canada historically has been conducted though protecting powers (such as the Finnish embassy, on behalf of Estonia, prior to World War II) or through Baltic missions within the United States.[36]

Canada's response toward Baltic diplomacy has been, in its own way, both unique and unprecedented. The presence of honorary consuls is not an especially unusual occurrence. However, the presence of honorary diplomatic representatives on behalf of defunct governments and countries that no longer enjoyed political independence certainly was unorthodox. The fact that these officials were appointed by other diplomats (particularly by diplomats serving within other countries whose own status was highly unusual, unprecedented, and inconsistent with the normal expectations of conventional international law) made this situation especially notable.

These honorary consuls general fulfilled their functions on a part-time basis, since they were compelled to earn a living by conventional means as members of Canadian society. They continued to function in this way, even after the restoration of Estonian, Latvian, and Lithuanian sovereignty, primarily for reasons of fiscal constraint regarding their respective governments. Nonetheless, they have served as important symbols of a larger effort that advanced the cause of Baltic independence and undermined the legitimacy of the Soviet Union, in general, and of its annexation of the Baltic region, in particular.

These diplomats also have provided practical support for the political and cultural endeavors of their respective ethnic communities within Canada, especially in terms of coordination and information services. Since the restoration of Baltic independence, these officials have provided additional consular services, especially in terms of processing visa applications and providing other notarial services. They also have served the function of political, economic, and cultural liaison between Baltic nationals in Canada and their respective homelands and, occasionally and informally, between Canadian governmental officials and their Baltic counterparts.[37]

The highly unusual nature of this diplomatic situation produced another unique response by a Western nation. This response was influenced by Canada's own political heritage and practical considerations of international relations and theoretical considerations of international law. It is another piece in the puzzle of Estonian, Latvian, and Lithuanian diplomacy during the "years of dependence" that followed the end of World War II.

Notes

1.   This diplomatic condition that Canada experienced as part of the British Empire is addressed in John S. Galbraith, *The Establishment of Canadian Diplomatic Status at Washington* (Berkeley: University of California Press, 1951), pp. 42–77.

2.   Rosario Bilodeau, Robert Comeau, André Gosselin, and Denise Julien, *Histoire des Canadas* (Montréal: Editions Hurtubise HMH, 1970), pp. 530–533.

3.   This inter-war diplomatic situation is described in general terms in McHugh interview with Ilmar Heinsoo, honorary consul general of Estonia in Toronto, March 17, 1992, and McHugh interview with Grazina Lappas, consular secretary to Haris Lappas, honorary consul general of Lithuania in Toronto, March 18, 1992.

4.   Interview with Heinsoo; Interview with Lappas.

5.   Peter Lyon, "Britain and Canada since the Second World War: Two Much Mutually Entangled Countries," in *Britain and Canada in the 1990s*, D. K. Adams, ed. (Halifax, NS: Institute for Research on Public Policy, 1992), pp. 13–25; Gordon T. Stewart, *The American Response to Canada since 1776* (East Lansing: Michigan State University Press, 1992), pp. 175–205.

6.   London, December 31, 1952, "Statement: Recognition of the Baltic States," FO/371/106115-NB1901/4, with emphases in the original document. This statement was a response to inquiries Fleming made at a meeting of "this Committee" that had been held on March 2.

7.   London, December 31, 1952, "Statement: Recognition of the Baltic States," FO/371/106115-NB1901/4.

8.   Arthur Andrew, *The Rise and Fall of a Middle Power* (Toronto: James Lorimer, 1993), pp. 85–108.

9.   Jean R. Burnet and Howard Palmer, *Coming Canadians: An Introduction to a History of Canada's Peoples* (Toronto: McClelland and Stuart, 1988), pp. 39–45, 164–171; Statistics on Baltic immigration patterns to Canada prior to the 1960s are located in *Royal Commission on Bilingualism and Biculturalism: Final Report* (Hull, QC: Queen's Printer for Canada, 1965), Book I, p. 32.

10.   These categories were informally described in interview with Heinsoo and interview with Lappas.

11.   *Vienna Convention on Consular Relations*, 1963, Chapter 3, Articles 58, 63, 65, 68.

12.   Grant V. McClanahan, *Diplomatic Immunity: Principles, Practices, Problems* (New York: St. Martin's Press, 1989), pp. 69–70.

13.   Interview with Lappas.

14.   Biswainath Sen, *A Diplomat's Handbook of International Law and Practice*, 3d ed. (Dordrecht, The Netherlands: Martinus Nijhoff, 1988), p. 259.

15.   Interview with Lappas.

16.   Interview with Heinsoo.

17.   This specific policy is articulated in a British "Foreign Office Minute," London, June 1, 1950, FO372/7063-T107/1903/1, and in a correspondence from K. A. Neil of the Soviet Department of the British Foreign and Commonwealth Office, March 12, 1986.

18.   This general tendency of British foreign policy during this period is discussed in Geoffrey McDermott, *The Eden Legacy* (London: Leslie Ferwin, 1969), pp. 95–104 and Keith Robbins, *The Eclipse of a Great Power* (London: Longman, 1983), pp. 172–181.

19.   This idealistic approach to Canadian foreign policy is addressed in Andrew F. Cooper, Richard A. Higgott, and Kim Richard Nossal, *Relocating Middle Powers: Australia and Canada in a Changing World Order* (Vancouver: University of British Columbia, 1993), pp. 12–32.

20.   This theme and a good overview of the concept of multiculturalism in Canada are addressed in Raymond Breton, "Multiculturalism and Canadian Nation-Building," in *The Politics of Gender, Ethnicity and Language in Canada*, Alan C. Cairns and Cynthia Williams, eds. (Toronto: University of Toronto Press, 1985), pp. 27–66.

21.   An excellent overview of the considerable amount of literature that has addressed this controversy can be found in Kenneth McRoberts, *Misconceiving Canada: The Struggle for National Unity* (Toronto: Oxford University Press, 1997), pp. 2–76.

22.   An important expression of these beliefs are provided in Léon Dion, *A la recherche du Québec* (Montréal: Editions Québec/Amérique, 1987), pp. 109–129.

23.   Many of these objections were related to a desire to maintain "national" standards of rights, liberties, and political status as expressed within the Canadian Charter of Rights and Freedoms and other constitutional documents, as enunciated in Alan C. Cairns, "Reflections on the Political Purposes of the Charter:

The First Decade," in *Reconfigurations*, Douglas E. Williams, ed. (Toronto: McClelland and Stewart, 1995), pp. 194–214.

24.   *Royal Commission on Bilingualism and Biculturalism*, Book I, pp. 50–51.

25.   Sylvia B. Bashevkin, *True Patriot Love: The Politics of Canadian Nationalism* (Oxford: Oxford University Press, 1991), p. 171.

26.   A good review of this debate can be found in McRoberts, pp. 125–133.

27.   An overview of governmental policies related to Canadian multiculturalism is provided in Leslie A. Pal, *Interests of State: The Politics of Language, Multiculturalism, and Feminism in Canada* (Montreal and Kingston: McGill-Queen's Universities Press, 1993), pp. 189–215.

28.   This theme is addressed in J. W. Holmes, *Canada and the United States: Political and Security Issues* (Toronto: Canadian Institute of International Affairs, 1970), pp. 1–12.

29.   This issue is addressed in John G. Diefenbaker, *One Canada*, vol. 1, *The Crusading Years, 1895-1956* (Toronto: Macmillan, 1975), pp. 218–223, 252–254.

30.   H. Basil Robinson, *Diefenbaker's World: A Populist in Foreign Affairs* (Toronto: University of Toronto Press, 1989), p. 271.

31.   "Baltic Community Vote," *Globe and Mail*, Toronto, June 16, 1962, p. A17.

32.   In fact, there is no official record of this recognition having occurred, although it was promised, publicly, and it has been acknowledged, generally, both by Baltic honorary consuls and Canadian Government officials. This situation was confirmed by the interview with Ilmar Heinsoo and the interviews with Haris and Grazina Lappas.

33.   Interview with Haris Lappas, March 18, 1992.

34.   Interview with Heinsoo, March 17, 1992.

35.   Interview with Heinsoo, March 17, 1992.

36.   Interview with Heinsoo, March 17, 1992; Interview with Haris Lappas, March 19, 1992.

37.   Interview with Heinsoo, March 17, 1992; Interview with Grazina Lappas, March 19, 1992.

Chapter 7

Australian Interlude

The history of the diplomatic activities of the Baltic states in Australia is best understood in terms of that continent's own domestic policy history regarding ethnic issues and its foreign policy history regarding the Cold War. Despite the apparent remoteness of Estonia, Latvia, and Lithuania from the political and economic experiences of the South Pacific, the Soviet annexation of those countries and the ordeals of the Baltic peoples as immigrants and exiles proved to be relevant to Australia. In particular, it would invoke (as it did in terms of Canada) an interesting interrelationship between internal and external themes of Australian politics and society.

Australia provides, perhaps, the most conspicuous example of a Western country that, ultimately, rejected Baltic attempts to gain diplomatic standing and, instead, recognized the Soviet domination of those three countries de jure, as well as de facto. However, prior to its decision to do so, the Australian government had adopted a policy toward Baltic diplomatic representation that was similar to the Canadian approach toward this issue. The change in policy was the result of specific pressures and desires that occurred against a general background of cultural and broadly civic interests.

There was no significant emigration from the Baltic states to Australia prior to World War II. That pattern was not unusual; the nonaboriginal population had remained predominantly British in origin, with the exception of groups of immigrant workers who had arrived upon that continent from China and other parts of Asia and the Pacific. That pattern changed dramatically during the middle of the twentieth century, particularly because of the relatively large numbers of refugees who had fled Europe during, and after, the war. The relocation of Estonian, Latvian, and Lithuanian people from the overcrowded refugee centers of Europe to Australia (which became a popular alternative to North America) made a significant contribution to that migratory situation.[1]

Both Liberal and, especially, Labour governments sought to place greater controls upon immigration during the early years of the Commonwealth of Australia in the interest of protecting white working–class Australians from competing with the cheap labor that new arrivals would present. The most notorious product of that concern was the "White Australia" policy that formally was introduced, first, by the Labour government of Prime Minister John C. Watson in 1904.[2] However, a general lack of immigration into Australia during the first half of the twentieth century contributed to a lack of development, a labor shortage, and a general problem of underpopulation in many parts of the continent that became very noticeable during World War II.[3]

Therefore, another Labour government, under Prime Minister Joseph B. Chifley, aggressively addressed this issue. The Ministry of Immigration was created in 1945, and it was led first by Arthur A. Calwell. One of the first tasks of the new minister was the encouragement of immigration in order to augment the need for a larger workforce in Australia. A likely source for this new population was the displaced persons camps of Europe, especially those camps that contained Baltic refugees who were unwilling, or unable, to return to their Soviet-occupied homelands. Calwell negotiated an agreement with the United Nations Preparatory Commission of the International Refugee Organization in 1947 that enabled thousands of Estonians, Latvians, and Lithuanians to be resettled in Australia, where many of the refugees undertook bonded-labor contracts. This agreement and subsequent Australian policy were not as supportive of Baltic émigrés as had been the American Displaced Persons Act of 1948. Nonetheless, it was attractive enough to encourage the migration of thousands of these people from Europe to Australia.[4]

There appears to have been little diplomatic representation of the Baltic states within Australia prior to this time, primarily because of the cost that such activity would entail and the lack of compelling economic or political interest for any of the countries involved. There appeared to be only two consular officials overseeing Baltic interests within Australia by the end of World War II, and both of them represented Latvia. It is interesting to note that the surnames of both of these diplomats do not appear to be of Latvian origin; it is possible that these officials were, in fact, local inhabitants of this continent who had political, cultural, or, more likely, economic ties to Latvia and who initially were appointed upon that basis. This observation is supported further by the fact that these consuls were assigned specific regions of responsibility that corresponded, roughly, to the most important economic centers of Australia. No consular official appears to have been assigned responsibility for the entire country, and, in general, economically underdeveloped parts of Australia appear to have been diplomatically ignored by the Baltic states.[5]

R. G. McComas was listed, in 1946, as being the Latvian consul at Melbourne, with responsibility for the states of Victoria and Tasmania. Norman McLeod was listed as being the Latvian "senior consul" in Sydney, with responsibility for Queensland.[6] However, later accounts refer to these officials as "honorary consuls," which would support the hypothesis that they were Australian nationals.[7] That situation would be similar to the status of the Baltic honorary consuls found within Canada. The only other diplomats who appear to have represented the Baltic states within the Pacific rim were James F. Mackley, a Latvian acting consul at Auckland, Alfred Pure, who served as a Latvian acting consul at Shanghai, and Reginald Temple Stevens, who served as a consul for Latvia in Brisbane. Kārlis Zariņš, Latvian minister in London, also served as consul general for the British Empire, especially Australia and New Zealand.[8] It is unlikely that Pure continued to function in that post after the fall of the Kuomintang Government and the establishment of the People's Republic of China in 1949. However, there is no apparent indication regarding whether or not he continued to function diplomatically within Taiwan after that date.

One difference between the Baltic diplomats assigned to Canada and Australia was the origin of their respective appointments. Baltic honorary consuls within Canada were appointed by their respective legations in Washington and the Estonian consul general in New York, while the Latvian honorary consuls within Australia were appointed by the Latvian Legation in London. Despite the fact that both countries were members of the Commonwealth of Nations, Australian appointments were regarded as part of the Latvian representation within the "British Empire," while Latvian and other Baltic appointments to Canada were not treated, apparently, in the same way.[9]

This development provides an interesting example of another, specific anomaly of the broadly anomalous condition of Cold War Baltic diplomacy. Normally, a consulate or consular official symbolizes an extension of an embassy that is located within the host country's capital city. There is no formal proscription within international law against the presence of a consul or consulate without the benefit of an embassy or legation, but such a condition sometimes has not been accepted as consistent with the theory and practice of diplomacy, since consulates generally are expected to perform specific diplomatic functions (such as providing regional representation within a host country or focusing upon economic activities and relationships), while embassies are expected to perform general diplomatic functions.[10] However, since this practice is not unique to the Baltic states, and since it apparently was done during, and prior to, World War II, it probably was pursued as a result of financial considerations as much as a result of the general circumstances under which Estonian, Latvian, and Lithuanian political leaders-in-exile conducted this extremely unusual version of international diplomacy.[11]

The next official correspondence regarding the general situation of Latvian diplomats within Australia that has been discovered occurred in 1952. The third secretary of the Latvian legation to the Court of St. James's, Olgerts Rozìtis, was appointed by the chief of that legation, Kãrlis Zariņš (who also claimed to be the "Senior Latvian Representative Abroad"[12]), as the "carrière consular representative in Australia" in order to augment the activities of those honorary consuls.[13] The British Foreign Office previously had rejected Zariņš' request that Roberts Kampus (a former counselor at the Latvian Legation in Sweden) be placed in London's diplomatic list as Rozìtis' replacement, but it did not comment upon the latter diplomat's appointment to Australia.[14] Evidence that would indicate the Australian government's reaction to this appointment does not appear to be readily available. It is difficult to find evidence that mentions his relationship to the regional Latvian honorary consuls within Australia or comments upon his activities within that country. The next readily available reference to any Baltic diplomatic activity within Australia occurs more than twenty years later. This reference is made in connection with the Australian government's decision to alter its entire direction in foreign policy regarding the Cold War, in general, and the Soviet Union, in particular.

In 1972, Edward Gough Whitlam led the Labour Party to victory in a general election. The ability of that party to win a majority of seats in the Australian House of Representatives, after many years in opposition, signaled the start of a profound shift in domestic and foreign policy for that country. In particular, Prime Minister Whitlam was determined to promote a foreign policy that would establish a role for Australia that was independent of traditional American and British policies, especially within the context of the Cold War.[15] Australia's participation in the Vietnam War had been particularly controversial, and it seemed to symbolize a foreign policy that had become archaic, especially in terms of its seemingly stout support of Western policies and positions that often appeared to affect Australian interests only marginally.[16] Therefore, the impetus toward radical change seemed to be strong.

> To friends as well as critics of the Prime Minister, these euphoric early days of the new Government were taken for a period of almost spectacular rapid change, a wholesale sweeping away of the policies of the previous twenty-three years.   On   retrospective examination, what seems to have been swept away were mostly the dead shells of policies that had quietly expired sometime in the previous five years, rather than actual living policies. And where the policies were alive, those discarded were mostly what may be called 'declaratory' policies, such as the stances taken by Australian representatives in UN [United Nations] voting. So, without undue cynicism, one might say that the changes in rhetoric and attitude and image were a good deal larger than those in substance. Some of the Whitlam initiatives (such as extending *de jure* recognition to the incorporation of the Baltic Republics into the Soviet   Union,   and   an   ill-requited establishment of diplomatic relations with North Korea) perhaps gave a faintly fellow-traveling look to policy as a whole.[17]

The motivation behind the de jure recognition of the Soviet annexation of Estonia, Latvia, and Lithuania by the Whitlam government was declared to be based upon "realism" and "pragmatism." Prior to that decision, Australia followed a policy that resembled the general British attitude toward the Baltic states and their diplomatic representatives. The refusal to acknowledge officially the Soviet control of the region and the inability to proceed accordingly posed, in the opinion of this government, a supercilious and, arguably, silly obstacle to the smooth pursuit of Australia's independent foreign policy. Therefore, on August 3, 1974, the de jure recognition of the Soviet annexation officially was announced. It actually had been accomplished a month earlier by the Prime Minister, in his capacity as acting foreign minister, without the benefit of the formal advice or consent of either the cabinet or Parliament.[18] This decision was formally defended in Parliament on August 13 by the new minister for foreign affairs, Senator Donald R. Willesee.

> The Australian Government decided last month to accord *de jure* recognition of the incorporation of the Baltic states into the Union of Soviet Socialist Republics. This action was a logical step following the *de facto* recognition successive Australian governments have extended for over 20 years. This decision represented a logical application to these states of the principle the Government has adhered to firmly since it came into office, that is, the recognition of existing realities in the world whether or not we like or approve of those realities. This policy has been criticised by the Opposition from the beginning—over China, over North Vietnam and over North Korea . . . . All these decisions are consistent . . . with the Government's view that one has to recognise and deal with existing realities regardless of ideological preconceptions.
>
> The realities in the Baltic states are quite evident from a number of points of view. The Baltic states of Estonia, Latvia and Lithuania have been part of the U.S.S.R. for 34 years. Before 1915, they had formed part of Russian territory for over 100 years. At present they have the status of republics within the Soviet federation. It is unlikely that the Soviet Government will grant independence to these territories.[19]

Senator Willesee acknowledged that this decision differed from the policy of North Atlanta Treaty Organization [NATO] members, but he insisted that "the interests of these governments in Europe [and North America] are not the same as those of the Australian Government, and the Australian Government need not wait for these countries to move before taking action itself."[20]   Clearly, the establishment of an independent foreign policy upon such issues was as important a consideration to the Labour Government as was "the recognition of existing realities." One of the most important of these "realities," according to the minister, was the facilitation of consular and other diplomatic activities.

> Recognition will facilitate the carrying out of certain consular activities, including matters relating to the reunion of families and settlement of estates which require contact with the governments in the Baltic states. It will also be easier to offer any consular assistance to members of the Baltic communities in Australia to visit their family homeland. The Australian Ambassador in Moscow is now able to visit the republics and observe developments there at first hand. It is instructive to recall the practice of the previous Liberal/Country Party Government on this and related questions. Under its administration, Australian officials in Moscow—but not the Ambassador—and some parliamentarians had visited the Baltic states. The Leader of the Opposition (Mr. Snedden), when Attorney-General, himself accepted during a debate in Parliament on extradition treaties that Estonia, Latvia and Lithuania no longer existed as independent nations--a fact pointed out in another place by the present Prime Minister as long ago as 20 October 1966 (Hansard p. 2037).[21]

Discussion appears to be absent, within this statement and elsewhere, of the diplomatic consequences for Baltic representatives functioning within Australia on behalf of their formerly independent nations. It may have been regarded, perhaps, as a moot point, since that representation practically had disappeared within that country. Nonetheless, that presence had persevered, so the Australian government needed to respond to this new "reality." Indeed, the Labour government acted quickly, in this respect. On August 15, 1974, the chief of protocol for the Ministry of Foreign Affairs, H. Neil Truscott, sent a letter to the sole remaining diplomatic representative of a "sovereign" Baltic state, the Latvian honorary consul at Melbourne, R. G. McComas.

> The Australian Government has recently announced its recognition of the

> incorporation of the Baltic States of Estonia, Lithuania and Latvia into the Soviet Union.
>
> Accordingly, I am writing to inform you that recognition of your consular status as Honorary Consul of Latvia in Victoria with jurisdiction throughout the States of Victoria and Tasmania has been withdrawn, and the relevant Federal and State authorities have been notified of this, and of the deletion of your name from the Consular and Trade Representatives handbook.[22]

However, despite the popularity of this policy among many people and politicians within Australia, a vocal opposition to this action also developed quickly and, to a certain extent, effectively. Important reasons for this opposition included the attitudes and policies toward immigrant and minority groups that had been evolving within Australia since the end of World War II. Baltic immigrants, in particular, had been a prime motivating force behind this evolution.[23] Therefore, policies that affected Estonians, Latvians, and Lithuanians adversely were especially prone to criticism and political difficulty.

Australians had become increasingly sensitive to issues of multiculturalism during the latter part of the twentieth century, despite a legacy that included the "White Australia" policies of the early part of the century. Three identifiable phases indicate the development of these attitudes, and they were very relevant to the status of the Baltic peoples within Australia. In fact, because of the large numbers of Baltic immigrants and displaced persons who arrived in Australia during and after World War II (especially among the first transport ships of that era), European immigrants and refugees generally became known among many native, White Australians (unfortunately, often as an epithet), regardless of their actual national origins, simply as "Balts."[24]

The three phases have been labeled as "assimilation," "integration," and "multiculturalism." Each phase represents a progression of national attitudes and policies regarding the acceptance of non-British ethnic minorities within Australian society. The first phase, which occurred during the 1950s and early 1960s, emphasized the economic benefits of immigration through the filling of labor shortages, especially within agriculture and emerging manufacturing industries. It was intended to influence Australians to be more accepting of immigrant minority groups and to lead these immigrants, in turn, to become "good

Australians." The second phase, which occurred during the late 1960s and 1970s, rejected the homogeneous image of the "good Australian" in favor of a pluralist concept that would influence Australians of British descent to become more tolerant of immigrants who did not fit the traditional image of an "Australian." It also would influence, consequently, new, non-British immigrants to remain in Australia (rather than continuing the trend towards returning to their countries of origin) so they could continue to contribute to the country's economic development.

The third phase predominated after the late 1970s, but it was initiated by the Whitlam government in 1972. It moved beyond mere tolerance and promoted, instead, an embracing of pluralism within Australia. It sought to replace the traditional, British–oriented image of Australian identity with one that was consistent with national and international concerns regarding race, gender, ethnicity, and social justice.[25] However, in terms of his decision to recognize, de jure, the incorporation of the Baltic states into the Soviet Union, Whitlam's active promotion of a domestic policy of multiculturalism presented a problem that would undermine the popularity of the Labour Government's foreign policy decision within this area.

> Ethnics and multiculturalism were central to the message delivered by E.G. Whitlam in what remains a key statement on later migrant issues. Addressing the National Citizenship Convention in 1970, the then leader of the Labor Opposition dwelt at considerable length on the disadvantages experienced by migrants . . . . There was a strong suggestion in the statement that migrants had rights as well as obligations; that, maybe, it was time to transfer some attention to the 'needs' which went with rights, and away from the ever-ready alert to press the terms of the Australian Way of Life.
>
> The address is significant for several reasons, not the least being that it accorded with the Australian Labor Party's current stance on allied issues which led to its election to government in 1972. It enabled migrants to 'come out' and assume an active role in the political process and not to languish in the shadows until they plucked up enough

> courage to lay claim to membership in the
> Australian Way of Life club. The 'ethnic
> vote' was born at the time. But the Whitlam
> statement was also an exercise in pragmatism:
> situations were named, disadvantages
> enumerated and goals defined. 'Ethnics' had
> a programme. The 'rights' were presented as
> achievable and they were made to appear as
> solidly Australian. The inference was that not
> to take up the challenge would have been
> tantamount to engaging in un-Australian
> activities.[26]

The political climate that resulted from these policies was managed, with some success, by leading Baltic (particularly Latvian) political leaders within Australia. These forces were not strong enough to force the government to reverse its policy, nor were they able to inflict immediate political damage upon it. However, they did provide the opposition Liberal and Country Parties with an opportunity to embarrass the government. Furthermore, other ethnic groups could identify with their plight, and this identification could influence the general "ethnic vote." Baltic voters constituted a sizable proportion of that segment of the voting population within Australia. Their influence, while it certainly was not great, was not insignificant.[27]

The Labour Party did not control a majority of seats in the Senate, and the foreign minister sat in that chamber, so it provided a productive setting for the Opposition to pursue this matter. Questions and statements that were critical of the decision were made in both houses of Parliament.[28] In particular, Opposition leaders and members in the House of Representatives insisted that the government was "appeasing" the Soviet Union at the expense of the Baltic peoples.[29] But it was in the Upper House that a motion to censure the Government over the issue (where it had a reasonable chance of success) was introduced. The official reasons behind the motion of September 18, 1974, which was made by the deputy leader of the Opposition in the Senate, Ivor John Greenwood, emphasized the foreign policy dimensions of this issue, even though it was motivated, in large part, by domestic considerations regarding Australians of Baltic origin.

> (i) in denial of human rights and contrary to
> the rule of law and in order to appease the
> Government of the U.S.S.R. he [Senator
> Willesee] organized the surreptitious

departure of Georgi Ermolenko [a Russian musician who had contemplated defection to Australia during a music festival in Perth] from Australia when doubt existed as to whether he was departing under duress and when that issue was being considered by the Supreme Court of Western Australia;

(ii) in breach of a clear undertaking to the contrary given by the Prime Minister the Government shamefully and furtively extended recognition to the incorporation of the Baltic States in the U.S.S.R., the Minister withholding any announcement or explanation of the decision;

(iii) the foreign policy alignments he is promoting will not serve Australia's national interest.[30]

The debate upon the motion of censure reiterated the arguments on both sides. Willesee raised, again, arguments in favor of the policy that revolved around the theme of "pragmatism," including the contention that the Government merely was imitating the policy that the Liberal Party had adopted in 1961, when it recognized de jure, as well as de facto, the forcible incorporation of the Portuguese territory of Goa into India while continuing to condemn the action. The Opposition continued to contend that this policy undermined efforts to improve human rights abroad and the general cause of the Baltic peoples residing within Australia and elsewhere.[31] Finally, the censure motion was passed regarding the second part, which was regarded as a vote of no confidence in the foreign minister, in particular, and the government, in general.[32]

The vote had no immediate, practical effect, since only an action of the Lower House could force the government to resign—although a Senate rejection of the government's 1975 budget did prompt the governor general, Sir John Kerr, unilaterally to dissolve Parliament and call new elections.[33] However, it may have contributed to the decline in the Labour Party's popularity; in 1975, the Liberals were returned to power (helped, in part, by the support of the "ethnic" vote) and, in 1976, that Government reversed the earlier decision and withdrew Australia's de jure recognition of the incorporation of the Baltic states into the Soviet Union. In taking this action, the Australian government reinstated the previous policy of extending only de facto recognition to the Soviet annexation of the Baltic states while maintaining de jure recognition of, and official support for, the political sovereignty and independence of Estonia, Latvia, and Lithuania.[34]

That reversal apparently did not result in a revival of Latvian or any other Baltic diplomatic activity. The fact that Australia was regarded as too small and too remote to contribute effectively to this Cold War issue probably contributed to the lack of emphasis upon this symbolic struggle, despite the significant presence of a community of Baltic displaced persons and other immigrants throughout that continent. Nonetheless, it is an incident worth noting, for it demonstrates some of the consequences that a change in de jure recognition might have posed for Canada, the United Kingdom, or, perhaps, even the United States.

Furthermore, this episode may provide some insights, at least indirectly, into the rationale and effect that the refusal to extend de jure recognition of the Soviet annexation and incorporation of the Baltic states may have posed for the governments and Baltic residents of other democratic countries. The situation for Baltic diplomats and activists within Australia may have been, at one level, frustrating, but it also, at another level, was not without a certain amount of success, even though that success was limited and largely symbolic. This Australian response may be indicative of the intangible, yet purposeful, role that this unusual diplomatic strategy promoted and the possibilities that similar strategies potentially can offer.

Notes

1.   Brian Murphy, *The Other Australia: Experiences of Migration* (Cambridge: Cambridge University Press, 1993), pp. 124–128.

2.   Trevor Reese, *Australia in the Twentieth Century* (London: Paul Mall Press, 1964), pp. 38–39; A. Wyatt Tilby, *The English People Overseas* (London: Constable and Co., 1912), pp. 499–503.

3.   Russell Ward, *The History of Australia: The Twentieth Century* (New York: Harper and Row, 1977), pp. 275–283.

4.   Aldis L. Putnins, *Latvians in Australia* (Canberra: Australian National University Press, 1981), pp. 11–21.

5.   This fact is interesting, since large numbers of displaced Baltic persons migrated to less populous regions of the country (such as South Australia) that provided employment opportunities within emerging manufacturing enterprises,

as explained in Edgars Dunsdorfs, *The Baltic Dilemma* (New York: Robert Speller & Sons, 1975), pp. 28–36, and Murphy, pp. 133–135.

In fact, one of the most active and influential of the Baltic political and cultural institutions was the South Australian chapter of the Latvian Federation in Australia and New Zealand, as suggested in Dunsdorfs, pp. 218–219. There is no indication that Baltic diplomatic representatives within Australia worked actively with organizations such as the Baltic Council of Australia, which, if that observation is accurate, would resemble the relationship between Baltic diplomats and Baltic political and cultural organizations within other countries, also.

6.   London, December 9, 1946, letter from Kārlis Zariņš, Latvian minister in London, to R. M. A. Hankey, British Foreign Office, FO371/55973-N15833/112/59, which document includes a list of Latvian diplomatic representatives throughout the world as of December 1, 1946.

7.   Dunsdorfs, p. 71.

8.   London, December 9, 1946, letter from Kārlis Zariņš, Latvian minister in London, to R. M. A. Hankey, British Foreign Office, FO371/55973-N15833/112/59; FOLD, 1950–1953.

9.   London, December 9, 1946, letter from Kārlis Zariņš, Latvian minister in London, to R. M. A. Hankey, British Foreign Office, FO371/55973-N15833/112/59.

10.   Ludwik Dembinski, *The Modern Law of Diplomacy* (Dordrecht, The Netherlands: Martinus Nijhoff, 1988), pp. 44–48.

11.   Financial considerations often result in creative adaptations of the international conventions that govern diplomatic practice, especially for purposes of symbolism and prestige, as noted in Hans J. Morgenthau and Kenneth W. Thompson, *Politics among Nations* (New York: Alfred A. Knopf, 1985), pp. 87–92, 566–569.

12.   London, December 9, 1946, letter from Kārlis Zariņš, Latvian minister in London, to R. M. A. Hankey, British Foreign Office, FO371/55973-N15833/112/59.

13.   London, April 3, 1952, letter from Kārlis Zariņš, Latvian minister in London, to Marcus Cheke, British Foreign Office, with response FO372/7174-T66/1.

14.   London, April 3, 1952, letter from Kārlis Zariņš, Latvian minister in London, to Marcus Cheke, British Foreign Office, with response FO372/7174-T66/1.

15.   This policy is discussed in Henry S. Albinski, *Australian External Policy under Labor* (Vancouver: University of British Columbia Press, 1977), pp. 152–172.

16.   An overview of this general assessment of the history of Australian foreign policy is offered in Cora Bell, *Dependent Ally* (Melbourne: Oxford University Press, 1988), pp. 1–20.

17.   Bell, p. 122.

18.   Albinski, pp. 155–156; Betty Birskys, Antanas Birskys, Aldis L. Putnins, and Inno Salasoo, *The Baltic Peoples in Australia* (Melbourne: Australasian Educa Press, 1986), pp. 43-47.

19.   *Commonwealth Parliamentary Debates*, Senate, August 8, 1974, p. 781. New Zealand adopted, at this time, an almost identical policy regarding the de jure recognition of the incorporation of the Baltic states into the Soviet Union, although it appears that there were no longer any Baltic diplomats functioning within that country by this time, as reported in Dunsdorfs, pp. 100–102.

20.   *C.P.D.*, Senate, August 13, 1974, p. 781.

21.   *C.P.D.*, Senate, August 13, 1974, p. 782.

22.   Quoted in Dunsdorfs, pp. 71, 73.

23.   Murphy, pp. 124–128.

24.   Murphy, p. 124.

25.   Murphy, pp. 133–209.

26.   Murphy, pp. 193–194.

27.   Murphy, pp. 193–201.

28.   Examples are provided in *C.P.D.*, Senate, August 13, 1974, pp. 784–788, August 16, 1974, pp. 1055–1057, September 18, 1974, pp. 1165–1166, October 15, 1974, House of Representatives, pp. 2283–2286, October 31, 1974, pp. 3276–3277.

29.   A commentary upon these proceedings, as well as other correspondence relating to this issue, can be found in Dunsdorfs, pp. 75–156.

30.   *C.P.D.*, Senate, September 18, 1974, p. 1167.

31.   *C.P.D.*, Senate, September 18, 1974, pp. 1167–1229.

32.   This debate and its consequences are analyzed in Dunsdorfs, pp. 157–219.

33.   The "Governor–General's Crisis" is addressed, in this respect, in Ward, pp. 406–419.

34.   Betty Birskys et al., p. 46; Bell, pp. 139–142; The Australian Labour Party, while serving as the official Opposition, also reversed its official party policy upon this matter in 1978, as noted in Birskys et al., p. 46.

Chapter 8

Conclusion:
Diplomacy as the "Art of the Possible"

The conflicts that emerged from the Cold War resulted from a more abstract confrontation between polar entities: the United States and the Soviet Union (as the most recent representatives of a perceived Western tradition of bipolar conflicts extending back as far as the romanticized struggle between Athens and Sparta); the North Atlantic Treaty Organization and the Warsaw Pact; "democracy" and "dictatorship"; "freedom" and "tyranny"; "good" and "evil." The Baltic states were both "pawns" and victims of that grand confrontation. Therefore, the diplomatic representatives of these states, regardless of their true status, were well placed to become characters (albeit minor ones) upon the stage of this international, and often skewed, "morality play."[1] Diplomacy is a major component of a "cold" war, since it seeks, as much as armed conflict, to promote the interests of the state that it represents.[2] Nonetheless, the saga of Estonian, Latvian, and Lithuanian diplomacy has appealed to a universal dream of self-determination and freedom that ennobles this enterprise beyond the normally self-interested calculations that can be associated with diplomacy. It is this ennobling feature that ultimately makes this study so appealing.

However, the fact that the example of Baltic diplomacy during the Cold War era is so unusual raises a challenge regarding its larger relevance and utility. It is easy to argue that the conditions and attitudes that were responsible for the perpetuation (and, in some cases, even creation) of

Baltic diplomatic missions following the annexation of Estonia, Latvia, and Lithuania were unique and, therefore, not replicable. That contention may be true, in a strict sense, but it is not unrealistic to argue that aspects of this diplomatic experience could find applications within the dynamic, post–Cold War period of the post–industrial world.

In order to make such an argument, the lessons learned from this Baltic experience need to be compared to this post–industrial context. Two patterns appear to have emerged most prominently from the international situation that succeeded the periods of "confrontation," "containment," and "coexistence" between East and West: the globalization of economic activity and the global decentralization of political identity.   The first pattern has increased the importance of diplomatic presence and activity; the second pattern has increased a desire among nonindependent cultural and political communities to attain a political "voice" in the pursuit of political autonomy.[3]

One of the most noticeable developments in world politics in the last quarter of the twentieth century (especially since the end of the 1980s) has been the proliferation of "ethnic" and other nationalist movements. This development can be related to the collapse of the Soviet Union and the Western "victory over Communism." As the diplomatic emphasis upon this overarching relationship between "East" and "West" disappeared, it was replaced by an emerging movement toward greater international cooperation, especially under the aegises of formal trading blocs and other international conventions and organizations. This trend has paralleled an increasing economic globalization, in which a movement toward the diminution of differences among nations has contributed to a growing uniformity in economic structures and mores.   This growing uniformity, in turn, has contributed to a perception among many ethnic groups and nationalities that cultural differences have been, or will be, suppressed by this new "world order."[4]

Several political movements have sought greater autonomy for such groups. Some of these movements have been relatively, though not entirely, peaceful, such as the efforts of the Welsh and Scottish nationalists of the United Kingdom,[5] the Flemish and Walloon activists of Belgium,[6] and the Québécois separatists of Canada.[7]   Other movements have been violent (sometimes devastatingly), such as the Basque militants of Spain,[8] Irish terrorists in Ulster,[9] Chechen rebels in Russia,[10] and the various ethnic groups of the Balkans.[11] However, a necessary emphasis, with all of these cases, has been placed upon a presentation of the perspective of the ethnic or national group for the purpose of influencing world opinion, as well as foreign governments.   This aspect of these movements, whether they take the form of negotiation or propaganda, assumes the rudimentary forms of diplomacy.[12] It seems natural that these movements might wish to formalize such a process for enhancing the image and legitimacy of their respective causes.

In many cases, these movements lack a true government from which this sort of political activity can be coordinated. Even in the case of those movements that are supported by a governmental structure, a lack of full sovereignty inhibits the creation and implementation of a conventional foreign relations regime. This deficiency makes the historic example of the activities of Estonian, Latvian, and Lithuanian diplomats abroad particularly relevant to these trends within the current world order. A good example of this potential can be observed in connection with the developing separatist movement in Quebec.

Much of Canada's history has been affected by linguistic, cultural, and nationalist conflicts, especially between English–speaking and French–speaking inhabitants of that country. The institutional evolution of Canada has reflected, in large part, that focus. This conflict has been most relevant in terms of the political struggles between the federal Canadian government and the provincial government of Quebec, where the majority of North America's French–speaking population lives. Periodically, movements and rebellions have supported Quebec's cultural and political separation from the rest of Canada within a climate of general tension between that province and both the predominantly anglophone provinces and the federal government. Since the 1960s, much of the agitation for separation has been supported, and even initiated, by Quebec's political leadership—particularly the governments of the Parti Québécois. These separatist movements have culminated in rebellions and, more recently, referendums on the subject, but institutional responses in support of these objectives also have occurred, including within the realm of diplomacy.[13]

The Quebec government was not able to establish embassies in foreign capitals, but it did establish political, cultural, and trade centers that represented its interests abroad. These centers (often known as *"les Maisons Québec"*) promote trade, enhance commercial relationships, establish lines of communication, and assist Quebec businesses abroad. However, the perspective of Quebec governments that have pursued the goal of increased political autonomy regards the symbolic function of a "Quebec House" as extremely important. These units serve the role of potential "embassies," but they also represent the "idea" of an independent Quebec. They promote the image of Quebec as the authentic representative of francophone Canadians, so they are an institutional tool

in the quest for political legitimacy.[14] Therefore, they are part of a larger
institutional presence that separatist governments have sought to develop
in support of a movement toward political and cultural sovereignty. The
general significance of such institutions has not been lost upon Quebec
politicians and scholars.

> C'est le Québec qui prit la tête en ajoutant un
> service de coopération extérieure à ses
> ministères de l'Education et des Affaires
> culturelles au début des années soixante. Le
> ministère de l'Industrie et du Commerce avait
> un service étranger qui porta différents noms
> tout au long des années soixante. En 1965,
> un comité inter-ministériel pour les affaires
> inter-gouvernementales   fut   établi   pour
> coordonner les affaires extérieures de ces
> ministères.   En   1967,   les   relations
> internationales   furent   ajoutées   aux
> responsabilités du ministère des Affaires
> fédérales-provinciales. Les services politiques
> de la direction internationale dans le nouveau
> ministère des Affaires intergouvernementales
> furent initialement conçus comme système de
> bureau   régional.   Plus   récemment,   la
> Direction de la Coopération internationale
> fut réorganisée selon des linges fonctionnelles
> comprenant des missions dans les domaines
> des affaires sociales, économiques, éducatives,
> culturelles et institutionnelles. La direction
> des   relations   internationales   prit   la
> responsabilité des maisons du Québec à
> l'étranger, des organisations internationales et
> du développement international.[15]

Of course, these institutions represent an actual government, even
if it is not recognized internationally as being an independent and fully
sovereign one. However, it is not the sovereign government of Quebec but
the concept of such a government that is represented by these institutions.

A Baltic diplomat of the Cold War era did not represent a country;
that person represented the *idea* of a country. Simultaneously, it is both
easier and more difficult to conduct diplomatic affairs under such
circumstances. Baltic diplomats of this era did not need to defend, or even
explain, the actions and policies of their respective nongovernments. They
were free to conduct diplomatic negotiations in a manner of their own

choosing, within the limits imposed by the host nations and the realities of both international politics and international law.

However, they were forced to defend and promote the interests of something that was intangible. They rejected the legitimacy of the Estonian, Latvian, and Lithuanian Soviet Socialist Republics, but they offered no legitimate candidates in lieu of them. Their proper role was as vague and elusive as the states they claimed to represent. Yet none of these representatives nor any correspondence or other evidence that emanated from their respective missions ever registered any sentiment of incongruity. The idea of a free Baltic people who were legitimate subjects of international law was not, for them, an academic or political abstraction, regardless of its appearance to a disinterested observer. So, as a result of their commitment and faith, some members of the community of nations began to accept, to a limited extent, this unique interpretation of "reality."

One practical benefit of this episode of diplomatic history was the relative ease of transition these missions experienced as they were converted into fully recognized and functional embassies and consulates. It was an advantage that other emerging (or reemerging) independent countries normally lack, including the other, former "republics" of the Soviet Union. A tremendous amount of work necessarily had to be performed in this respect but, at least, the foreign ministries of these three countries were spared the daunting task of beginning "from scratch." The relative rapidity of the reestablishment of Baltic diplomats in foreign capitals offers testimony to this advantage.

In some cases, persons who already had functioned in that capacity during the Cold War era continued to serve as the diplomatic representatives of a fully sovereign Estonia, Latvia, and Lithuania. Ernst Jaakson provides an admirable example of that transition. His long service as "Consul General in New York" was traded for the unambiguous appointment as Estonian ambassador to the United States.[16] Likewise, Dr. Anatol Dinbergs continued his diplomatic activities of 21 years when his official status was changed from chargé d'affaires of the Latvian Legation in Washington to Latvian ambassador to the United States.[17] A similar occurrence marked the career of Stasys Lozoraitis, Jr. when he ceased being chargé d'affaires of the Lithuanian Legation in Washington and became head of the Lithuanian Embassy, with the rank of ambassador.[18]

In this Lithuanian case, as in many of the parallel examples, the physical resources of these diplomatic missions increased, but they were simply added to institutions that already existed. Of course, in many instances, these Baltic governments were compelled to establish completely new diplomatic missions, including compounds and staff, where none had existed for over 50 years, if ever. However, many of the missions to the most significant host countries (especially the United States) enjoyed this advantage and, therefore, both an easier transition and a sense of continuity that reinforced the legitimacy of the respective governments that they represent and the positive nature of those relations.[19]

Many peoples and political movements might benefit, in terms of potential political strategy, from the example of Estonian, Latvian, and Lithuanian activity during the years of Soviet annexation. However, despite everything that has been mentioned regarding this unique precedent of diplomatic law and practice, the extent to which the Baltic diplomacy of the Cold War era offers a useful model for other, expectant states remains dubious. The Baltic states had been able to rely upon the presence of both fully functioning and fully recognized diplomats and diplomatic missions prior to the era that has been emphasized. There had existed legitimate states of Estonia, Latvia, and Lithuania that made the subsequent diplomatic drama of the Cold War feasible.

For example, if the Kurdish people chose to adopt this strategy, it would be necessary for a recognizable authority, of some sort, to make the initial diplomatic appointments. This authority would not need to be, necessarily, a sovereign government. However, it would need to be accepted as a legitimate source of political autonomy by political authorities that also qualify as subjects of international law, whether those authorities are independent governments or a significant international institution, such as the United Nations.[20]

A Kurdish association of some sort would be necessary for achieving that purpose. It would need to consist of Kurdish political elites who can demonstrate a certain acceptance, by Kurdish people, of their claim to represent a Kurdish nation. Possibly, this association could be located within one or more countries. It also is possible that this association could declare itself to be a diplomatic mission and, thus, assume a dual role. Nonetheless, these missions, in either case, could not be self-generating; they would require a distinctly identifiable political entity as an ultimate source for their existence.

Furthermore, this "source" would require the achievement of legitimacy; it would need to be accepted by sovereign subjects of international law as the true representative of Kurdish people who are, or who deserve to be, politically sovereign. These are the fundamental conditions. There must be a connection between these hypothetical Kurdish diplomats and this political reality as an essential commencement. However, once those origins have been established, it is possible that this recognized Kurdish association could become disbanded or nonfunctioning. The novel example of Baltic diplomatic activity during the Cold War era might provide, at that point, an appropriate precedent for these Kurdish diplomats to emulate.

The diplomats and the missions that represented the idea of independent Estonia, Latvia, and Lithuania during the period of Soviet control also required this initial source of internationally recognized sovereign authority as an essential component of their existence. The representatives of the Quebec government, who function through the various *Maisons Québec*, also would require a recognition of the full independence of that Canadian province to assume a true diplomatic status. A connection must exist, at some point, between diplomats and some sort of fully sovereign authority. Baltic diplomats may have operated without the benefit of having fully sovereign states to represent, but that initial relationship, in fact, *did* exist.

The example of Quebec and the hypothetical example of the Kurdish people are instructive in that respect. It is necessary, in practical terms, for diplomats to represent, or have represented, an actual, functional institution of government in order for them to achieve a sense of purpose.[21] Furthermore, modern diplomacy is, by its nature, frequently complex and elaborate. Baltic missions of the twentieth century enjoyed the advantage of having been relatively well developed and sophisticated. Therefore, they were positioned, already, to function among the international community when circumstances compelled them to establish the highly unusual and, in some respects, imaginative precedent that has been the ultimate subject of this study.

The Baltic states had struggled very hard to achieve recognition of their sovereign status after achieving independence in the wake of World War I. The saga of Estonia from 1918 throughout the 1920s is indicative of the hard work, expense, and personal sacrifice required of such a small country that had only recently reestablished its independence. The transitory diplomatic missions that were created for the purpose of establishing *permanent* diplomatic missions within other countries (including neighboring East European countries) represented, in themselves, enormous efforts.[22] The Estonian experience was familiar to the Latvians and Lithuanians, also.[23] The diplomatic struggle of Baltic diplomats during the Cold War era may have served a practical purpose, in this respect, as well as an inspirational one, in terms of keeping the idea of Estonian, Latvian, and Lithuanian sovereignty alive. Certainly, these struggles finally achieved positive results, despite all of the interim suffering.

Other countries would experience a certain level of inconvenience in establishing their missions within these Baltic states, especially since they had been dismantled so completely by the Soviet forces that annexed these three countries during World War II. States that maintained the diplomatic status of Estonia, Latvia, and Lithuania (especially, but not exclusively, the United States) may not have achieved practical advantages from doing so, particularly from an infrastructural perspective.[24] However, the feeling of appreciation and goodwill that these countries have earned from their participation in this unusual episode of diplomatic history is bound to produce good and honorable, though intangible, results. The benefits of their position, in this respect, may not be measurable, but it is not unreasonable to assume that those countries that supported the struggles of the Baltic states in such a visible manner will be remembered and honored within those countries. That reaction is bound to make this international loyalty seem to have been, in some measure, worthwhile.

There are, and have been, stateless peoples and nations, in addition to political movements and organizations, that might have found, or might still find, relevance within the history of Baltic diplomacy. The Zionist movement that preceded the establishment and international recognition of the State of Israel had its "representatives" who conducted negotiations and served as "points of contact" between that movement and various sovereign governments.[25] The Palestine Liberation Organization, which also has achieved international recognition (even prior to achieving full political sovereignty) has experienced a similar series of "diplomatic" relationships.[26] If either of these political entities had ceased to exist, it is doubtful that their respective representatives would have continued to function in any sort of capacity; they almost certainly would not have achieved, let alone have maintained, a diplomatic status or appearance. Their political existence, to that extent, simply would have ended.

The Baltic experience demonstrated the extent to which diplomacy is an integral part of a larger political process and environment. It also may underscore the fact that all political activity necessitates interaction and presentation, both of which actions are, by their nature, diplomatic.[27] These diplomats exploited the power of the political symbolism that lies at the core of diplomatic activity. Their perseverance seemed to be, alternately, admirable, misguided, a subject for pathos, and absurd. Ultimately, it also seemed to be vindicated; the symbolic became real, and that objective is a central preoccupation of all diplomatic activity.

This experience underscores the classic contention that politics is the "art of the possible." The Baltic diplomats of the Cold War era never lost sight of that belief; as a result of their own faith, they helped to achieve the inconceivable. Perhaps, the greatest example that they have provided to other people who are engaged in pursuing a similarly desperate political objective is persistence, innovation, and the refusal to abandon hope, regardless of the seemingly insurmountable obstacles they must confront. These representatives were a small and largely symbolic part of a larger process, but they became (in terms of foreign support for that process) a catalyst for it, nonetheless.

These Baltic diplomats serve as a stirring and, potentially, popular example to anyone who seeks to promote the cause of self-determination and freedom in an often volatile and, seemingly, ruthless world of international relations. These relatively powerless persons were engaged in the almost hopeless process of defying the will of states and their own lack of legal "personality" within the context of an immense and dangerous world order. Ultimately, the only thing that mattered was the facilitation of the goal of Estonian, Latvian, and Lithuanian independence. Apparently, no effort is too small to contribute toward such a process.

Notes

1.   This theme is explored in Vernon V. Aspaturian, "Eastern Europe in World Perspective," in *Communism in Eastern Europe*, Teresa Rakowska-Harmstone and Andrew Gyorgy, eds. (Bloomington: Indiana University Press, 1979), pp. 1–36.

2.   This interpretation is suggested in Charles O. Lerche, Jr. and Abdul A. Said, *Concepts of International Relations* (Englewood Cliffs, NJ: Prentice-Hall, 1970), pp. 79–83.

3.   A significant manifestation of that trend is assessed in Alec Stone Sweet and Thomas L. Brunell, "Constructing a Supranational Constitution: Dispute Resolution and Governance in the European Community," *American Political Science Review* 92, no. 1 (March 1988), pp. 63–81.

4.   This emerging situation is discussed in Donald M. Snow, *The Shape of the Future: The Post-Cold War World* (Armonk, NY: M. E. Sharpe, 1995), pp. 112–116, 187–190.

5.   The development of twentieth century Scottish nationalism is addressed in Christopher T. Harvie, *Scotland and Nationalism: Scottish Society and Politics, 1707–1994* (London: Routledge, 1994), pp. 198–219. Interesting commentary on the eighteenth century origins of, and influences upon, modern Welsh nationalism can be found in Gwyn A. Williams, *The Search for Beulah Land: The Welsh and the Atlantic Revolution* (New York: Holmes & Meier, 1980), pp. 7–26.

6.   This contentious Belgian issue is summarized in Ronald Eckford Mill Irving, *The Flemings and Walloons of Belgium* (London: Minority Rights Group, 1980), pp. 7–13.

7.   A good appraisal of this aspect of the Quebec nationalist movement is offered in Dominique Clift, *Quebec Nationalism in Crisis* (Montreal and Kingston: McGill-Queen's University Press, 1989), pp. 86–108.

8.   An overview of the Basque nationalist movement, in all of its manifestations, is offered in Cyrus Ernesto Zirakzadeh, *A Rebellious People: Basques, Protests, and Politics* (Reno: University of Nevada Press, 1991), pp. 1–16.

9.   The cause of Irish nationalism has gone through many phases. During the late twentieth century, the majority of Irish nationalists (including nationalist residents of Ulster) have supported the non-violent efforts of the Social Democratic Labour Party, although more international attention has been focused upon the radical (including terrorist) approach of Sinn Fein and the Irish Republican Army. These conflicts are addressed in Donald P. Doumitt, *Conflict in Northern Ireland: The History, the Problem, and the Challenge* (New York: Peter Lang, 1985), pp. 25–36.

10.   The origins and early growth of this very old nationalist struggle are discussed in M. Gammer, *Muslim Resistance to the Tsar: Shamil and the Conquest of Chechnia and Daghestan* (London: F. Cass, 1994), pp. 113–121.

11.   These developments are summarized in W. Raymond Duncan, "Yugoslavia's Breakup," in *Ethnic Nationalism and Regional Conflict: The Former Soviet Union and Yugoslavia*, W. Raymond Duncan and G. Paul Holman, Jr., eds. (Boulder, CO: Westview Press, 1994), pp. 19–51.

12.   This political and "diplomatic" manifestation of post–Cold War nationalist movements is discussed in Walker Connor, *Ethnonationalism: The Quest for Understanding* (Princeton, NJ: Princeton University Press, 1994), pp. 166–191.

13.   That process has been a focal point of federal conflict between Canada and Quebec, as noted in Andre Bernard, *Problèmes politiques: Canada et Québec* (Ste. Foy: Les Presses de l'Université du Québec, 1993), pp. 141–170. Examples of other institutional approaches toward achieving this goal are addressed in James T. McHugh "The Quebec Constitution," *Quebec Studies*, 28 (Fall/Winter 2000), pp. 3–26.

14.   The Quebec government has been particularly active and relatively successful, in that respect, in its formal relationships with the members of the European Community, as noted in Louise Beaudoin, "Origines et développement du rôle international du Gouvernement du Québec," in *Le Canada et le Québec sur*

la scène internationale, Paul Painchaud, ed. (Montréal: Les Presses de l'Université du Québec, 1977), pp. 458–461.

15.   Thomas Allen Levy, "Le rôle des provinces," in Painchaud, pp. 141–142.
    "It is Quebec which took the lead in adding the administration of external cooperation to its ministries of Education and Cultural Affairs at the beginning of the 1960s. In 1965, an interministerial committee for intergovernmental affairs was established for the purpose of coordinating foreign affairs for these ministries. In 1967, international relations was added to the responsibilities of the Ministry of Federal–Provincial Affairs. Internationally–directed policy administration within the new Ministry of Intergovernmental Affairs initially was conceived as a system of regional offices. More recently, the direction of international cooperation was reorganized along functional lines encompassing missions in the domains of social, economic, educational, cultural, and institutional affairs. The direction of international relations was assigned responsibility for the Quebec Houses abroad, international organizations, and international development" (translation provided by McHugh).

16.   USDL, November 1993.

17.   USDL, November 1970; USDL, February 1992; USDL, May 1992.

18.   USDL, May 1992.

19.   McHugh interview with Victor Nakas, political and press officer, Lithuanian Embassy, Washington, March 16, 1992.

20.   Many of the actual political and "diplomatic" developments that have occurred within the modern Kurdish nationalist movement are discussed in Nader Entessar, *Kurdish Ethnonationalism* (Boulder, CO: Lynne Rienner, 1992), pp. 159–169.

21.   This difficulty is addressed in Louis Henkin, Richard C. Pugh, Oscar Schacter, and Hans Smit, *International Law: Cases and Materials* (St. Paul, MN: West, 1980), pp. 199–200.

22.   Malbone W. Graham, *The Diplomatic Recognition of the Border States. Part II: Estonia*, Publications of the University of California at Los Angeles in the Social Sciences, vol. 3, no. 3 (Berkeley: University of California Press, 1942), pp. 231–238; Eric A. Sibul, "The Origins of Estonian Diplomacy, 1917–1922: The Roles of Kaarel Robert Pusta, Antonius Piip, and Jaan Poska" (master's thesis, San Jose State University, 1989), pp. 36–38.

23.   Malbone W. Graham, *The Diplomatic Recognition of the Border States. Part III: Latvia*, Publications of the University of California at Los Angeles in the Social Sciences, vol.3, no. 4, 1941 (Berkeley: University of California Press, 1942), pp. 404–409; Georg von Rauch, *The Baltic States, the Years of Independence: Estonia, Latvia, Lithuania, 1917–1940* (Berkeley: University of California Press, 1942), p. 258; Alfred Erich Senn, "The Formation of the Lithuanian Foreign Office, 1918–1921," 21 *Slavic Review*, (September 1962), pp. 501, 503; Alfred Erich Senn, *The Emergence of Modern Lithuania* (New York: Columbia University Press, 1959), pp. 237–238; Janis A. Samts, "The Origins of Latvian Diplomacy, 1917–1925: The Role of Zigfrids Anna Meierovics in the Formulation of Latvian Foreign Policy" (master's thesis, San Jose State University, 1975), p. 29 et seq.

24.   Nonetheless, American embassies were established in all three Baltic capitals as early as October 2, 1991, as reported by information provided to the authors by Andrew Silski, Office of Nordic and Baltic Affairs, Department of State, Washington, DC, August 16, 1996.

25.   An important aspect of the political history of the Zionist nationalist movement is explored in Jehuda Reinharz, "Chaim Weizmann as Political Strategist: The Initial Years, 1918–1920," in *Essays in Modern Jewish History*, Frances Malino and Phyllis Cohen Albert, eds. (East Brunswick, NJ: Association of University Presses, 1982), pp. 271–294.

26.   These relationships have proven to be more successful than, and consequently have supplanted, earlier Palestinian militancy (although not without, ironically, terrorist opposition), and they are examined in Rashid Khalidi, "The PLO as Representative of the Palestinian People," in *The International Relations of the Palestine Liberation Organization*, Augustus R. Norton and Martin H. Greenberg, eds. (Carbondale: Southern Illinois University Press, 1989), pp. 59–73.

27.   The symbolic role of diplomatic activity as part of the "policy of prestige" is discussed in Hans J. Morgenthau and Kenneth W. Thompson, *Politics among Nations* (New York: Alfred A. Knopf, 1985), pp. 86–92.

Appendix A

Biographical Sketches of Estonian Diplomats

DR. FRIEDRICH K. AKEL

Born on September 5, 1871. Earned a doctorate at Tartu University and studied, as well, at Riga, Warsaw, and in Germany.[1] Minister to Finland, 1922–1923. Left Helsinki to become Estonian Foreign Minister in August 1923. Became premier on March 26, 1924 and served as such until December 16, 1924. He had a narrow escape from being murdered in the communist insurrection of December 1, 1924. Thereafter, he eventually resigned and resumed, for a time, the profession of oculist, which he had practiced in Tallinn, 1902–1922.[2] He was Estonian Foreign Minister, 1926–1927.[3] On May 12, 1928, he presented credentials as minister to Sweden and also assumed duties as minister to Denmark and Norway,

---

[1]   RHA; Tallinn, June 30, 1939, W. H. Gallienne, FO371/23609-N3306/3306/59, Records of Leading Personalities in Estonia.

[2]   HVL;   Georg von Rauch, *The Baltic States, The Years of Independence: Estonia, Latvia, Lithuania, 1917–1940* (Berkeley: University of California Press, 1974), pp. 111–114; Stockholm, February 12, 1929, Sir J. C. T. Vaughan, FO371/14053-N1430/400/42; Riga, January 17, 1934, Hughe M. Knatchbull-Hugessen, FO371/18236-N463/463/59.

[3]   HVL.

resident in Stockholm.[4] He presented credentials in Copenhagen on June 9, 1928.[5] He was minister to Germany from 1934 to1936, simultaneously being accredited to Vienna, Budapest, and The Hague. He again was Estonian Foreign Minister, 1936–1938,[6] retiring from public service because of ill health in May 1938. He was deported to the Soviet Union in 1940.[7] Died on July 3, 1941.[8]

ADO BIRK

Born on November 2, 1883. Lawyer.[9] Foreign Minister for two Estonian governments of Prime Minister Jan Tõnisson, 1919–1920.[10] Presented credentials as minister to the Soviet Union on July 13, 1922—the same day as the distinguished Lithuanian minister, Jurgis Baltrusaitis.[11] Birk served in Moscow when relations between Estonia and the Soviet Union were in a delicate state as a result of the execution of the Estonian communist, Viktor Kingissepp (1888–1922) and the prosecutions

---

[4]   Stockholm, February 12, 1929, Sir J. C. T. Vaughan, FO371/14053-N1430/400/42; Stockholm, January 1, 1932, Archibald Clark-Kerr, FO371/16342-N187/187/42.

[5]   Copenhagen, 1932, Sir Thomas B. Hohler, FO371/16280-N4/4/15.

[6]   HVL; Riga, January 17, 1934, Hughe M. Knatchbull-Hugessen, FO371/18236-N463/463/59.

[7]   William J. H. Hough, III, "The Annexation of the Baltic States and Its Effect on the Development of Law Prohibiting Forcible Seizure of Territory," *New York Law School Journal of International and Comparative Law* 6 (Winter 1985), pp. 485–486.

[8]   RHA.

[9]   RHA;   [Tallinn], June 4, 1931, [author unknown], FO371/15538-N3925/273/59, List of Leading Personalities in Estonia.

[10]   HVL; Eric A. Sibul, "The Origins of Estonian Diplomacy, 1917–1922: The Roles of Kaarel Robert Pusta, Antonius Piip, and Jaan Poska" (master's thesis, San Jose State University, 1989), p. 198.

[11]   Moscow, *Le Corps diplomatique à Moscou, juillet 1925*, FO371/11789-N568/568/38.

for speculation and espionage which the Soviets periodically brought against Estonian subjects in the Soviet Union. It was reported that Birk was "pleasant and agreeable" in his dealings, and, through his tact and moderation, he had been able to maintain his position as representative of a small country that, "as [Soviet foreign minister] Chicherin pointed out in his speech of January 1925 at Tiflis, 'must understand that it depends for its existence upon the loyalty and respect for treaties (of Soviet Russia), and not upon the protection of western Powers.'" Birk had "definite anglophile sympathies," a fact which did not ease his task when it was "remembered that Estonia is, among the Baltic States, the one which the Soviet Government is wont to regard as being the most firmly enmeshed in the web of British imperialist aspirations."[12] In June 1926, the Estonian government asked for Birk's resignation. There followed one of diplomacy's most bizarre episodes. Caught in the net of a Soviet attempt to discredit Britain, Birk was detained in the Soviet Union for nine months until he managed, with the aid of the Norwegian minister in Moscow, Andreas Urbye, to return to Estonia in early March 1927. There he was arrested, imprisoned, tried for high treason, and acquitted on November 4, 1927.[13] He died on February 2, 1942.[14]

ALEKSANDER HELLAT

Born on August 8, 1881. Lawyer. First Estonian representative to Latvia, serving as *Délégué Diplomatique* from 1920 to 1921. Was named minister on March 22, 1921, serving until January 20, 1922.[15] Assigned to Poland in 1922, with the title of diplomatic representative, he was

---

[12]   Moscow, February 18, 1926, Sir R. M. Hodgson, FO371/11793-N1064/1064/38.

[13]   August Rei, *The Drama of the Baltic Peoples* (Stockholm: Kirjastus Vaba Eesti, 1970), pp. 199–203; *Times* (London), November 5, 1927; [Tallinn], June 4, 1931, [author unknown], FO371/15538-N3925/273/59, List of Leading Personalities in Estonia.

[14]   RHA.

[15]   RHA; [Tallinn], June 4, 1931, [author unknown], FO371/15538-N3925/273/59, List of Leading Personalities in Estonia; LAM, pp. 57–58.

replaced in April 1923.[16] He assumed the position of Estonian foreign minister in 1923, until his posting as minister to Finland in September of that year.[17] Thus, in 1923, he was stationed in Poland, foreign minister in Tallinn, and went on to duty in Helsinki. In 1926, he was Estonian delegate to nonaggression pact negotiations with the Soviet Union.[18] Became Estonian foreign minister, again, for a short time in November and December 1927.[19] He left Helsinki on January 31, 1931 and became the secretary-general of the Estonian Foreign Ministry.[20] Simultaneously, minister to Hungary, 1925–1927, presenting credentials in June 1925. Died on November 28, 1943.[21]

HERMAN HELLAT

Born January 13, 1872.[22] Chargé d'affaires in Rome, 1923–1925,[23] between the departure of the Estonian minister, Kaarel Robert Pusta, in 1923, and the assignment of a new chargé, Aleksander Jurgenson, in 1925.[24]

---

[16]   Warsaw, January 2, 1922, W. G. Max Muller, FO371/8132-N491/491/55; Warsaw, February 15, 1924, W. G. Max Muller, FO371/10455-N1643/1643/55.

[17]   Helsinki, January 1, 1926, Ernest A. Rennie, FO371/11751-N177/177/56.

[18]   Helsinki, January 1, 1927, Ernest A. Rennie, FO371/12564-N225/225/56.

[19]   Helsinki, January 9, 1928, Ernest A. Rennie, FO371/13295-N569/569/56.

[20]   Helsinki, February 5, 1931, Rowland A. C. Sperling, FO371/15562-N990/990/56. Helsinki, November 26, 1931, Vivian Burbury, FO371/15562-N7670/990/56.

[21]   Budapest, January 18, 1927, Sir Colville Barclay, FO371/12182-C703/195/21; RHA.

[22]   RHA.

[23]   HVL.

[24]   Noted in biographical sketches of Pusta and Jurgenson.

ERNST JAAKSON

Born of Estonian parents on August 11, 1905, in Riga, Latvia. After graduation from the Gymnasium, studied at the University of Latvia and, later, at Tartu University. Began his diplomatic career with a posting to the Estonian Legation in Riga and, thereafter, at the Estonian Foreign Ministry in Tallinn. Appointed secretary of the Estonian Consulate in San Francisco in 1929. Transferred to New York City in 1932. Graduated from Columbia University in 1934, with a B.S. in economics. Served in New York as vice-consul and consul.[25] Upon Johannes Kaiv's death on November 21, 1965,[26] Jaakson succeeded Kaiv, first as acting consul at New York City in charge of legation on December 15, 1965,[27] then as consul general at New York City in charge of legation in 1968.[28] Upon the reestablishment of Estonian independence on August 20, 1991, he became the permanent representative (ambassador) to the United Nations, serving until August 1994.[29] He presented credentials as ambassador to the United States on November 25, 1991, and served until succeeded by Eerik-Niiles Kross as chargé d'affaires on April 5, 1993.[30] Jaakson has been a special adviser to the Estonian Mission to the United Nations since August 1994.[31]

---

[25]   Ernst Jaakson, "A Short Biography of Ernst Jaakson," personal to the authors, June 6, 1996.

[26]   RHA.

[27]   USDL, February 1966.

[28]   USDL, August 1968.

[29]   Jaakson, "Short Biography."

[30]   USDL, May 1993. The new ambassador, Toomas Hendrik Ilves, was appointed on May 20, 1993, and presented credentials on September 3, 1993, USDL August 1993, USDL, November 1993. Grigore Kalev Stoicescu succeeded Ilves, presenting credentials on May 14, 1997, USDL, summer 1997. Sven Jürgenson replaced Stoicescu in June 2000.

[31]   Jaakson, "Short Biography."

DAVID JANSON

Born on July 28, 1880.[32] Served as chargé d'affaires in Rome, 1934–1936[33] between the departure of Estonian minister August J. Schmidt-Torma in 1934 and the presentation of credentials as minister to Italy by Johan Leppik on November 5, 1936.[34]

RICHARD JÖFFERT

Born on October 7, 1900.[35] Served as Estonian chargé d'affaires in Hungary between the cessation of accreditation there of nonresident Estonian minister Karl Menning in 1933 and the presentation of credentials of Menning's successor as nonresident Estonian minister, Johan Leppik, on May 24, 1937.[36] Died on June 7, 1953.[37]

ALEKSANDER JURGENSON

Born on August 8, 1882.[38] Served as chargé d'affaires in Rome, 1925–1926[39] between the departure of chargé Herman Hellat in 1925 and the presentation of credentials as minister to Italy by Karl Tofer on May 21, 1927.[40] Died on November 11, 1936.[41]

---

[32]   RHA.

[33]   Janson was accredited to Rome as chargé on November 22, 1934, Rome, February 22, 1936, Sir E. Drummond, FO371/20413-R1092/230/22.

[34]   Noted in biographical sketches of Schmidt-Torma and Leppik.

[35]   RHA.

[36]   Noted in biographical sketches of Leppik and Menning. Jöffert also is mentioned in Budapest, January 3, 1936, Sir G. Knox, FO371/20395-R152/152/21.

[37]   RHA.

[38]   RHA.

[39]   HVL.

[40]   Noted in biographical sketches of Herman Hellat and Tofer.

[41]   RHA.

JOHANNES KAIV

Born July 8, 1897.[42] Became consul in New York City in charge of legation on April 1, 1939[43] until he was named acting consul general in New York City in charge of legation during the 1940s. He served with the acting consul general title until he appeared in the *U.S. Diplomatic List* of February 1965 as consul general at New York City in charge of legation, with the date of this appointment also cited as April 1, 1939.[44] He died on November 21, 1965,[45] and was listed in the *U.S. Diplomatic List* for the last time that month.[46] He was succeeded by Ernst Jaakson.[47]

DR. OSKAR KALLAS

Born on October 25, 1868. Graduated in philosophy from Tartu University in 1893 and earned a doctorate from Helsinki University. Was chargé d'affaires in Finland, 1919–1920. Became minister to Finland in 1920.[48] Presented credentials as the first Estonian minister to Britain on March 28, 1922, replacing the person serving as chargé d'affaires, Jaan Kopwillem.[49] Served as minister to The Netherlands, resident in London,

---

[42]   RHA.

[43]   USDL, May 1939.

[44]   USDL, February 1965. Listed as acting consul general in the *U. S. Diplomatic List* for the last time in the issue of November 1964.

[45]   RHA.

[46]   USDL, November 1965.

[47]   Noted in biographical sketch of Jaakson. An interesting item on Kaiv's relationship with Estonian diplomat Kaarel Robert Pusta and his son, K. R. Pusta, Jr., can be found in Washington, February 10, 1943, Elbridge Durbrow, USNA701.60i 11/2-1043.

[48]   ENE-2, 4, p. 254; Tallinn, June 30, 1939, W. H. Gallienne, FO371/23609-N3306/3306/59, Records of Leading Personalities in Estonia; Helsinki, November 17, 1920, George J. Kidston, FO371/5389-N3487/3487/56.

[49]   FOLD, 1922; FOLD, 1923.

1925–1934. Left this post in 1934.[50] Died at Stockholm, January 26, 1949.[51]

RICHARD M. KÄSPER [KASPERIS, KESPER]

Born on February 25, 1910.[52] Named minister to Lithuania on July 12, 1940. There appears to be no record that he ever served there and, given the Soviet occupation, whether he ever reached his post.[53]

JAAN KOPWILLEM

Born on July 12, 1885.[54] Was the first Estonian chief of mission in London to appear in the British *Foreign Office List*. He was listed as the chargé d'affaires in the 1922 issue, which covered the year 1921. No specific dates were cited for his tenure. It was the only issue in which he was mentioned.[55] He was a specialist in oil shale.[56] Died on May 13, 1956.[57]

CHARLES KUSIK [KUUSIK]

Born on October 17, 1900, in Estonia. Came to the United States in 1921 and received his education at New York University. He earned an M.A. in 1926 and completed his residence requirements for the doctorate at the

---

[50]   FOLD, 1935.

[51]   ENE-2, 4, p. 254.

[52]   RHA.

[53]   Heini Vilbiks, Librarian, Estonian Foreign Ministry, letter to Pacy, May 4, 1995; A book by the last American minister to Lithuania before Sovietization notes: "July 10, 1940. A new Estonian Minister to Lithuania has been named. His name is R. Kasperis," asa reported in Owen J. C. Norem, *Timeless Lithuania* (Chicago: Amerlith Press, 1943), p. 295. Kasperis is the Lithuanian version of Käsper.

[54]   RHA.

[55]   FOLD, 1922.

[56]   Sibul, p. 80.

[57]   RHA.

School of Business of Columbia University in 1931.[58] Named acting consul general in charge of legation, on June 21, 1928. He served in New York intermittently until 1939. Colonel Victor Mutt and Ernst Jaakson also had been principal officers there between 1928 and 1939.[59] Kusik returned to Estonia with his wife, Mary Jackson Kusik, and two children in 1940, where he served at the Estonian Foreign Ministry. They fled Estonia in 1941. He died on March 3, 1992, at Oak Ridge, Tennessee, and was buried in the Richmond Center Cemetery, Richmond, Massachusetts.[60]

HEINRICH LARETEI
Born on January 4, 1892.[61] Served as an officer in the czar's army. He was a former minister of the interior and was named minister to the Soviet Union in 1926.[62] He was reassigned from the Soviet Union in 1928 to be minister to Lithuania, presenting credentials on May 14, 1928.[63] Departing Lithuania on May 5, 1931,[64] he served in the Foreign Ministry in Tallinn as head of the Political Department and, later, as assistant minister[65] until 1936, when he was sent to be minister to Denmark, Norway, and Sweden, resident in Stockholm. He presented credentials at Stockholm on September 21, 1936, and at Copenhagen on December 9,

---

[58]   Obituary in *The Oak Ridger*, Oak Ridge (Tennessee), March 4, 1992.

[59]   USDL, July 1928, October 1928, April 1932, October 1936, December 1936. The appointment of Johannes Kaiv is noted in USDL, May 1939.

[60]   Obituary in *The Oak Ridger* [Oak Ridge, TN], March 4, 1992.

[61]   ENE-2, 5, p. 408.

[62]   Moscow, January 14, 1927, Sir R. M. Hodgson, FO371/12597-N315/315/38.

[63]   Riga, January 25, 1929, Joseph Addison, FO371/13985-N948/380/59.

[64]   Kovno, May 18, 1931, Hugh S. Fullerton, USNA701.60i 60M/3.

[65]   Tallinn, June 30, 1939, W. H. Gallienne, FO371/23609-N3306/3306/59, Records of Leading Personalities in Estonia.

1936.[66] After the closing of the Baltic legations in 1940, he settled in Sweden and ran a market garden.[67] Died in Stockholm on April 3, 1973.[68]

REV. JAAN LATTIK

Born on October 10, 1878. Studied theology at Tartu University. Member of the Estonian delegation to the League of Nations in 1921. Became minister of education in 1925. Estonian foreign minister from 1928 to his resignation on February 12, 1931.[69] Presented credentials as minister to Lithuania on September 20, 1939.[70] The American minister to Lithuania feared for Lattik when the latter diplomat was recalled on July 10, 1940,[71] but Lattik survived until June 27, 1967, dying in Stockholm.[72] He had fled to Sweden in the fall of 1944 and worked there as a pastor until his death.[73]

DR. JOHAN LEPPIK

Born on July 16, 1894. Studied medicine at Tartu University. Served as a physician in the czar's navy and, later, with the Estonian army during the Estonian War of Independence. Attended the peace conference following World War I and remained in Paris until 1923 as counselor of

---

[66]   Stockholm, January 4, 1937, Michael Palairet, FO371/21109-N5551/129/42; Copenhagen, January 1, 1938, Sir Patrick Ramsay, FO371/22259-N118/118/15; Stockholm, February 25, 1938, Sir Edmund Monson, FO371/22302-N1294/243/42.

[67]   Stockholm, July 9, 1941, A. W. M. Ross for Victor A. L. Mallet, FO371/29681-N3910/882/42.

[68]   ENE-2, 5, p. 408.

[69]   [Tallinn], June 4, 1931, [author unknown], FO371/15538-N3925/273/59, List of Leading Personalities in Estonia.

[70]   Riga, October 9, 1939, Charles W. Orde, FO371/23609-N5349/3449/59.

[71]   Norem, pp. 179, 295.

[72]   Heini Vilbiks, librarian, Estonian Foreign Ministry, letter to Pacy, May 4, 1995.

[73]   ENE-2, 5, p. 426.

the Estonian Legation. During April 1923, was made chargé d'affaires in Poland. Promoted to minister, August 1924.[74] Also served, resident in Warsaw, as chargé to Czechoslovakia, 1925–1927, and as minister to Romania, 1924–1927. Assigned to the Foreign Ministry, 1927–1931. Presented credentials as minister to Lithuania on May 11, 1931.[75] Accredited to Italy on November 5, 1936,[76] he was, simultaneously, minister to Austria, 1937–1938, and to Hungary, 1937–1939, resident in Rome. Presented credentials in Vienna on June 3, 1937,[77] and in Budapest on May 24, 1937.[78] Transferred to Budapest in June 1939.[79] Died in Sweden on January 25, 1965.[80]

JOHANNES E. MARKUS [HANS MARKUS]

Born on August 18, 1884. Chief of the Administrative Department of the Foreign Ministry, 1921–1927. Thereafter, he served as consul general in Berlin until March 1931. Served both as counselor and consul general at the Estonian Legation in London, 1931–1934.[81] He subsequently presented

---

[74]   RHA;   Warsaw, January 15, 1925, W. G. Max Muller, FO371/11002-N716/716/55; Warsaw, February 15, 1924, W. G. Max Muller, FO371/10455-N1643/1643/55;   Tallinn, June 30, 1939, W. H. Gallienne, FO371/23609-N3306/3306/59, Records of Leading Personalities in Estonia.

[75]   Riga, January 16, 1932, Hughe M. Knatchbull-Hugessen, FO371/16286-N567/238/59 — a rewrite of N238/238/59.

[76]   Rome, April 5, 1937, Sir E. Drummond, FO371/21180-R2486/1040/22.

[77]   Vienna, January 1, 1938, Michael Palairet, FO434/5-R121/121/3.

[78]   Budapest, January 7, 1938, Sir G. G. Knox, FO371/22376-R177/177/21.

[79]   Tallinn, June 30, 1939, W. H. Gallienne, FO371/23609-N3306/3306/59, Records of Leading Personalities in Estonia.

[80]   *Vaba Eesti Sona*, New York, February 4, 1965.

[81]   RHA; FOLD, 1932-1935; Tallinn, June 30, 1939, W. H. Gallienne, FO371/23609-N3306/3306/59, Records of Leading Personalities in Estonia.

credentials as minister to Poland, January 18, 1935.[82]   He also was Estonian minister to Czechoslovakia and Romania, resident in Warsaw. Presented credentials in Prague on October 14, 1935,[83] and in Bucharest on June 28, 1935.[84] After the fall of Poland, he was assigned as minister to Hungary, resident in Budapest, in November 1939.[85] Emigrated to the United States, where he worked with the Estonian community until the early 1950s, eventually becoming informal Estonian honorary consul general in Toronto.[86] Died on September 26, 1969.[87]

KARL MENNING

Born on May 11, 1874 at Tartu.[88] Studied theology at Tartu University. Served as a Lutheran pastor, but left the church for the stage, becoming director of the new Estonian Theatre until 1914. Among those persons who sought early recognition for Estonia, he was a member of the Estonian delegation at the Paris Peace Conference. Represented Estonia in Scandinavia from 1918 to 1921, mainly residing in Copenhagen.[89] Chargé d'affaires in Germany, 1921–1923, and, simultaneously, chargé in Austria, 1921–1925, Czechoslovakia, 1921–1925, and Hungary, 1921–1922, resident in Berlin. Named minister to Germany in 1923, minister to Austria in 1925, minister to Hungary in 1931 (presenting

---

[82]   Warsaw, January 1, 1936, Sir Howard W. Kennard, FO371/19958-C53/53/55.

[83]   Prague, January 4, 1938, B. C. Newton, FO434/5-R165/165/12.

[84]   Bucharest, January 1, 1936, Sir R. H. Hoare, FO434/3-R150/150/37.

[85]   HVL;   Tallinn, November 16, 1939, John C. Wiley, USNA7001.50i 67/2.

[86]   McHugh interview with Ilmar Heinsoo, Estonian consul general, Toronto, March 17, 1992.

[87]   RHA.

[88]   ENE-2, 6, p. 264.

[89]   [Tallinn], June 4, 1931, [author unknown], FO371/15538-N3925/273/59, List of Leading Personalities in Estonia; Riga, January 17, 1934, Hughe M. Knatchbull-Hugessen, FO371/18236-N463/463/59; Sibul, pp. 29, 80.

credentials in Budapest on July 2, 1931[90]), and chargé d'affaires in Switzerland, 1924–1929, with all posts served from Berlin.[91] Appointed minister to Latvia on November 18, 1933, presented credentials on January 17, 1934, and ended his service there on November 17, 1937.[92] Died on March 5, 1941, at Tartu.[93]

JAAN M. MÖLDER

Born on October 19, 1880.[94] Served as Estonian chargé d'affaires in Latvia, between the departure from there of Estonian minister Eduard Virgo, August 8, 1931, and the presentation of credentials of Virgo's successor as Estonian minister, Karl Menning, on January 17, 1934.[95] Died on March 22, 1942.[96]

RUDOLF MÖLLERSON

Born on July 27, 1892 at Tartu. During the Estonian War of Independence, he served in the Estonian navy as a liaison officer to the British naval squadron operating in Estonian waters.[97] One of the first

---

[90]   Budapest, August 4, 1931, Nicholas Roosevelt, USNA701.60i 64/2.

[91]   HVL.

[92]   HVL; LAM, p. 58; Riga, January 17, 1934, Hughe M. Knatchbull-Hugessen, FO371/18236-N463/463/59; an American dispatch, dated August 28, 1937, claimed that he was recalled to Tallinn and was "now at the Ministry of Foreign Affairs," in Tallinn, August 28, 1937, William C. Trimble, USNA701.60i 60P/6.

[93]   ENE-2, 6, p. 264.

[94]   RHA.

[95]   Noted in biographical sketches of Menning and Virgo. Mölder is mentioned in Riga, January 15, 1932, Hughe M. Knatchbull-Hugessen, FO371/16263-N542/7/59, and in Riga, January 2, 1933, Hughe M. Knatchbull-Hugessen, FO371/17180-N62/62/59.

[96]   RHA.

[97]   RHA; Tallinn, June 30, 1939, W. H. Gallienne, FO371/23609-N3306/3306/59, Records of Leading Personalities in Estonia.

diplomats to serve at the Estonian Legation in London, he began as secretary and vice-consul, became first secretary, and, on May 9, 1925, became counselor and consul general, serving until 1930.[98] Successively appointed chief of the Administrative Department of the Estonian Foreign Ministry, 1931, chief of the Political Department of the Foreign Ministry, 1934, and counselor of the Estonian Legation in Paris, September 1936. Presented credentials as minister to Finland on December 15, 1937.[99] Became minister to Germany in fall 1939, serving in that post until 1940.[100] Died in November, 1940.[101]

COLONEL VICTOR (WIKTOR) MUTT

Born on May 25, 1886.[102] Ants Piip presented credentials as Estonian minister to the United States on December 31, 1923.[103] Colonel Mutt was listed in the *Register of the Department of State* as being in Washington with Piip, Mutt serving as secretary of legation and military attaché.[104] Upon Piip's departure from the United States on December 18, 1925, Colonel Mutt was listed as secretary of legation in charge of consulate,[105] acting military attaché, and chargé d'affaires,[106] with the latter posting dated from December 28, 1925.[107] In 1925, Mutt was listed as secretary of legation in charge of consulate, resident in New York City, while Piip was listed as resident at 1618 18th Street, Washington, D. C.

---

[98]   FOLD, 1922–1931.

[99]   Helsinki, January 26, 1938, Thomas M. Snow, FO371/22269-N1077/710/56.

[100]   HVL.

[101]   RHA.

[102]   RHA.

[103]   Discussed in biographical sketch of Piip.

[104]   USRD, January 1, 1924, p. 248.

[105]   USRD, January 1, 1926, p. 284.

[106]   USRD, January 1, 1926, p. 269.

[107]   USRD, January 1, 1926, p. 269.

In 1926, both Mutt and the departed Piip were listed at 38 Park Row, New York, N. Y.[108] Mutt received consular status on December 6, 1926.[109] He was titled Consul General in New York City in charge of Legation on November 17, 1927.[110] He retained that title until Charles Kusik succeeded him as acting consul general in New York City in charge of legation, on April 1, 1932.[111] Colonel Mutt's name no longer appeared in the *U.S. Diplomatic List*, beginning with the May 1932 issue. Died on April 30, 1942.[112]

COLONEL ARTUR NORMAK
Born on September 5, 1895. Served in World War I. Studied at a military academy in France, 1930-1932.[113] Appointed Estonian diplomatic agent to Franco's Spain in February 1939 by the Estonian foreign minister, Karl Selter, rather than by the president of Estonia. Selter emphasized the source of the appointment in order to make clear the fact that Normak's appointment did not constitute de jure recognition of Franco's government.[114] Normak was given the status of chargé d'affaires at Burgos in March 1939.[115] By October 26, 1939, Normak was

---

[108]   USRD, January 1, 1926, pp. 269, 284; USRD, January 1, 1927, p. 263.

[109]   USRD, January 1, 1928, p. 289.

[110]   USRD, January 1, 1928, p. 273.

[111]   USDL, May 1932.

[112]   RHA.

[113]   Typed file provided by Estonian Archives in the United States, Inc., Lakewood, NJ.

[114]   Tallinn, February 23, 1939, Walter A. Leonard, USNA701.60i 52/3.

[115]   Tallinn, March 13, 1939, Walter A. Leonard, USNA701.60i 52/4.

recalled from that post.[116] Deported to Siberia on June 14, 1941, he returned to Estonia in 1957 and died there on August 18, 1975.[117]

OSKAR ÖPIK

Born on June 8, 1895. Studied law at Tartu University. Entered Ministry of Foreign Affairs in 1921. Sent to Berlin as attaché. Later assigned as secretary at Stockholm and, then, at Warsaw. Returned to the Foreign Ministry in 1923, where he served as head of the Political Department and, thereafter, head of the Administrative Department. In 1926, he was, for a short time, chargé d'affaires at Moscow, before being transferred to Berlin as first secretary. He was chargé d'affaires in Lithuania, 1927–1928, counselor at Moscow, 1928–1931, and counselor at Berlin, 1931–1934. He was named counsellor at Paris, in 1934.[118] Presented credentials as minister to Lithuania on October 23, 1936.[119] In December 1937, he was selected to be vice minister at the Estonian Foreign Ministry, with assumption of duties on January 15, 1938.[120] He served as Estonian minister to France in 1940,[121] until the Vichy French government closed all Baltic legations on August 15, 1940.[122] Died on November 20, 1974, in Northern Ireland.[123]

---

[116]   Riga, October 28, 1939, Charles W. Orde, transmitting dispatch of W. H. Gallienne, Tallinn, October 26, 1939, FO371/23608-N5993/2726/59.

[117]   Typed file provided by Estonian Archives in the United States, Inc., Lakewood, NJ.

[118]   RHA; Tallinn, June 30, 1939, W. H. Gallienne, FO371/23609-N3306/3306/59, Records of Leading Personalities in Estonia.

[119]   Kaunas, October 30, 1936, C. Porter Kuykendall, USNA701.60i 60M/5.

[120]   Kaunas, December 28, 1937, Owen Norem, USNA701.60i 60M/7.

[121]   HVL.

[122]   Hough, p. 430, n. 451.

[123]   *Vaba Eesti Sona*, New York, December 12, 1974.

PROFESSOR ANTS [ANTON, ANTONIUS, ANTHONY] PIIP

Born on February 28, 1884. Politician, lawyer, journalist, diplomat. Studied at the University of St. Petersburg and the University of Berlin. Had been employed in the czarist Ministry of the Interior.[124] Active in party politics and organization with future diplomats Julius Seljamaa and Otto Strandmann. Became chief editor of Labor Party newspaper, *Vaba Maa*, in 1923.[125] Member, along with Kaarel Robert Pusta and others, of the Estonian delegation traveling abroad to seek recognition of Estonia.[126] Accepted as informal representative of the Estonian government in London on May 3, 1918.[127] Member of the Estonian delegation at the Paris Peace Conference following World War I.[128] Served as prime minister, October 26, 1920 to January 4, 1921, and as foreign minister in 1919, 1922, 1926, 1933, and 1939–1940.[129] Became the first Estonian minister to the United States on December 31, 1923. Departed the United States on December 18, 1925.[130] When not in the

---

[124]   RHA; Sibul, p. 31; [Tallinn], June 4, 1931, [author unknown], FO371/15538-N3925/273/59, List of Leading Personalities in Estonia; Tallinn, June 30, 1939, W. H. Gallienne, FO371/23609-N3306/3306/59, Records of Leading Personalities in Estonia.

[125]   Vincent E. McHale, "Historical Estonia," in *Political Parties of Europe: Albania-Norway*, Vincent E. McHale, ed. (Westport, CT: Greenwood Press, 1983), pp. 382–384, 389–390, 393; [Tallinn], June 4, 1931, [author unknown], FO371/15538-N3925/273/59, List of Leading Personalities in Estonia.

[126]   Sibul, pp. 29–32 and passim; [Tallinn], June 4, 1931, [author unknown], FO371/15538-N3925/273/59, List of Leading Personalities in Estonia.

[127]   Albert N. Tarulis, *American–Baltic Relations, 1918–1922: The Struggle over Recognition* (Washington, DC: Catholic University Press, 1965), p. 83.

[128]   Sibul, p. 80; [Tallinn], June 4, 1931, [author unknown], FO371/15538-N3925/273/59, List of Leading Personalities in Estonia; Tallinn, June 30, 1939, W. H. Gallienne, FO371/23609-N3306/3306/59, Records of Leading Personalities in Estonia.

[129]   HVL; Rauch, p. 256.

[130]   USRD, January 1, 1924, p. 248; Departure date is found in a letter from the Estonian Minister of Foreign Affairs to the Secretary of State, October 11, 1927, USNA701.60i 11/26; Evan E. Young, American commissioner to the Baltic provinces, wrote that Piip was "unquestionably the best qualified man

service of his government, he was a professor of international law at Tartu University, a subject he utilized most effectively on behalf of Estonian statehood. He was arrested in July 1940 and deported to the Soviet Union following the Soviet occupation of Estonia.[131] Died on October 1, 1942.[132]

KAAREL [CHARLES] ROBERT PUSTA

Born on February 17, 1883. Active during the 1904–1905 Russian Revolution, fled abroad, settled, for a time, in Paris. Returned to Estonia where, with the future diplomat, Eduard Virgo, he published a weekly newspaper, *Tallinna Elu*. While Estonians sought independence toward the end of World War I, he became one of Estonia's first diplomats, going to Scandinavia and Western Europe and serving as a member of the Estonian delegation at the Paris Peace Conference following the end of the war. Remained in Paris as Estonian representative where, upon French recognition of Estonia, he was named minister. While minister to France, 1921–1932, he was, simultaneously, accredited to Italy (first as chargé d'affaires, then as minister), 1921–1923, Belgium, 1921–1932, Spain, 1928–1932, and was absent from Paris while serving as Estonian foreign minister in Tallinn, 1924–1925. Served as minister to Poland and, simultaneously, assigned as minister to Czechoslovakia and Romania, 1932–1934, resident in Warsaw. Transferred as minister to Denmark, Norway, and Sweden, resident in Stockholm, in 1935.[133] Presented credentials in Stockholm on September 19, 1935, but was removed from his post in December, 1935 when his government associated him with an attempted coup d'etat. Nonetheless, he was one of the most famous

---

in Esthonia [*sic*] to fill the position of Minister to the United States," as quoted in Washington, October 29, 1923, Evan E. Young, USNA701.60i 11/9.

[131]   Sibul, pp. 189–190.

[132]   RHA.

[133]   HVL; Sibul, pp. 29–38, 168, 191–193; Riga, December 4, 1926, Sir T. Vaughan, FO371/11736-N5500/5097/59, Notes on the Leading Personalities in Estonia; [Tallinn], June 4, 1931, [author unknown], FO371/15538-N3925/273/59, List of Leading Personalities in Estonia; Tallinn, June 30, 1939, W. H. Gallienne, FO371/23609-N3306/3306/59, Records of Leading Personalities in Estonia.

Estonian diplomats, if not *the* most famous one.[134] Sent on a special mission to Paris, 1940. Left for the United States following the German invasion of France.[135] Died on May 4, 1964, in Madrid.[136]

HANS REBANE

Born on December 24, 1882. Journalist. Studied at Tartu University and in Berlin. Joined the staff of the Tallinn newspaper *Postimees* in 1906, remaining until 1918, when he became chief editor of *Paevaleht* in Tallinn. Foreign Minister of Estonia, 1927–1928, and member of the Estonian Parliament, serving on the Parliamentary Committee for Foreign Affairs. Presented credentials as minister to Finland in April 1931.[137] It was communicated that he had made a good position for himself with the Finns, having the advantage that the Finnish language came easily to him.[138] Presented credentials as minister to Latvia on November 17, 1937.[139] Recalled by the new Estonian government that

---

[134] Stockholm, February 3, 1936, Michael Palairet, FO371/20356-N933/581/42; Stockholm, December 17, 1935, G. G. M. Vereker, FO371/19397-N6631/222/59; one report noted that no less a person than the permanent head of the French Foreign Ministry, Alexis Saint-Léger Léger, privately requested information from the French minister in Tallinn of the whereabouts of Pusta and inquired whether or not he had been arrested. The Institute of International Law in Paris, sent a telegram to the president of Estonia, asking that every possible facility be afforded Pusta for his defense, as reported in Paris, December 23, 1935, Charles B. P. Peake, FO371/19402-N6702/6702/59.

[135] Sibul, p. 191.

[136] *Vaba Eesti Sõna*, New York, May 7, 1964.

[137] RHA; Helsinki, January 28, 1932, Rowland A. C. Sperling, FO371/16289-N1138/1138/56; [Tallinn], June 4, 1931, [author unknown], FO371/15538-N3925/273/59, List of Leading Personalities in Estonia; Tallinn, June 30, 1939, W. H. Gallienne, FO371/23609-N3306/3306/59, Records of Leading Personalities in Estonia.

[138] Helsinki, January 16, 1934, Rowland A. C. Sterling, FO371/18276-N452/452/56.

[139] Riga, January 4, 1938, P. W. Scarlett, FO371/22226-N185/185/59.

had been formed after the occupation of Soviet forces, on June 30, 1940.[140] Died on December 16, 1961, in Sweden.[141]

AUGUST REI

Born on March 10, 1886. Politician, lawyer, journalist, diplomat. Displayed activity in political circles early in his career, and also was engaged in journalism. He graduated with a degree in law from St. Petersburg University in 1911. Served as an officer in the czarist army during World War I. Played a leading role in organizing an Estonian army. A founder of the Estonian Social Democratic Party. Minister of labor and social welfare, 1918–1919. President of the first Constituent Assembly, 1919. Parliamentarian. Leader of the Estonian delegation to the plenary session of the League of Nations in Geneva, 1925. Engaged as defense counsel in political trials, including the trial of diplomat Ado Birk. Premier of Estonia, December 4, 1928, to July 2, 1929. He welcomed the king of Sweden on a state visit in June 1929. Foreign minister, November 1932 to May 1933.[142] Candidate for Estonian presidency, 1934. Presented credentials as minister to the Soviet Union on February 9, 1938, after previously serving as assistant minister of foreign affairs. Went to Moscow with background of having begun his life as a Russian subject and being comfortable with the language.[143] Last Estonian envoy in Moscow before Sovietization. Estonian president Konstantin Päts nominated Rei to be the new prime minister, but the director of the Soviet occupation,

---

140   Riga, July 1, 1940, Charles W. Orde, FO371/24765-N6491/6491/59.

141   "In Memoriam" material from the Swedish press [undated], provided by Estonian Archives in the United States, Inc., Lakewood, NJ.

142   Riga, December 4, 1926, Sir T. Vaughan, FO371/11736-N5500/5097/59, Notes on the Leading Personalities in Estonia; [Tallinn], June 4, 1931, [author unknown], FO371/15538-N3925/273/59, List of Leading Personalities in Estonia; Tallinn, June 30, 1939, W. H. Gallienne, FO371/23609-N3306/3306/59, Records of Leading Personalities in Estonia.

143   Moscow, July 5, 1939, Sir William Seeds, FO371/23686-N3287/281/38.

Andrei Zhdanov, rejected this suggestion.[144] Went to Sweden in 1940. Died on March 29, 1963, in Stockholm.[145]

ALEKSANDER F. RENNING

Born on July 24, 1903.[146] Named minister to Latvia on July 12, 1940. There appears to be no record that he ever served there and, given the Soviet occupation, whether or not he ever reached his post.[147]

AUGUST J. SCHMIDT-TORMA [AUGUST J. SCHMIDT, AUGUST J. TORMA]

Born on February 19, 1895. Educated at St. Petersburg University. Attended Vladimir Military Academy and served as an officer in the czarist army during World War I. Was badly wounded in Galicia. Upon recovery, served with the Allies at Archangel in 1918 and, then, as Estonian military representative. Went to Lithuania as military attaché in December 1919, was appointed chargé d'affaires there in 1921, remaining until September 1923, when he returned to Tallinn and became director of the Political Department of the Foreign Ministry. Served temporarily as chargé d'affaires in Paris and Moscow during 1924–1926. Appointed assistant foreign minister, September 1927. It was reported that he "speaks many languages, and English well."[148] Presented credentials as minister to Italy on February 28, 1931.[149] Also accredited as representative to the League of Nations and minister to Switzerland,

---

[144]   David M. Crowe, *The Baltic States and the Great Powers: Foreign Relations, 1938–1940* (Boulder, CO: Westview Press, 1993), p. 169.

[145]   ENE-1, 6, p. 452; *New York Times*, April 2, 1963.

[146]   RHA.

[147]   Heini Vilbiks, librarian, Estonian Foreign Ministry, letter to Pacy, May 4, 1995.

[148]   RHA; Tallinn, June 30, 1939, W. H. Gallienne, FO371/23609-N3306/3306/59, Records of Leading Personalities in Estonia.

[149]   Rome, January 1, 1932, Sir R. Graham, FO371/15978-C154/154/22.

1931–1934, resident in Rome.[150] Presented credentials in Berne on August 14, 1931.[151] He transferred from Italy and presented credentials to King George V in London on December 18, 1934. While resident in London, he continued as Estonian representative to the League of Nations until 1939 and minister to Switzerland until 1940.[152] Died on March 12, 1971, in London.[153]

JULIUS F. SELJAMAA

Born on March 27, 1883. Presented credentials as minister to Latvia on January 25, 1922.[154] During his tenure in Latvia, he was made chargé d'affaires and, later, minister to Lithuania, resident at Riga.[155] He left Latvia and Lithuania in 1926.[156] Presented credentials as minister to the Soviet Union on May 31, 1928. Reports from Moscow declared that he was an ex-clerk, factory worker, schoolmaster, and journalist, had been elected to the Russian Duma as a Social Democrat in 1917, and helped to found the Estonian Labor Party. His diplomatic background included conducting important negotiations, prior to his country's independence, with representatives of the Allied powers and, thereafter, with the

---

[150]   HVL.

[151]   Berne, January 1, 1935, Sir Howard W. Kennard, FO425/412-W125/125/43.

[152]   HVL; FOLD, 1935; Schmidt-Torma appeared as August Schmidt in the *Foreign Office List* from 1935 (covering 1934) until 1941 (covering 1940), when he began to be listed as August Torma. In addition to presenting credentials to George V, he presented them again on May 5, 1936, and March 1, 1937, upon the accessions of King Edward VIII and King George VI, respectively.

[153]   *Times* (London), March 24, 1971.

[154]   Riga, May 21, 1928, F. W. B. Coleman, USNA701.60i 61/12; Riga, February 8, 1924, J. C. T. Vaughan, FO371/10375-N1626/1626/59.

[155]   Riga, March 2, 1925, J. C. T. Vaughan, FO371/10982-N1303/1303/59.

[156]   Riga, January 3, 1927, J. C. T. Vaughan, FO371/12545-N117/117/59.

Soviets.[157] Served as Estonian minister of foreign affairs, 1933–1936, resigning from that position on June 2, 1936.[158] Regarded as being very friendly to the United States. Cited as being very reliable, influential, highly respected, very helpful, and a trustworthy colleague.[159] Died on June 7, 1936.[160]

KARL SELTER

Born on June 24, 1898.[161] His studies in Tallinn were interrupted by his participation in World War I and the Estonian War of Independence. Graduated in law from Tartu University, 1925. Legal adviser to the defense, interior, and justice ministries until 1927. He was a member of the Anglo-Estonian Cultural Society.[162] Estonian foreign minister, 1938–1939, with duties including the conclusion of the mutual assistance pact with the Soviet Union, which served as a prelude to Sovietization.[163] Thereafter, appointed permanent representative of Estonia to the League of Nations, 1939, which was the first permanent Estonian assignment there at the ministerial level. The previous Estonian minister to the League of Nations, August J. Schmidt-Torma, was resident in Rome, 1931–1934, and, then, resident in London, 1934–1939. Prior Estonian representatives to the League of Nations, resident in Geneva, had been appointed below the ministerial level. Selter simultaneously was accredited to the Holy See, 1939–1940, and accredited to Switzerland,

---

157   Moscow, November 24, 1930, Sir Esmond Ovey, FO371/14885-N8355/5828/38; Moscow, January 4, 1932, Sir Esmond Ovey, FO371/16327-N150/150/38; Rauch, pp. 48, 178-179, 187; Evald Uustalu, *The History of Estonian People* (London: Boreas, 1952), p. 162.

158   Tallinn, June 3, 1936, Harry E. Carlson, USNA701.60i 65/2.

159   Riga, May 21, 1928, F. W. B. Coleman, USNA701.60i 61/12.

160   RHA.

161   ENE-1, 7, p. 130.

162   Tallinn, June 30, 1939, W. H. Gallienne, FO371/23609-N3306/3306/59, Records of Leading Personalities in Estonia.

163   Toivo U. Raun, *Estonia and the Estonians*, 2d ed. (Stanford, CA: Hoover Institution Press, 1991), pp. 140–141.

1940, resident in Geneva.[164] Reportedly, Selter wanted to be posted to Berlin, rather than Geneva, but was denied such a posting.[165] Died on January 31, 1958.[166]

OTTO STRANDMAN

Born on November 30, 1875. Educated at Tartu University and St. Petersburg University. Politician, lawyer, diplomat. Premier of Estonia, May 8, 1919 to November 11, 1919,[167] Foreign minister in 1920 and 1924.[168] Minister to Poland, 1927–1929.[169] Also served as minister to Czechoslovakia and Romania, resident at Warsaw, 1927–1929. Presented credentials in Warsaw on June 3, 1927 and in Prague on November 11, 1927.[170] Premier, again, July 9, 1929, to February 3, 1931.[171] Minister to France, 1933–1939, presenting credentials on January 20, 1933.[172] Served, simultaneously, as minister to Belgium, Luxembourg,

---

164   HVL;   Tallinn, November 16, 1939, John C. Wiley, USNA701.60i 64/4.

165   Riga, November 14, 1939, Charles W. Orde, transmitting dispatch of Wilfred H. Gallienne, Tallinn, November 10, 1939, FO371/23608-N6944/2726/59.

166   RHA.

167   RHA; Rauch, p. 256; Tallinn, June 30, 1939, W. H. Gallienne, FO371/23609-N3306/3306/59, Records of Leading Personalities in Estonia.

168   HVL.

169   Warsaw, January 23, 1928, R. A. Leeper, FO371/13307-N508/508/55; Warsaw, January 29, 1929, Sir William Erskine, FO371/14023-N743/743/55.

170   HVL; Warsaw, June 4, 1927, John B. Stetson, Jr., USNA701.60i 60c/orig.; Prague, November 14, 1927, John S. Gittings, USNA701.60i 60f/orig.

171   Rauch, p. 256.

172   Paris, January 1, 1935, Sir George R. Clerk, FO371/18797-C56/56/17.

Spain, and the Holy See, resident in Paris, 1933–1939.[173] Presented credentials as the first Estonian minister at the Holy See on September 30, 1933.[174] Deported by Soviet authorities. Died on February 5, 1941.[175]

KARL TOFER

Born on August 11, 1885. Studied at Riga Polytechnic. Began his career as consul at Riga, then Berlin and, in 1923, was assigned to the Estonian Foreign Ministry as assistant minister of foreign affairs.[176] Had a remarkable career while serving as Estonian minister to states of particular importance to a Baltic country, such as Germany, the Soviet Union, and Poland.   His service also included accreditation to Czechoslovakia, Hungary, The Netherlands, and Romania. Presented credentials as minister to Italy on May 21, 1927,[177] where he was posted until 1930.   He also was minister to Hungary, resident in Rome, 1928–1929, having presented credentials in Budapest in March, 1928.[178] Presented credentials as minister to Poland on January 21, 1930, and, resident in Warsaw, he also was accredited as minister to Czechoslovakia and Romania, presenting credentials in Prague on March 19, 1931.[179] Presented credentials as minister to the Soviet Union on August 28,

---

[173]   HVL.

[174]   Holy See/Rome, January 1, 1934, Sir R. H. Clive, FO371/18427-R163/163/22.

[175]   RHA; Hough, pp. 485–486.

[176]   RHA;   Moscow, January 1, 1934, Viscount Chilston, FO371/18321-N137/137/38;   Tallinn, June 30, 1939, W. H. Gallienne, FO371/23609-N3306/3306/59, Records of Leading Personalities in Estonia.

[177]   Rome, February 3, 1928, Sir R. Graham, FO371/12955-C922/583/22.

[178]   Budapest, January 16, 1929, Viscount Chilston, FO371/13664-C546/546/21.

[179]   Warsaw, January 5, 1931, Sir W. Erskine, FO371/15580-N218/216/55.

1933.[180] Following his tour in Moscow, he was assigned to Germany and presented credentials on October 6, 1936.[181] Served, simultaneously, as minister to The Netherlands, 1936–1939.[182] Died on December 31, 1942.[183]

COLONEL AUGUST TRAKSMAA

Born on August 27, 1893. Served in the Estonian War of Independence. Attended courses in military science in Paris. Author of several works on military education and training.[184] A military officer since age 20. Had been an officer of the General Staff and commander of the 2d Division. Presented credentials as minister to the Soviet Union on September 21, 1936. Transferred from Moscow to the Estonian Foreign Ministry on August 25, 1937.[185] Named chief of the State Defense Training Institute at Tartu University, 1938. Promoted to the rank of *général de brigade* in February 1939.[186] Died on July 16, 1942.[187]

---

[180]   Moscow, January 1, 1934, Viscount Chilston, FO371/18321-N137/137/38.

[181]   Berlin, January 1, 1939, Sir George Ogilvie-Forbes, FO371/23042-C170/170/18.

[182]   HVL.

[183]   RHA.

[184]   RHA.

[185]   Tallinn, June 30, 1939, W. H. Gallienne, FO371/23609-N3306/3306/59, Records of Leading Personalities in Estonia; Moscow, January 19, 1937, Viscount Chilston, FO371/21099-N505/249/38; Moscow, January 10, 1938, Viscount Chilston, FO371/22293-N198/196/38; Tallinn, August 25, 1937, William C. Trimble, USNA701.60i 60P/6.

[186]   Tallinn, June 30, 1939, W. H. Gallienne, FO371/23609-N3306/3306/59, Records of Leading Personalities in Estonia.

[187]   RHA.

TÕNIS VARES

Born on December 11, 1859.[188] "Plenipotentiary representative" to the Russian Socialist Federative Soviet Republic by February 14, 1921. Name appears as Dionisi Georgievich Vares.[189] Cited as Dionis Vares in the Moscow diplomatic list of February 1, 1922, with the title of envoy extraordinary and minister plenipotentiary.[190] Replaced during summer of 1922.[191] Died on June 26, 1925.[192]

EDUARD VIRGO [WIRGO]

Born on October 4, 1878. Journalist. Studied from 1903 to 1906 at the Russian High School in Paris, while, simultaneously, Paris correspondent for the Estonian newspaper *Teataja*. Returned to Estonia in 1906, banished from Estonia, summer 1907, and lived, successively, in Finland, Paris, and London. Returned to Estonia, 1909. Traveled abroad with K. R. Pusta and others, seeking recognition for Estonia, 1918. Member of the Estonian delegation at the Paris Peace Conference. While in Rome for about a year, 1918–1919, he helped obtain de facto recognition of Estonia from the pope. Served as secretary of the Estonian delegation during peace negotiations with the Soviet Union at Tartu, fall 1919. Sent on a mission to London, early 1920. Acted as chief of the Political Department of the Estonian Foreign Ministry, May 1920–April 1921.[193] Assumed the duties of chargé d'affaires in Denmark, Norway, and Sweden, resident in Stockholm, 1921. Previously had visited Sweden and

---

[188]   RHA.

[189]   London, May 28, 1921, Department of Overseas Trade to Foreign Office, "Diplomatic Corps accredited [*sic*] to the Government of the Russian Socialist Federative Soviet Republic," FO371/6913-N6215/6215/38. This document refers to the RSFSR as shown here, and not as the Russian Soviet Federated Socialist Republic.

[190]   Moscow, RSFSR, *Corps diplomatique et missions étrangères, le 1er février, 1922*, FO371/8215-N4412/4412/38.

[191]   Moscow, February 23, 1923, R. M. Hodgson, FO371/9361-N2107/2107/38.

[192]   RHA.

[193]   Sibul, pp. 29, 80; [Tallinn], June 4, 1931, [author unknown], FO371/15538-N3925/273/59, List of Leading Personalities in Estonia.

reportedly was well acquainted with that country and its language.[194] Evan
E. Young, American commissioner to the Baltic provinces, 1920–1922,
wrote negatively of Virgo as a potential Estonian minister to the United
States. In a note to the American diplomat D. C. Poole, Young stated that
Virgo's appointment would be "unfortunate," but he doubted that it would
be "wise or expedient" to reject him.[195] Served as minister to Latvia,
1928–1931, presenting credentials on May 18, 1928, and departing Riga
by August 8, 1931.[196] Died on April 28, 1938.[197]

ALEKSANDER WARMA [VARMA]

Born on June 21, 1890.[198] Chief of naval staff during the Estonian
War of Independence, 1918–1920. Counselor of Estonian Legation in
Moscow, 1931–1933. Consul-general in Leningrad, 1933-1938.[199]
Presented credentials as minister to Lithuania on March 16, 1938.[200]
Arrived in Finland on November 29, 1939, and presented credentials on
December 2, 1939.[201] The American Legation in Helsinki reported, on

---

[194]   Stockholm, May 6, 1921, Colville A. Barclay, FO371/6948-
N6031/83/42.

[195]   Washington, March 28, 1923, Poole repeating Young's note to
Robert Woods Bliss in USNA701.60i 11/6.

[196]   LAM, p. 58.

[197]   RHA.

[198]   RHA.

[199]   Aleksander Warma, *In the Shadow of Communist Pressure: Finno-
Soviet Relations, 1938-1962* (Stockholm: Scandinavian Youth Service, 1962),
biographical sketch, unpaginated.

[200]   Riga, July 11, 1939, Thomas H. Preston, Kovno, to Charles W.
Orde, Riga, FO371/23609-N3449/3449/59.

[201]   Aleksander Warma, *Lähettiläänä Suomessa, 1939–1944* (Helsinki:
Kustannusosakeyhito Otava, 1973), pp. 98–99. Reference to Warma as Estonia
minister to Italy can be found in Kaunas, September 8, 1939, Owen J. C. Norem,
USNA701.60i 60M/9 and 701.60i 65/6, but, although appointed, he never served
there. The Estonian minister to Rome during 1939–1940 was Johann Leppik, as
reported in Italy. *Ministero Degli Affari Esteri. I Documenti Diplomatici Italiani.*

August 7, 1940, that Warma had suspended the operation of the Estonian Legation in Finland.[202]   Left Turku, Finland, by boat for Stockholm, September 23, 1944.[203] Died on December 23, 1970.[204]

Nona Serie 1939-1943, 4, Maggio 1940, 1960, p. 652. Leppik appears in the May 1940 Italian listing, while Warma is cited in the Helsinki diplomatic list of May 1940, as reported in Finland. *Corps diplomatique accrédité à Helsinki, mai 1940*, p. 14.

[202]   Helsinki, August 7, 1940, H. F. Arthur Schoenfeld, USNA701.60i 60P/7.

[203]   Warma, *Lähettiläänä*, p. 294.

[204]   RHA.

Appendix B

Biographical Sketches of Latvian Diplomats

HERMAN ALBĀTS

Born on August 23, 1879. Husband of Berta Bēkis. Attended university at Moscow, Paris, and Heidelberg.[1] Assistant minister of foreign affairs, July 23, 1920–April 1, 1923. Secretary-general of the Foreign Ministry, April 1, 1923–July 16, 1933. Foreign Minister, December 23, 1925–May 7, 1926.[2] Minister to the Holy See, resident at Riga, while serving as Secretary-General of the Foreign Ministry, presenting credentials on December 24, 1927.[3] Lecturer in international law, University of Riga.[4] Deported to the Soviet Union, where he died.[5]

---

[1] LKV, p. 238; EVP, pp. 25–26.

[2] LAM, pp. 102–103.

[3] Holy See/Rome, June 10, 1939, D. G. Osborne, FO371/23822-R4917/631/22.

[4] Riga, July 7, 1939, C. W. Orde, FO371/23609-N3444/3444/59, Records of Leading Personalities in Latvia.

[5] LES, 1, p. 496; LEA 1, p. 21; The Latvian minister in London, Kārlis R. Zariņš, reported that, according to Albāts' son, Albāts died in the Soviet Union, September 25, 1950, as recorded in FO371/86215-NB1903N.

PROFESSOR ANTONS BALODIS

Born on January 15, 1880. Participated in anti-Russian political movements and was forced into exile to Switzerland and France. Studied at Zurich and Grenoble, mastering the French language. Served as a professor at the University of Riga and taught among the Latvian colony in Baku. Was in charge of the Baltic Section of the Latvian Foreign Ministry in the early 1920s.[6] Presented credentials as minister to Lithuania on July 23, 1924. Foreign minister of Latvia, January 27, 1928–February 5, 1930.[8] While serving, simultaneously, as Latvian foreign minister and minister to Lithuania, resident in Riga, he delivered a speech, at Geneva, concerning the Liepāja-Romny railway and was, thereupon, declared persona non grata by Lithuania.[9] Presented credentials as minister to Finland on May 26, 1930.[10] Deported to the Soviet Union in 1941.[11]

DR. ALFREDS BĪLMANIS

Born on February 2, 1887 in Riga. Received a degree in history from Moscow University, 1910, studied at Strasbourg, and earned a doctorate from Vilnius University.[12] Married Halina Salniece.[13] Headed the Press Section of the Latvian Foreign Ministry, 1920–1932.[14] Presented credentials as

---

[6]   LKV, 1, p. 1,628; Helsinki, June 4, 1930, Arthur Bliss Lane, USNA701.60p 60d/3.

[7]   Kovno, February 8, 1924, J. C. T. Vaughan, FO371/10375-N1627/1627/59.

[8]   LAM, p. 102.

[9]   Riga, October 22, 1928, E. H. Carr, FO371/13273-N5139/674/59. A quick insight into the Balodis railway speech is provided in Hugh I. Rodgers, *Search for Security: A Study in Baltic Diplomacy, 1920–1934* (Hamden, CT: Archon Books, 1975), p. 75.

[10]   Helsinki, February 5, 1931, R. Sperling, FO371/15562-N990/990/56; Helsinki, January 11, 1933, R. Sperling, FO371/17204-N806/34/56.

[11]   LES, 1, p. 182.

[12]   LKV, 2, pp. 2398–2400.

[13]   EVP, p. 76.

[14]   LES, 1, p. 268.

minister to Moscow on July 5, 1932.[15] Presented credentials as minister to Washington on November 20, 1935.[16] The American Ambassador to Moscow, William C. Bullitt, called him "an enthusiastic admirer of the US and of all things American" and stated that Bīlmanis' father was an American citizen.[17] Indeed, in 1919, Bīlmanis spent his honeymoon at Niagara Falls, New York.[18] Bīlmanis was named as the successor (should the need arise) to Kārlis Zariņš, the Latvian minister to London, who, during World War II, was decreed to be "the Bearer of the Emergency Power of the Latvian National Government" on May 17, 1940.[19] Bīlmanis never needed to serve in that capacity, for he died before Zariņš, on July 26, 1948.[20] He was a prolific writer.[21]

---

[15]   Moscow, January 27, 1933, Sir Esmond Ovey, FO371/17255-N739/120/38; Riga, June 13, 1932, Felix Cole, USNA701.60P 61/12; Moscow, January 1, 1934, Viscount Chilston, FO371/18321-N137/137/38; Moscow, January 7, 1935, Viscount Chilston, FO371/19462-N306/306/38.

[16]   USDL, November 1935.

[17]   Moscow, April 29, 1935, William C. Bullitt, USNA701.60P 11/40.

[18]   Riga, August 24, 1938, E. L. Packer, USNA701.60P 11/66. Bīlmanis' tenure in Washington is addressed in Washington, January 1, 1936, Sir R. C. Lindsay, FO371/19832-A309/309/45, and George Abell and Evelyn Gordon, Let Them Eat Caviar (New York: Dodge, 1936), pp. 95–98. State Department reaction to Bīlmanis can be found in Washington, December 15, 1936, Robert F. Kelley, USNA701.60P 11/57, and Riga, February 5, 1937, Arthur Bliss Lane, USNA801.60P 11/59.

[19]   The document naming Zariņš and Bīlmanis is found in Third Interim Report of the Select Committee on Communist Aggression, 83d Congress, 2d Session (Washington, DC, 1954), p. 433. The original document, in Latvian, is reproduced in Arturs Bērzinš, Kārlis Zariņš Dzīvē un Darbā (London: Rūja, 1959), p. 226.

[20]   LES, 1, p. 268.

[21]   A partial list of the incredible number of his publications, with commentary, is provided in Adolf Sprudzs and Armins Rusis, eds., Res Baltica: A Collection of Essays in Honor of the Memory of Dr. Alfred Bilmanis, 1887–1948 (Leyden: A. W. Sijthoff, 1968), pp. 286–301.

GEORGS BISENIEKS [GEORGES BISSENEEK]

Born on December 19, 1885. Member of the Social Democratic Party from 1902. Arrested for revolutionary activity. Taught himself English while in Riga prison. Exiled to Irkutsk. Escaped to Belgium and Britain, 1911. Informal Latvian representative in London from December 1918. Stationed in London until 1924,[22] having presented credentials as the first Latvian minister to Britain on November 28, 1921. Returned to Riga in 1924 to succeed his father as managing director of the Latvian Economic Society, an agricultural cooperative organization.[23] Served as consul in Leningrad, where he was accused of being associated with the famous murder, on December 1, 1934, of Sergei M. Kirov.[24] He became a banker.[25] He was married to Lotija Hanney.[26] Deported to the Soviet Union in 1941.[27]

HŪGO CELMIŅŠ

Born on October 30, 1877. Agronomist and politician. Studied at Riga Polytechnic Institute, 1899-1903, and Berne, Switzerland, 1913–1914. Reserve soldier in the Czarist army, 1914–1918.[28] Latvian Agriculture Minister, 1920–1921 and 1924–1925. Latvian Education Minister, 1923–1924. Premier of Latvia, December 19, 1924–December 23, 1925, and December 1,

---

[22]   LES, 1, p. 276; LKV, 2, pp. 2477–2478.

[23]   FOLD, 1922-1925; [Riga], January 3, 1931, [author unknown], FO371/15538-N273/273/59, List of Leading Personalities in Latvia.

[24]   LES, 1, p. 276; no less a Soviet luminary than Vyacheslav M. Molotov spoke of a "foreign consul," while advancing a Soviet propaganda theme of a foreign link to the murder. The assassin, Leonid V. Nikolayev, was married to a *Latvian* woman, Milda Draula, whom Kirov reportedly liked. Bisenieks left Moscow on January 1, 1935. This particular episode is addressed in Moscow, 1935, Lord Chilston, FO371/19449-N6/N50/N313/N404/N428/N525/N1311/6/38; Arkady Vaksberg, *Stalin's Prosecutor: The Life of Andrei Vyshinsky*, Jan Butler, trans. (New York: Grove Weidenfeld, 1991), pp. 67–69, 79, and Robert Conquest, *Stalin and the Kirov Murder* (New York: Oxford University Press, 1989), pp. 11, 56, 67, 72.

[25]   EVP, p. 82; LES, 1, p. 276.

[26]   EVP, p. 82.

[27]   LES, 1, p. 276.

[28]   LKV, 3, pp. 3485–3486.

1928–March 26, 1931.[29] Latvian Foreign Minister, August 23, 1925–December 23, 1925 and February 5, 1930–March 26, 1931.[30] Mayor of Riga, 1931–1935.[31] Presented credentials as minister to Berlin on October 13, 1935.[32] Simultaneously, accredited as minister to Austria, resident in Berlin. Presented credentials at Vienna on December 17, 1935.[33] Later accredited to The Netherlands, resident in Berlin. Relieved of his duties, at his own request, in 1938.[34] Married to Marta Ġailīte.[35] Deported to the Soviet Union in 1941.[36]

FĒLIKSS CIELĒNS

Born on February 7, 1888. Politician and writer. Attended the University of St. Petersburg. Emigrated to Paris, 1910. Wrote in legally sanctioned and unsanctioned press. Returned to Latvia, March 1917. Member of the Latvian delegation to the Paris Peace Conference, following World War I. Social Democratic Member of the Saeima (parliament), 1923–1933.[37] Vice minister for foreign affairs, January 27, 1923–June 27, 1923. Foreign minister of Latvia, December 18, 1926–January 23, 1928.[38] Minister to France, Spain, and Portugal, resident in Paris, 1933–1934.[39] Recalled from

---

29   LES, 1, p. 373.

30   LAM, p. 102.

31   LES, 1, p. 373.

32   Berlin, [day and month unknown] 1938, [author unknown], FO371/21671-C80/80/18.

33   Vienna, January 1, 1938, Michael Palairet, FO434/5-R121/121/3.

34   Riga, September 19, 1938, E. L. Packer, USNA701.60P 55/2.

35   EVP, p. 111.

36   LEA, 1, p. 258; LES, 1, p. 373.

37   LES, 1, p. 396.

38   LAM, pp. 102–103.

39   LES, 1, p. 396. He presented credentials in Lisbon on November 7, 1933, as reported in Lisbon, November 11, 1933, R. G. Caldwell, USNA701.60P 53/4.

Paris on account of his alleged complicity in the purchase of arms found in the house of Dr. Pauls Kalniņš, president of the Saeima, 1925–1934, at the time of the Latvian coup d'etat of 1934.[40]   He wrote under several pseudonyms, including seven plays written under the pseudonym *Baltezers*.[41] He sent a memorandum to President John F. Kennedy in 1961, and Secretary of State Dean Rusk in 1963, encouraging American action against the Soviet Union. He became blind and died on July 10, 1964, in Stockholm.[42]

DR. ANATOL DINBERGS

Born in 1911 in Riga. Studied at the French Institute, in Riga, and earned a law degree at the University of Latvia. His early diplomatic career, begun in 1932, included service at the Latvian Foreign Ministry at Warsaw and as a diplomatic courier. Vice-consul in New York during 1940, when the Soviet Union annexed Latvia.[43]   First appeared in a *U. S. Diplomatic List* in February, 1941, ranked as an attaché.[44]   Named chargé d'affaires at Washington on July 26, 1948,[45] but reverted to the rank of attaché, upon the arrival of Julijs Feldmanis as chargé d'affaires (with the personal rank of minister plenipotentiary) on June 28, 1949.[46]   Became first secretary and assumed, again, the duties of chargé d'affaires upon the death of Feldmanis on August 16, 1953.[47]   Dr. Arnolds Spekke became chargé d'affaires (with the personal rank of minister plenipotentiary) on May 24, 1954,[48] serving until 1970, when Dr. Dinbergs, counselor of the Washington Legation, assumed

---

[40]   Paris, January 1, 1935, Sir George R. Clerk, FO371/18797-C56/56/17. Further detailed coverage of Cielēns can be found in Rodgers, passim.

[41]   LES, 1, p. 396.

[42]   LEA, 1, p. 265.

[43]   Obituary, *Washington Post*, November 11, 1993.

[44]   USDL, February 1941.

[45]   USDL, September 1948.

[46]   USDL, July 1949.

[47]   USDL, September 1953.

[48]   USDL, June 1954.

duties as chargé d'affaires on October 1, 1970.[49] Twenty-one years later, he was appointed Latvian ambassador to the United States, December 6, 1991,[50] and presented credentials on March 11, 1992.[51] Ojars Eriks Kalnins was appointed ambassador on February 4, 1993,[52] and officially succeeded Dinbergs when he presented credentials on April 14, 1993.[53] He was cited for the last time in the *U. S. Diplomatic List*, as a counselor in November 1993.[54] During the years of the Soviet occupation of Latvia, Dr. Dinbergs engaged in lobbying and public relations work, seeking and preserving Latvian assets, maintaining an information service, publishing a newsletter, issuing passports to Latvian exiles, and remaining in contact with Latvians, world wide. He returned to Latvia for the first time in 54 years in 1991. After over 60 years as a Latvian diplomat, he died on November 11, 1993, in Washington. He was survived by his wife of 44 years, Ruth B. Dinbergs.[55]

KĀRLIS DUCMANIS [CHARLES DUZMANS]

Born on November 10, 1881. Diplomat, publicist, and humorist. Law graduate of St. Petersburg University, 1913. Began legal practice, in Riga, 1914. Served in the czarist army during World War I. First diplomatic posting was to Copenhagen, 1919, followed by service as consul general and chargé d'affaires in Stockholm, April 1, 1923–September 1, 1925. Thereafter, he became Latvian representative at the League of Nations and also was accredited to Czechoslovakia and Yugoslavia, resident in Geneva. Wrote in several languages, including Latvian, English, French, German, Russian, and Swedish.[56] Headed the Legal Section of the Latvian Foreign Ministry, 1933–1934. Given his legal background from 1934 to 1936, he rendered international service for the League of Nations in the Saar Territory

---

49   USDL, November 1970.

50   USDL, February 1992.

51   USDL, May 1992.

52   USDL, February 1993.

53   USDL, May 1993.

54   USDL, November 1993.

55   Obituary, *Washington Post*, November 11, 1993.

56   LKV, 3, pp. 6003–6005.

controversy between France and Germany. Elected Latvian senator, 1936, serving until 1940. His name as a humorist was Atskabarga, which is Latvian for "Splinter." Married to Alma Vitola. Deported to the Soviet Union, 1941.[57]

LUDVIGS ĒĶIS

Born on September 11, 1892. Married to Alma Fūrmane. Studied economics at the University of Latvia. Entered the Latvian Foreign Ministry, 1920.[58] After assignments in Berlin and Helsinki, he became chief of protocol in 1925 and, then, chief of the Western Section of the Latvian Foreign Ministry. Counselor of the Latvian Legation in London, 1928. Named minister to Lithuania, 1934.[59] Latvian minister of finance, May 16, 1934–June 15, 1938.[60] During that tenure, he also was foreign minister, April 17, 1936–July 16, 1936.[61] Presented credentials as minister to Poland on September 7, 1938. Reportedly, he had a good knowledge of the English language, was an agreeable colleague, and was popular with the Poles, because he was a good sportsman. But, since relations between "Latvia and Poland are never unduly cordial," he had a "somewhat difficult task" in Warsaw.[62] Simultaneously accredited to Hungary, resident in Warsaw, he presented credentials in Budapest on September 24, 1938.[63] After Poland fell

---

[57]   EVP, pp. 141–142; LES, 1, pp. 528–529.

[58]   EVP, p. 154.

[59]   EVP, p. 154; LES, 1, p. 594; Warsaw, June 30, 1939, Sir H. W. Kennard, FO371/23144–C9681/1109/55.

[60]   EVP, p. 154.

[61]   LAM, p. 103.

[62]   Warsaw, June 30, 1939, Sir H. W. Kennard, FO371/23144–C9681/1109/55.

[63]   Budapest, July 3, 1939, Owen O'Malley, FO371/23115–C9505/3004/21.

in 1939, he was transferred to Romania, presenting credentials on October 18, 1939.[64] Died on July 7, 1943, in the United States.[65]

ĒRIKS MARTINS FELDMANIS

Born on September 12, 1884. Married to Ija Chreščaticka. Graduated with a degree in law from Tartu University. Served as Latvian minister of war.[66] Presented credentials as minister to Moscow on July 16, 1921. Withdrawn from Moscow with the more important members of his staff, 1923, when a lady typist of the Latvian Legation was "treated abominably by the secret police." His protest "met with a reply from the Commissariat for Foreign Affairs of so unpleasant a nature that [he] had no option but to leave his post."[68] Thereafter, he engaged in the practice of law and wrote for the press.[69] Deported to the Soviet Union, 1945, where he died.[70]

JŪLIJS FELDMANIS [FELDMANS]

Born on July 21, 1889. Married to Marianna Robina. Graduated with a degree in law from Moscow University. Chaired the Latvian National Committee at Omsk. Entered the Latvian Foreign Ministry, 1919.[71] Served as secretary, Latvian Legation in Paris, 1921–1923. Chief of the League of Nations section of the Latvian Foreign Ministry, 1923–1925. Returned to the Legation in Paris, 1925–1927. Chief of the Western Section of the Foreign Ministry, 1928–1930. Named Latvian representative to the League of

---

64   Bucharest, December 2, 1939, Franklin M. Gunther, USNA701.60P 71/2.

65   LES, 1, p. 594.

66   EVP, p. 163.

67   Moscow, RSFSR, *Corps diplomatique et missions étrangères, le 1er février 1922,* FO371/8215-N4412/4412/38.

68   Moscow, February 23, 1923, R. M. Hodgson, FO371/9361-N2107/2107/38.

69   EVP, p. 163.

70   LES, 1, p. 630.

71   EVP, p. 163.

Nations, 1930.[72] Presented credentials as minister to Switzerland on January 20, 1933.[73] Accredited to Denmark, resident in Geneva, 1939.[74] After the Swiss closed the Latvian Legation, he worked at the International Refugee Organization, created in 1947. The Latvian minister in London, Kārlis Zariņš, named him representative in Washington in 1949, succeeding Dr. Alfreds Bīlmanis, who died in 1948.[75] Feldmanis served in Washington as chargé d'affaires (with the personal rank of minister plenipotentiary), from June 28, 1949, until his death on August 16, 1953.[76]

FRĪDRICHS GROSVALDS

Born on December 13, 1850. Studied law in the 1870s at St. Petersburg. Served in the czarist judiciary. Practiced law, in Riga. Chair of the Latvian Association, 1885–1919. Deputy of the first Russian Duma, 1906. One of those Latvian diplomats abroad, from January 1919, seeking recognition for their state. Unofficial representative, from June 1919, in Stockholm, eventually becoming minister there and, simultaneously, accredited to Denmark and Norway.[77] It was reported from Stockholm, where he had presented credentials in May 1921, that, in addition to the Latvian language, he spoke only German, but his wife and daughter spoke English and French and professed "strong British sympathies." It was added that his daughter was a "very intelligent and capable young lady who

---

[72]   LES, 1, pp. 630–631.

[73]   Berne, January 1, 1935, Sir H. W. Kennard, FO425/412-W125/125/43.

[74]   Denmark. *Corps diplomatique accrédité à Copenhague, octobre 1939*, p. 27. This Copenhagen diplomatic list cited the Hotel d'Angleterre as his residence, when on duty in that city.

[75]   LES, 1, "*Diplomātiskais korpuss*," pp. 494–496. Upon the closing of the Baltic legations, in 1941, the Swiss government allowed the Baltic chiefs of mission to receive personal diplomatic privileges, as an act of courtesy, as reported in Hough, pp. 435–436, and Berne, January 31, 1946, British Legation to Northern Department, Foreign Office, FO371/55971-N1900/112/59.

[76]   EVP, p. 565; USDL, July 1949.

[77]   EVP, p. 192; LKV, 6, pp. 10878–10879.

practically runs the legation." His son, Oļģerts, was Latvian minister in Paris at this time.[78] Died on April 8, 1924 in Riga.[79]

DR. OLĢERTS GROSVALDS [OLGERD GROSVALD]

Born on April 25, 1884, in Riga. Son of Frīdrichs Grosvalds. Studied at Tartu, Paris, and Munich, receiving a doctorate in Munich in 1912. Lived in Riga until 1917, working as a journalist and art critic. Entered the foreign department of the Latvian National Council, 1917, working for the recognition of Latvia's independence. Secretary to the Latvian Delegation at the Paris Peace Conference following World War I.[80] Appointed Latvian diplomatic representative to France, July 1919. Later, presented credentials as minister to France, serving until August 1, 1924. Simultaneously employed as minister to Belgium and The Netherlands.[81] Chief of the Western Section, Latvian Foreign Ministry, 1924–1925.[82] Minister to Finland, October 1925–1930.[83] Presented credentials as minister to Poland on May 20, 1930.[84] Accredited, as well, to Austria, Hungary, and Romania, resident in Warsaw.[85] Presented credentials in Bucharest on June 20, 1930 and in Budapest on May 5, 1933.[86] Presented credentials as minister to France on

---

[78] Stockholm, January 9, 1922, Sir Colville Barclay, FO371/8231-N739/739/42.

[79] EVP, p. 192.

[80] LKV, 6, p. 10883; Helsinki, March 18, 1930, Alfred J. Pearson, USNA701.60p 60d/2.

[81] Helsinki, March 18, 1930, Alfred J. Pearson, USNA701.60p 60d/2.

[82] LKV, 6, p. 10883.

[83] Helsinki, January 1, 1927, Ernest Rennie, FO371/12564-N225/225/56.

[84] Warsaw, January 5, 1931, Sir W. Erskine, FO371/15580-N218/216/55.

[85] LES, p. 730; LKV, 6, p. 10883.

[86] Bucharest, January 4, 1934, Michael Palairet, FO434/1-R195/195/37; Budapest, January 26, 1934, Sir Patrick Ramsay, FO371/18410-R515/515/21.

October 29, 1934,[87] and also was accredited to Portugal and Spain, resident in Paris.[88] The Vichy French government closed all Baltic legations in Paris on August 15, 1940, and gave the buildings to the Soviet government, which had demanded them.[89] Eventually, Portugal and Spain also ceased relations with Latvia.[90] Married to Fannija Kuferate.[91] Died on September 12, 1962, in Paris.[92]

FRICIS KOCIŅŠ

Born in Jelgava[93] on May 10, 1895. Married to Emilija Grinberga.[94] Entered the czarist army in 1916, joining the Latvian army after the Russian Revolution. Participated actively in the struggle for Latvian independence. Upon the conclusion of peace, he completed his education at the University of Latvia and returned to the Latvian army. Appointed military attaché to the Latvian Legation in Lithuania, 1932,[95] serving until 1936.[96] Presented credentials as minister to the Soviet Union on January 4, 1937. Reportedly, he had the advantage of knowing Russia during his youth, having studied

---

[87]   Paris, January 1, 1935, Sir George R. Clerk, FO371/18797-C56/56/17.

[88]   Grosvalds presented credentials to the "Head of State" of Spain, as recorded in Riga, May 23, 1939, E. L. Packer, USNA701.60P 52/3. He presented credentials in Lisbon on November 5, 1935, as reported in Lisbon, November 6, 1935, R. G. Caldwell, USNA701.60P 53/5.

[89]   Hough, p. 430, n. 451.

[90]   LES, 1, "Diplomātiskais korpuss," pp. 494-496.

[91]   EVP, pp. 192-193.

[92]   LEA, 1, p. 524.

[93]   Riga, November 24, 1936, Arthur Bliss Lane, USNA701.60P 61/18.

[94]   EVP, pp. 259-260.

[95]   Riga, November 24, 1936, Arthur Bliss Lane, USNA701.60P 61/18.

[96]   LES, 2, p. 1030.

at the Moscow Commercial Institute and the Odessa Military School.[97] Upon the closing of the Latvian Legation in 1940, he was arrested and, presumably, died in the Soviet Union.[98] One source cited the year of his death as 1949.[99]

EDGARS KRIEVIŅŠ [EDGAR KREEWINSCH]

Born on June 1, 1884. Studied agronomy and economics at Tartu University. Also, studied at Grenoble, Leipzig, and Berlin. Earned a degree in Germanic and Roman philology at Moscow University, 1916, where he was a lecturer, 1914–1919. A lecturer at Riga University in 1920, when he entered the Latvian Foreign Ministry. Became first secretary at the Latvian Legation in Berlin. He engaged in consular duties there and at the Latvian Legation in Paris. Served as consul general and counselor in Berlin, 1924–1932. Minister to Germany, 1932–1935, and accredited, simultaneously, as minister to Austria and The Netherlands, having presented credentials in Vienna in May 1933[100] and at The Hague on February 27, 1934.[101] Presented credentials as minister to Estonia on November 7, 1935, leaving Tallinn three years later to present credentials, a second time, as minister at Berlin on November 22, 1938.[102] He appears to have lived the rest of his life in Germany. Died on January 9, 1971, in Konstanz, Germany.[103]

---

[97]   Moscow, January 10, 1938, Viscount Chilston, FO371/11193-N198/196/38.

[98]   LES, 2, p. 1030.

[99]   Andrejs Plakans, *The Latvians: A Short History* (Stanford, CA: Hoover Institution Press, 1995), p. 144.

[100]   LKV, 9, pp. 18343–18344; Vienna, January 1, 1934, Sir W. Selby, FO371/18359-R229/229/3; Riga, July 7, 1939, C. W. Orde, FO371/23609-N3444/3444/59, Records of Leading Personalities in Latvia.

[101]   The Hague, January 1, 1935, Sir Hubert Montgomery, FO425/412-W119/119/29.

[102]   Tallinn, January 3, 1936, W. H. Gallienne, FO371/20308-N819/267/59; Berlin, January 1, 1939, Sir George Ogilvie-Forbes, FO371/23042-C170/170/18.

[103]   LES, 2, p. 1072; LPE, p. 194.

JĀNIS LAZDIŅŠ [JAN LASDIN, LASDINS, LAZDYNS]

Born on August 22, 1875. Studied music in St. Petersburg, finishing in 1898, and performed as a violinist, 1902-1917. Worked as a secretary to the Latvian finance minister, 1918. Joined the Latvian Foreign Ministry, 1920, where, among his duties, he accompanied the famous Latvian Foreign Minister, Zigfrīds A. Meierovics, on trips abroad to Berlin, Geneva, London, Paris, and other places. Assigned to Brussels as consul general, July 1924. Made chargé d'affaires there, 1927, and appointed minister in 1929, while accredited to Luxembourg, simultaneously.[104] It was reported from Brussels that he was a "very intelligent and pleasant man,"[105] and he also was "quiet and distinguished in manner, and an agreeable conversationalist, ready to discuss any question."[106] He was relieved of his Belgian post and assigned to the Foreign Ministry, in Riga "awaiting orders," in 1938.[107] Died in Brussels on March 10, 1953.[108]

ROBERTS LIEPIŅŠ

Born on September 2, 1890. Married to Elza Vikstrēma. Studied commerce at Riga Polytechnic. Entered the Latvian Foreign Ministry around 1920 and served as chief of the Administrative and Legal Department until 1928 — a year when he temporarily left the Foreign Ministry to serve as Latvian minister of finance from March to October. Presented credentials as minister to Lithuania on January 15, 1929, serving until 1933.[109] Presented credentials as minister to Estonia on September 21, 1933,[110] serving until 1935, when he was transferred to the Soviet Union. Presented credentials in

---

104   LKV, 12, pp. 22684–22685.

105   Brussels, January 14, 1930, Earl Granville, FO371/14894-W613/613/4.

106   Brussels, January 15, 1937, Sir Noel Charles, FO371/20680-C397/397/4.

107   Riga, August 16, 1938, E. L. Packer, USNA701.60P 60C/3.

108   LEA, 2, p. 460.

109   EVP, p. 313; Riga, January 28, 1930, Alan Walker, FO371/14783-N692/692/59.

110   EVP, p. 313; Riga, January 4, 1934, Hughe M. Knatchbull-Hugessen, FO371/18235-N333/333/59.

Moscow on November 15, 1935.[111] In a 1935 message to Washington, the American chargé d'affaires in Riga wrote that officials of the Latvian Foreign Ministry had said, informally, that Liepins was considered to be Latvia's most able foreign representative.[112] He left Moscow and the foreign service in 1936. Appointed mayor of Riga by the president of Latvia, Kārlis Ulmanis, July 1936.[113] Served as an unofficial Latvian "diplomatic representative" in Germany, where he died on September 16, 1978, in Ludwigsburg.[114]

ARTURS LŪĻE [ARTHUR B. LULE]

Born on January 6, 1882. Married to Irma Ozolina. Graduate of Grenoble University, France. A city elder of Riga. Entered the Latvian Foreign Ministry, 1920.[115] Became consul in New York City on November 4, 1922[116] and, thereafter, consul in New York City in charge of legation on May 20, 1923.[117] When Latvia upgraded its level of representation with Ludvigs Sēja's (Charles Louis Seya) presentation of credentials as minister to the United States, on June 17, 1925,[118] Lūļe reverted to consular status only, as consul general.[119] Upon Sēja's reassignment, Lūļe resumed his post as consul general in New York City in charge of legation, on May 7, 1927.[120] He was absent from that post in October, 1932 and in August, 1934. Vilibert Kalejs substituted for him as vice-consul in charge of legation. He returned in

---

[111]   EVP, p. 313; Moscow, January 11, 1926, Viscount Chilston, FO371/20349-N298/298/38.

[112]   Riga, September 27, 1935, Felix Cole, USNA701.60P 61/17.

[113]   EVP, p. 313; Riga, July 7, 1939, Charles W. Orde, FO371/23609-N3444/3444/59, Records of Leading Personalities in Latvia.

[114]   LEA, 2, p. 514.

[115]   EVP, p. 321.

[116]   USRD, January 1, 1926, p. 296.

[117]   USDL, June 1923.

[118]   USDL, July 1925.

[119]   USRD, January 1, 1927, p. 290.

[120]   USRD, January 1, 1928, p. 275.

September 1934[121] and was succeeded by Dr. Alfreds Bīlmanis, who presented credentials as minister on November 20, 1935. Deported to the Soviet Union in 1941.[122]

MĀRTIŅŠ NUKŠA

Born on September 29, 1878. Studied engineering and architecture at Riga Polytechnic, graduating in 1908. Worked in Riga until 1915, in Moscow, 1915–1916, served as city architect of Sevastapol, 1916–1918, and was the city architect's assistant in Marseilles, France in 1919. Named first secretary of the Latvian Legation in Paris on February 1, 1920, and promoted to counselor on June 21, 1920. Sent to Poland as minister on August 4, 1921, serving until 1930. Accredited, simultaneously, as minister to Austria and Romania.[123] Presented credentials as minister to Sweden on May 23, 1930.[124] Accredited, additionally, to Denmark and Norway, resident in Stockholm, presenting credentials in Copenhagen on July 30, 1930,[125] and Oslo on August 1, 1930.[126] Presented credentials as minister to Czechoslovakia on September 6, 1933,[127] and, simultaneously, accredited to Yugoslavia, where he presented credentials in February 1934,[128] and Romania, where he

---

[121]   USDL, October 1932, November 1932, August 1934, September 1934.

[122]   USDL, November 1935; .LES, 2, p. 1580.

[123]   LKV, 15, pp. 29440–29441.

[124]   Stockholm, January 2, 1931, Sir H. W. Kennard, FO371/15626-N250/250/42; Stockholm, January 1, 1932, Archibald Clark Kerr, FO371/16342-N187/187/42.

[125]   Copenhagen, 1932, Sir T. Hohler, FO371/16280-N4/4/15/N7702/4/15.

[126]   Copenhagen, August 15, 1930, Ralph H. Booth, USNA701.60P 57/1.

[127]   Prague, January 1, 1935, Sir Joseph Addison, FO371/19492-R233/233/12.

[128]   Belgrade, January 1, 1938, Sir R. H. Campbell, FO434/5-R145/145/92.

presented credentials on November 29, 1935.[129] Secretary-general of the Latvian Foreign Ministry, 1939–1940. Deported to the Soviet Union, 1941.[130] His wife was Marija Sostena.[131]

PĒTERIS Z. OLINŠ

Born on April 3, 1890. Studied philosophy at St. Petersburg University, 1910–1914. Served with the Latvian military during World War I. Began diplomatic career with posting to Warsaw, 1919–1921. Named chief of the Western Department of the Foreign Ministry in Riga, 1922. Served in London. Assigned as counselor to Washington, 1925. Returned to Riga as chief of the Western Department by 1927. Became director of the Trade and Industry Department of the Latvian Ministry of Finance.[132] Assigned to Moscow, 1929. Thereafter, sent to Argentina and Brazil, becoming chargé d'affaires in Rio de Janeiro on May 2, 1935,[133] and chargé d'affaires in Buenos Aires on May 21, 1935, where he was resident.[134] In 1946, with Latvia a Soviet republic, it was communicated from Buenos Aires that Olinš continued to be carried in that country's diplomatic list but was seldom seen, except at official functions. The communication added, "I don't know who pays him."[135] Argentina closed the Latvian mission on November 30, 1946. Olinš moved to Rio de Janeiro on December 5, 1946, where he remained accredited as chargé d'affaires. He tried to reestablish the mission in Buenos Aires in March 1956 but failed. Brazil closed the Latvian mission on March 11, 1961. Olinš tried to reopen that mission one year later but, again, there was no success. Although he was no longer a diplomat, he continued to look

---

[129]   Bucharest, January 1, 1937, Sir R. H. Hoare, FO371/21189-R467/467/37.

[130]   LES, 2, pp. 1791–1792.

[131]   EVP, p. 360.

[132]   LES, 2, p.1,802; LKV, 15, pp. 29779–29780; Riga, May 27, 1925, F. W. B. Coleman, USNA701.60p 11/19.

[133]   Rio de Janeiro, January 2, 1936, Sir Hugh Gurney, FO371/19765-A792/42/6.

[134]   Buenos Aires, January 5, 1937, Sir Nevile Henderson, FO371/20598-A791/696/2.

[135]   Buenos Aires, June 7, 1946, Sir R. K. Leeper, FO371/51788-AS3483/36/2.

after Latvians. Interestingly, he was carried in the Brazilian diplomatic list as late as October 23, 1962, but he had died in Rio de Janeiro on August 27, 1962.[136]

KĀRLIS OZOLS

Born on May 7, 1882. Graduate of Riga Polytechnic, 1914. Engineer in Russia, 1914–1915. Sent to the United States as an official of the czarist government. Organized a society for Russian engineers in the United States in 1918 and served as its president. In 1919, he was a member of the Latvian Delegation to the Paris Peace Conference, following the end of World War I. Became active in the United States. Notified the State Department that he was authorized as the Latvian commercial representative in the United States on May 26, 1920. This position never rose above informal representation. Presented credentials as Latvian minister in Moscow on September 14, 1923.[137] It was noted that his "task as representative of a Baltic State must necessarily be an unpleasant one, for, besides having to deal with an infinity of petty annoyances, he has ever present before him the fact that Bolshevik Russia finds it difficult to assimilate the theory that Latvia can remain outside" the Soviet Union.[138] A later assessment drew attention to "disagreeable incidents in view of the fact that Latvia and Soviet Russia have a common frontier" and that Soviet officials felt no need to moderate "their eloquence whenever they find it convenient to magnify a Russo-Latvian episode for public delectation."[139] Ozols, it was stated, "is wont to handle these awkward situations with considerable tact and dignity."[140] He was recalled in 1929, "whereupon the Soviet press opened a bitter campaign of

---

[136]   LEA, 3, pp. 275–276.

[137]   LKV, 15, pp. 30206–30207; Tarulis, pp. 300–301; Riga, September 28, 1923, F. W. B. Coleman, USNA701.60p 61/2.

[138]   Moscow, March 16, 1925, R. M. Hodgson, FO371/11026-N1879/1879/38.

[139]   Moscow, February 18, 1926, Sir R. M. Hodgson, FO371/11793-N1064/1064/38.

[140]   Helsinki, August 28, 1929, Vivian Burbury to Laurence Collier, Foreign Office, FO371/14050-N3955/3955/38.

cartoons and abuse against him as a smuggler." Deported to the Soviet Union, 1941.[141]

OLĢERTS ROZĪTIS

Born on July 2, 1912 in St. Petersburg. Studied law and English at the University of Latvia, graduating from there in 1935. Entered the Latvian Foreign Ministry, 1935,[142] and was posted to London, 1938, as third secretary of legation, serving in London until 1952. He was cited in the British *Foreign Office List* in 1943 with the unique title of "third counsellor," but this title disappeared in the 1952 issue, where he was listed as consul general and first secretary.[143] He was sent as honorary consul (a title usually held only by citizens of the host country) to Melbourne, Australia. He served in that capacity until 1974, when Australia granted de jure recognition to the Soviet absorption of the Baltic states, which recognition was revoked by a succeeding Australian government. He earned a law degree from Melbourne University in 1973. Died on March 23, 1984, in Melbourne.[144]

VOLDEMĀRS SALNAIS

Born on May 20, 1886. Participated in the Russian Revolution of 1905. Sentenced to hard labor in Siberia. Emigrated to the United States in 1913, where he participated in Latvian life, including journalism. After the Russian Revolution of 1917, he returned to Siberia and became a member of the Latvian National Council. Returned to Latvia, 1920. Served in Parliament, was vice director and, later, director of the State Statistical Office, welfare minister,[145] vice minister of foreign affairs, June 19, 1921–January 23, 1923, and Latvian minister of foreign affairs, March 24, 1933–March 7, 1934.[146] Presented credentials as minister to Stockholm on May 11, 1937 and also was accredited to Oslo and Copenhagen, presenting credentials in

---

141   LES, 2, p. 1821.

142   LEA, 4, pp. 143–144.

143   FOLD, 1939–1952.

144   LEA, 4, pp. 143–144.

145   LKV, 19, pp. 37416–37418.

146   LAM, pp. 102–103.

Copenhagen in 1937.[147] Relieved of duties in Denmark on September 22, 1939.[148] All Baltic legations in Stockholm were closed in 1940.[149] Salnais served there until July 23, 1940. Was married to Milda Klavina.[150] Died on August 4, 1948, in Stockholm.[151]

LUDVIGS SĒJA [CHARLES LOUIS SEYA, C. LOUIS SEYA]

Born on June 2, 1885. Married to Herta Ozola. Prior to Latvian independence, studied at Paris and Grenoble. Teacher and journalist. Joined the Latvian Foreign Ministry, 1919. Became Director of its Political and Administrative Department. Named first formal Latvian representative to the United States, when he served as chargé d'affaires in Washington from September 28, 1922 to mid-1923.[152] Presented credentials as minister to Lithuania in July 1923.[153] Served as Latvian foreign minister, January 30, 1924–December 18, 1924.[154] Presented credentials as minister to the United States on June 17, 1925. In December, 1927, became consul general in London, serving as chargé d'affaires in 1932.[155] Named minister to Lithuania, again, in September 1934, and was still serving in that post as of July 11, 1939.[156] Arrested by the Gestapo in Latvia and imprisoned. Freed in 1945,

---

147   Stockholm, February 25, 1938, Sir E. Monson, FO371/22302-N1294/243/42.

148   Riga, September 29, 1939, E. L. Packer, USNA791.60P 59/2.

149   Stockholm, July 9, 1941, A. W. M. Ross, FO371/29681-N3910/882/42.

150   EVP, p. 433.

151   LES, 3, p. 2247.

152   EVP, p. 437; LKV, 19, p. 37970; Riga, July 7, 1939, Charles W. Orde, FO371/23609-N3444/3444/59, Records of Leading Personalities in Latvia.

153   Riga, February 8, 1924, J. C. T. Vaughan, FO371/10375-N1627/1627/59.

154   LAM, p. 102.

155   LKV, 19, p. 37970; FOLD, 1928–1933.

156   Riga, February 3, 1936, C. W. Torr, FO371/20308-N820/165/59; Riga, July 11, 1939, C. W. Orde, FO371/23609-N3449/3449/59.

he lived in Poland until his deportation to the Soviet Union. Released in 1954, he returned to Latvia. Died on February 15, 1962, in Riga.[157]

PĒTERIS SĒJA [PIERRE SEYA]

Born on April 19, 1880. Emigrated in 1906. Studied history and economics, at Zurich, and worked there as a teacher. Entered the Latvian Foreign Ministry following World War I. After serving in Paris and Brussels, transferred to the Foreign Ministry in Riga, from which post he was sent as minister to Rome and accredited, simultaneously, as minister to Albania, Bulgaria, and Greece. Presented credentials in Rome, where he resided, on December 5, 1927.[158] Presented credentials in Tirana on April 3, 1928,[159] and Sofia, on June 21, 1928.[160] Left Rome for Scandinavia, 1933. Residing in Stockholm, he presented credentials there on August 28, 1933,[161] Copenhagen on September 20, 1933,[162] and Oslo on September 30, 1933.[163] Committed suicide on June 9, 1940, in Stockholm.[164]

JĀNIS SESKIS

Born on May 16, 1877. Married to Alma Sulca. Trained as a teacher. After the Russian Revolution of 1905, he studied at Basel, Berne, and Paris. Returned to Latvia by 1913 and was editor of a newspaper. Served in 1919 with the Latvian delegation at the Paris Peace Conference following World War I and became, eventually, the last head of the delegation. Latvian

---

[157] LEA, 4, pp. 255–256; LES, 3, p. 2260.

[158] LKV, 19, pp. 37970–37971;   Rome, February 15, 1929, Sir R. Graham, FO371/13687-C1338/122/22.

[159] Tirana, April 11, 1928, Charles G. Hart, USNA701.60p 75/1.

[160] Sofia, January 4, 1929, R. Sperling, FO371/13574-C357/357/7.

[161] Stockholm, January 1, 1934, A. Clark-Kerr, FO371/18334-N503/503/42.

[162] Copenhagen, January 2, 1934, Hugh Gurney, FO371/18263-N186/185/15.

[163] Oslo, October 4, 1933, Hoffman Philip, USNA701.60P 57/3.

[164] LES, 3, p. 2260.

diplomatic agent in Switzerland, 1920.[165] Minister to Estonia, 1921–1929.[166] Presented credentials as minister to Moscow on October 24, 1929.[167] Leaving Moscow in June 1932, he was named chief of the Press Department of the Latvian Foreign Ministry.[168] Latvian consul general at Memel (Klaipėda), Lithuania, 1934.[169] Deported to the Soviet Union sometime during 1940–1941.[170]

DR. ARNOLDS SPEKKE [ARNOLD SPEKE]

Born on July 14, 1887. Studied at Riga Polytechnic and Moscow University. Remained as a lecturer in Roman philology at Moscow University following graduation. Returned to Latvia around 1920 and taught at the University of Latvia as a professor of philology and philosophy. Earned a doctorate, held positions equivalent to dean and provost, was fluent in French and Italian, traveled abroad to do research on behalf of the Latvian government, and received a Rockefeller research grant.[171] Presented

---

165   EVP, p. 437; LKV, 19, pp. 38414–38415; Jānis J. Samts, "The Origins of Latvian Diplomacy, 1925–1927: The Role of Zigfrīds Anna Meierovics in the Formulation of Latvian Foreign Policy" (master's thesis, San Jose State University, 1975), pp. 29, 68.

166   Riga, February 8, 1924, J. C. T. Vaughan, FO371/10375-N1625/1625/50; Riga, January 25, 1930, from Alan Walker in Tallinn, FO371/14783-N596/596/59.

167   Moscow, November 24, 1930, Sir Esmond Ovey, FO371/14885-N8355/5328/38. Further details on Seskis' activities in Moscow can be found in Riga, February 8, 1924, J. C. T. Vaughan, FO371/10375-N1625/1625/50; Riga, January 25, 1930, from Alan Walker in Tallinn, FO371/14783-N596/596/59; Moscow, January 27, 1933, Sir Esmond Ovey, FO371/17255-N739/120/38; Riga, June 13, 1932, Felix Cole, USNA701.60P 61/12; Riga, November 4, 1929, F. W. B. Coleman, USNA701.60P 61/8.

168   LKV, 19, pp. 38414–38415.

169   EVP, p. 437.

170   LES, 3, p. 2272.

171   LKV, 20, pp. 40050–40053; Riga, July 7, 1939, Charles W. Orde, FO371/23609-N3444/3444/59, Records of Leading Personalities in Latvia.

credentials as minister to Rome on October 27, 1933.[172] Simultaneously, accredited to Albania, Bulgaria, and Greece, presenting credentials, in Albania, on May 16, 1934,[173] and in Bulgaria on June 22, 1934.[174] He was relieved of his responsibilities in Albania, effective April 15, 1939.[175] Became chargé d'affaires (with the rank of minister plenipotentiary) in Washington on May 24, 1954,[176] serving until he was succeeded by Dr. Anatol Dinbergs, who became chargé d'affaires on October 1, 1970.[177] Dr. Spekke had been nominated by the Latvian minister in London, Kārlis Zariņš, "the Bearer of the Emergency Power of the Latvian National Government," to be chargé d'affaires, in Washington.[178] Zariņš also proposed, in the event Zariņš could not continue to function as "Bearer of the Emergency Power," that Dr. Spekke should succeed to that task.[179] Dr. Spekke was married to Aleksandra Sterste.[180] Died on July 17, 1972, in Washington.[181]

VILIS SŪMANIS [WILLIS SUMANS, SCHUMANS, SHUMANS]
Born on April 24, 1887. Student of agriculture at Moscow University for a year, but he was exiled to Siberia during the Russian Revolution of

---

[172]   Rome, February 12, 1934, Sir Eric Drummond, FO371/18434-R1143/1143/22.

[173]   Durazzo, January 7, 1938, Sir Andrew Ryan, FO371/22307-R444/444/90.

[174]   Sofia, January 1, 1935, C. H. Bentinck, FO371/19488-R201/201/7.

[175]   Riga, May 23, 1939, E. L. Packer, USNA701.60P 52/3.

[176]   USDL, July 1954.

[177]   USDL, November 1970.

[178]   London, February 16, 1954, Kārlis Zariņš to John Foster Dulles, FO371/111382-NB1901/1.

[179]   London, December 15, 1954, Charles Zarine [Kārlis Zariņš] to H.A.F. Hohler, Foreign Office, FO371/111382-NB1901/9.

[180]   EVP, p. 452.

[181]   Report of death found in *Times* (London), July 31, 1972. Precise date of death provided by M. Bundza, Librarian, Latvian Studies Center, Kalamazoo, MI.

1905. Emigrated to Switzerland, where he studied political science and political economy at Zurich and St. Gall. Employed at the Russian consulate general in Marseilles until the start of World War I in 1914. Returned to Russia to fight against Germany and was pardoned. As an independent Latvia emerged, he worked in local government, 1917–1919, then entered the Latvian Foreign Ministry. Director of the Political Department, 1921–1924. Minister to Italy, 1924–1926. Became minister to France, fall 1926.[182] Simultaneously accredited to Spain[183] and Portugal,[184] resident in Paris. Transferred from Paris, 1933. Presented credentials as minister to Finland on July 10, 1933. It was reported, from Helsinki, that he had arrived there rather exhausted by a term of strenuous service at Paris, that he said the relations between his country and Finland were of no great importance, and that he regarded Helsinki as a "rest cure."[185] Leaving Finland in 1938, he presented credentials as minister to Estonia on November 3, 1938.[186] He left Tallinn in 1940 for Switzerland. Died on October 27, 1948, in Geneva — a city he had visited every year from 1921 to 1930 as a participant in the League of Nations assemblies.[187]

JĀNIS E. B. TEPFERS

Born on January 16, 1898. Fought in the Latvian War of Independence. Studied medicine at Tartu University and law at Riga University. Entered the Latvian Foreign Ministry and accompanied Foreign Minister Zigfrīds A. Meierovics abroad during the quest for recognition of Latvia. Appointed attaché in 1923 and first secretary in 1926, becoming director of the Administrative and Protocol Department in 1928, director of the Legal Department in 1934, secretary-general of the Foreign Ministry on

---

[182]   Riga, July 7, 1939, Charles W. Orde, FO371/23609-N3444/3444/59, Records of Leading Personalities in Latvia.; LES, 3, p. 2405.

[183]   Sūmanis presented credentials on May 12, 1928, as reported in Madrid, May 16, 1928, Ogden H. Hammond, USNA701.60p 52/1.

[184]   Sūmanis presented credentials on June 9, 1928, as reported in Lisbon, June 14, 1928, Fred M. Dearing, USNA701.60p 53/2.

[185]   Helsinki, January 16, 1934, R. Sperling, FO371/18276-N452/452/56.

[186]   Estonia. *Corps diplomatique á Tallinn, décembre 1939*, p. 2.

[187]   LES, 3, p. 2405.

September 9, 1936, and minister to Finland on February 16, 1939.[188] The years 1943–1946 found him living in Sweden and working in the Swedish Foreign Ministry as a translator. By 1947, he was employed at a Stockholm bank and active in Swedish refugee organizations.[189] Was married to Maija Pauluka.[190] Died on April 9, 1994, in Stockholm.[191]

DR. MIĶELIS VALTERS [MICHAEL WALTERS]

Born on April 25, 1874. Arrested in 1897 for political activity, he escaped the czar and went to Switzerland, where he studied law at Berne and, by 1903, founded an expatriate group with a Social Democratic platform. Also studied at Zurich. He earned a doctorate in political science. Latvia's first minister of the interior, November 19, 1918–December 8, 1919. Embarked on a diplomatic career, becoming minister to Italy, 1920–1924, and minister to France, November 1924–December 1925, when he was recalled.[192] Named consul at Konigsberg, Germany, by 1927.[193] Returned to the ministerial ranks, when he presented credentials on November 9, 1934, as minister to Poland,[194] where he served until 1937. Accredited, simultaneously, as minister to Hungary, presenting credentials at Budapest on June 5, 1936.[195] Presented credentials as minister to Belgium on October

---

188   LKV, 21, p. 42585;   Riga, July 7, 1939, Charles W. Orde, FO371/23609-N3444/3444/59, Records of Leading Personalities in Latvia.

189   LES, 3, p. 2464.

190   EVP, p. 489.

191   Brīvā Latvija, Catthorpe and London, May 2-9, 1994, p. 4.

192   LES, 3, pp. 2590–2591; Riga, November 6, 1926, E. H. Carr, FO371/11736-N5097/5097/59, Biographical Notes on the Leading Personalities in Latvia; [Riga], January 3, 1931, [author unknown], FO371/15538-N273/273/59, List of Leading Personalities in Latvia.

193   [Riga], January 3, 1931, [author unknown], FO371/15538-N273/273/59, List of Leading Personalities in Latvia. Königsberg has been called Kaliningrad since 1945, and lies in Russian territory.

194   LES, 3, p. 2591; Warsaw, January 1, 1936, Sir H. W. Kennard, FO371/19958-C53/53/55.

195   Budapest, January 5, 1937, Sir G. G. Knox, FO371/21151-R453/159/21.

14, 1938.[196] Simultaneously, accredited minister to Luxembourg, presenting credentials on October 31, 1938.[197] Returned to private life in 1940.[198] Died in 1968.[199]

FRĪDRICHS VESMANIS [FREDERICK VESMANS, WESMANS]

Born on April 15, 1875. Jurist. Edited a Latvian revolutionary newspaper and was arrested in 1897. Sentenced to be exiled to Russia but escaped to Britain and lived with Latvian exiles in Bournemouth. Returned to Russia after the Russian Revolution of 1905. Graduated in law from St. Petersburg University. Elected president of the first Latvian Parliament, November 1922. Presented credentials as minister to Great Britain on April 27, 1925, serving until 1931. Also served as one of the Latvian delegates to the League of Nations. Member of the Latvian Senate. [200] A document supplied by the Latvian (Zariņš) and Lithuanian (Balutis) ministers in London during 1942, listed Vesmanis as having been deported to the Soviet Union.[201] Died there in 1942.[202]

DR. OSKARS VOITS [WOIT]

Born on April 18, 1866. Married to Irmgarde Genca. Physician, with hospital administration experience.[203] Sent as minister to Germany in 1921 and, while resident in Berlin, was accredited, simultaneously, to Switzerland in 1922, The Netherlands in 1925, and Hungary, also in 1925.[204] Presented

---

196   Brussels, July 7, 1939, Sir R. H. Clive, FO371/22864-C9788/289/4.

197   Luxembourg, November 4, 1938, George P. Waller, USNA701.60P 50A/3.

198   LES, 3, p. 2,591.

199   Rauch, p. 11.

200   EVP, p. 523; FOLD, 1926–1932; Riga, July 7, 1939, Charles W. Orde, FO371/23609-N3444/3444/59, Records of Leading Personalities in Latvia.

201   London, 1942, Kārlis Zariņš and Bronius K. Balutis, FO181/965, item 2.

202   LES, 3, p. 2640.

203   EVP, p. 537.

204   LES, 3, p. 2763.

credentials at Berne on April 29, 1922,[205] The Hague on October 15, 1925,[206] and Budapest in December 1925.[207] Returned to Riga in 1932, was pensioned and, thereafter, lived in Germany.[208] Died on September 19, 1959.[209]

KĀRLIS ZARIŅŠ [CHARLES ZARINE]

Born on December 4, 1879. Studied in St. Petersburg. Worked there as a lawyer's clerk and was active in the Latvian community. Had some Estonian roots, spoke Estonian, and kept apprised of Estonian affairs. Actively engaged in refugee work during World War I. Member of the Latvian delegation to the Paris Peace Conference following World War I. Upon entering the foreign service, he served in Sweden, 1919, and was "representative," then minister, to Finland, 1919–1923.[210] Presented credentials as minister to Sweden on May 7, 1923,[211] also accredited, simultaneously, as minister to Denmark and Norway, resident in Stockholm.[212] Submitted recall from Stockholm on May 5, 1930,[213] and presented credentials as minister to Estonia on May 13, 1930.[214] Left Tallinn

---

[205]   Berne, January 3, 1925, R. Sperling, FO371/11101-W89/89/43.

[206]   The Hague, February 22, 1927, Earl Granville, FO371/11369-C1578/341/21.

[207]   Budapest, January 26, 1926, Sir C. Barclay, FO371/11369-C1578/341/21.

[208]   LES, 3, p. 2763; Berlin, January 2, 1933, Sir Horace Rumbold, FO371/16714-C308/308/18.

[209]   *Laiks*, Brooklyn, New York, September 26, 1959, p. 1.

[210]   LES, 3, pp. 2776–2777; Helsinki, January 31, 1922, Ernest Rennie, FO371/8101-N1674/1674/56; Riga, July 7, 1939, Charles W. Orde, FO371/23609-N3444/3444/59, Records of Leading Personalities in Latvia.

[211]   Stockholm, May 11, 1923, Hallett Johnson, USNA701.60p 58/orig.; Stockholm, January 2, 1930, Sir H. W. Kennard, FO371/14888-N224/224/42.

[212]   Stockholm, January 1, 1926, Sir A. C. Grant Duff, FO371/11805-N179/179/42.

[213]   Stockholm, May 16, 1930, John M. Morehead, USNA701.60p 60i/5.

[214]   Estonia. *Liste du corps diplomatique à Tallinn, novembre 1932*, p. 3.

on December 8, 1931,[215] and assumed post of Latvian foreign minister, serving December 9, 1931–March 24, 1933.[216] Retained appointment as minister to Estonia, where the Latvian Legation functioned under the direction of chargé d'affaires Charles Freimanis.[217] Returned to Tallinn after leaving the post of foreign minister, and, subsequently, was named minister to London, presenting credentials on July 20, 1933.[218] Represented Latvia in London throughout World War II, the Soviet annexation of Latvia, and the early years of the Cold War. Designated "the Bearer of the Special Emergency Power of the Latvian National Government" on May 17, 1940, giving him great authority over Latvia's resources and diplomats, abroad.[219] Married to Henriete Houpert.[220] Died on April 29, 1963.[221] His daughter, Marie-Anne, also has pursued a diplomatic career.

---

[215]   Tallinn, December 9, 1931, Harry E. Carlson, USNA701.60P 60i/7.

[216]   LES, 3, p. 2777.

[217]   Riga, December 16, 1931, Hughe M. Knatchbull-Hugessen transmitting dispatch of A. J. Hill, Tallinn, December 12, 1931, FO371/15541-8136/1667/59.

[218]   FOLD, 1934, 1937, 1938. In addition to presenting credentials during the reign of King George V he presented them, again, on May 5, 1936, and February 4, 1937, upon the accession of King Edward VIII and King George VI, respectively.

[219]   Les, 1, p. 268; The document assigning this authority to Zariņš (and designating Dr. Alfreds Bīlmanis as his future successor) is found in *Third Interim Report of the Select Committee on Communist Aggression*, 83d Congress, 2d Session (Washington, DC, 1954), p. 433. The original document, in Latvian, is reproduced in Bērziņš, p. 226.

[220]   EVP, p. 545.

[221]   Obituary, *Times* (London), May 2, 1963.

Appendix C

Biographical Sketches of Lithuanian Diplomats

JONAS AUKŠTUOLIS

Born on April 2, 1886.[1] Educated at Jelgava and St. Petersburg. Lawyer. Represented Lithuania in Sweden, prior to the Swedish de jure recognition of Lithuania, then moved to The Hague, in 1922.[2] Served as chargé d'affaires in Riga, February 13, 1923–December 22, 1924, and, simultaneously, as chargé d'affaires in Tallinn. Became minister to Latvia on December 22, 1924, and presented credentials as minister to Estonia, resident in Riga, on January 13, 1925. His assignment was terminated upon the appointment of a new Lithuanian minister to Estonia on September 9, 1927, and his residence now was Tallinn.[3] Presented credentials as minister to Finland, resident in Tallinn, on March 5, 1929.[4] Became doyen of the Diplomatic Corps in Tallinn on October 4, 1929. Left Tallinn on January 7, 1930 to become Director of the

---

[1]   ELI, 1, p. 215.

[2]   Riga, February 8, 1924, J. C. T. Vaughan, FO371/10375-N1626/1626/59.

[3]   LAM, p. 62;   Riga, February 8, 1924, J. C. T. Vaughan, FO371/10375-N1626/1626/59;   Riga, January 16, 1928, Sir J. C. T. Vaughan, FO371/13273-N419/419/59.

[4]   Helsinki, December 13, 1929, Vivian Burbury, FO371/14010-N6042/532/56.

Administrative Department of the Lithuanian Foreign Ministry.[5] Presented credentials as minister to Czechoslovakia on October 27, 1932.[6] Presented credentials as minister to Argentina on October 30, 1934,[7] as minister to Uruguay on January 31, 1935,[8] and as minister to Brazil on August 27, 1935, serving all posts while resident in Buenos Aires.[9] Upon the Soviet occupation of Lithuania, deported to the Soviet Union in 1940.[10]

DR. STASYS A. BAČKIS

Born in 1906. Earned a doctorate in international law at the University of Paris. Entered the Lithuanian Foreign Ministry in 1930, worked in the Political Department until 1934, then served as secretary to the foreign minister, until 1938. Also had duties as secretary-general of the Lithuanian Delegation to the League of Nations and alternate delegate. Became first secretary of the Lithuanian Legation in Paris on August 1, 1938 and was promoted to counselor on June 1, 1939. Lithuanian diplomatic representative in Paris, 1944–1960, where he was titled minister plenipotentiary from 1953. Became counselor at the Lithuanian Legation in Washington on June 20, 1960,[11] and was named chargé d'affaires on January 1, 1977.[12] He reverted to the role of political counselor on November 15,

---

5   Riga, January 25, 1930, from Alan Walker in Tallinn, FO371/1783-N596/596/59.

6   Prague, January 1, 1933, Joseph Addison, FO371/16659-C396/396/12.

7   Buenos Aires, October 31, 1935, H. G. Chilton, FO371/17473-A9460/435/2.

8   Montevideo, January 31, 1935, Leon Dominian, USNA701.60M 33/3.

9   Rio de Janeiro, September 14, 1935, Edward Coote, FO371/18653-A8627/946/6.

10   ELI, 1, p. 215. A more detailed account of Aukštuolis can be found in Riga, July 12, 1939, C. W. Orde, transmitting dispatch of Thomas H. Preston, Kovno, June 28, 1939, FO371/23609-N3452/3452/59, Records of Leading Personalities in Lithuania.

11   ELI, 1, p. 237.

12   USDL, February 1977.

1987, when Stasys Lozoraitis, Jr., previously counselor, was named chargé d'affaires.[13] Dr. Bačkis appeared as a counselor for the last time in the *U. S. Diplomatic List* of November, 1993. Residing in Lithuania, he was awarded the Order of Grand Duke Gediminas, First Class, in 1996.[14]

VINCAS BALICKAS

Born in 1904. Employed by the Bank of Lithuania, 1929–1931. Entered the Lithuanian Foreign Ministry and served as chief of section and counsellor of various departments, April 1931–April 1938. Became commercial counsellor at the Lithuanian Legation in London on April 20, 1938, where he would serve the remainder of his career.[15] Became acting counselor of the legation, 1941,[16] serving with that title until 1967. Assumed the role of chargé d'affaires on January 22, 1968.[17] Appointed Lithuanian ambassador to the United Kingdom on December 11, 1991.[18]

JURGIS BALTRUŠAITIS

Born on May 2, 1873. Graduate of Moscow University. A poet of note before World War I. Headed the Russian writer's union, 1919.[19] Described as "a bilingual Symbolist poet of the school of Alexander Blok."[20] Listed as "Temporary Acting Plenipotentiary Representative" of Lithuania

---

13   USDL, February 1988.

14   USDL, November 1993; award information provided by Arunas Zailskas, director of Research Services, Lithuanian Research and Studies Center, Chicago.

15   ELI, 6 (Supplement), pp. 379-380.

16   FOLD, 1942.

17   ELI, 6 (Supplement), pp. 379-380.

18   United Kingdom. *The London Diplomatic List* (London: Her Majesty's Stationery Office, June 1992).

19   ELI, 1, pp. 270–271; Alfred Erich Senn, *The Great Powers, Lithuania, and the Vilna Question, 1920–1928* (Leiden: E. J. Brill, 1966), p. 155.

20   Rauch, p. 118.

to Moscow, 1921.[21] Listed as "Plenipotentiary Representative" in 1922,[22] and presented credentials as minister on July 13, 1922.[23] The Soviet Commissariat for Foreign Affairs gave a dinner in his honor in October 1930, to mark the 10th anniversary of his arrival in Moscow.[24] It was reported in 1932 that he hoped to be assigned to Paris and that he had resigned from the Lithuanian Diplomatic Service in April 1931. However, he was at his Moscow post in December 1931 and showed no sign of early departure.[25] The American chargé d'affaires in Moscow imparted on April 3, 1939, that Baltrušaitis was relinquishing his post and leaving Moscow on April 6, 1939.[26] Dr. Ladas Natkevičius presented credentials as his replacement on May 19, 1939.[27] Baltrušaitis had been accredited, simultaneously, as minister to Turkey, presenting credentials on May 21, 1932,[28] and to Persia (Iran), presenting credentials on May 20, 1933, resident in Moscow.[29] Assigned as counselor at Paris in 1939. Died on January 3, 1944, in Paris.[30]

---

21   London, May 28, 1921, Department of Overseas Trade to Foreign Office, "Diplomatic Corps Accredited to the Government of the Russian Socialist Federative Soviet Republic," FO371/6913-N6215/6215/38.

22   Moscow, RSFSR, *Corps diplomatique et missions étrangères, le 1er février 1922*, FO371/8215-N4412/4412/38.

23   Moscow, *Le Corps diplomatique à Moscou, juillet 1925*, FO371/11789-N568/568/38.

24   Moscow, November 24, 1930, Sir Esmond Ovey, FO371/14885-N8355/5328/38.

25   Moscow, January 4, 1932, Sir Esmond Ovey, FO371/16327-N150/150/38.

26   Moscow, April 3, 1939, Alexander C. Kirk, USNA701.60M 61/4.

27   Moscow, July 5, 1939, Sir W. Seeds, FO371/23686-N3287/281/38.

28   Istanbul, June 17, 1932, Charles E. Allen, USNA701.60M 67/1.

29   Teheran, June 1, 1933, Charles C. Hart, USNA701.60M 91/2.

30   ELI, 1, pp. 270–271.

BRONIUS KAZYS BALUTIS

Born on December 29, 1879. Emigrated to the United States in 1905. Naturalized as an American citizen at Chicago, May 17, 1912. Received United States passport 80207 on May 10, 1919,[31] surrendering it in 1920, when he obtained naturalization as a Lithuanian citizen and entered the Lithuanian Foreign Ministry.[32] Member of the Lithuanian delegation at the Paris Peace Conference[33] and the delegation for negotiations on the Lithuanian/Latvian border. Appointed director of the Lithuanian Foreign Ministry's Political Department and, later, assumed duties as vice minister of the Foreign Ministry, participating in negotiations for the Vilna plebiscite, which never materialized. Named director of the Foreign Ministry's Eastern Department, March 1921, and, later, was a member of the delegation dealing with the Davis Commission over the issue of Memel (Klaipėda). Director of the Lithuanian Telegraph Agency "Elta" for some time in 1922. Attended several sessions of the League of Nations and, until 1927, was continuous director of the Lithuanian Foreign Ministry's Political Department. Became secretary-general of the Foreign Ministry, June 1927, and served 12 times as administrator for the ministry.[34] Presented credentials as minister to the United States on November 2, 1928.[35] Presented credentials as minister to Great Britain on June 12, 1934, where he would serve throughout World War II and during the period of Sovietization until his death.[36] Also presented

---

[31]   Washington, May 18, 1928, Robert F. Kelley, USNA701.60M 11/47.

[32]   Riga, August 30, 1928, W. B. Coleman, USNA701.60M 11/49.

[33]   Alfred Erich Senn, *The Emergence of Modern Lithuania* (New York: Columbia University Press, 1959), p. 239.

[34]   Riga, July 12, 1939, C. W. Orde, transmitting dispatch of Thomas H. Preston, Kovno, June 28, 1939, FO371/23609-N3452/3452/59, Records of Leading Personalities in Lithuania.

[35]   Washington, November 1, 1928, Bronius K. Balutis to Secretary of State Frank B. Kellogg, USNA701.60m 11/57.

[36]   FOLD, 1935. Balutis presented credentials, again, on May 5, 1936 and February 4, 1937, upon the accession of King Edward VIII and King George VI, respectively, as reported in FOLD 1937 and 1938.

credentials as minister to The Netherlands, resident in London, on July 6, 1935.[37] Died on December 30, 1967, in London.[38]

KAZYS BIZAUSKAS

Born in 1893. Graduate from the Kovno Gymnasium in 1913 and was admitted to Moscow University to study law. Among the signatories of the Lithuanian Declaration of Independence, February 6, 1918. Appointed counselor to the Lithuanian delegation to London on February 1, 1919 and was secretary-general of the Lithuanian Peace Delegation to Russia in 1920. Lithuanian Minister of Education, 1922.[39] Later that year, appointed chargé d'affaires at the Vatican, leaving that post in 1923[40] to become chargé d'affaires in Washington, effective December 11, 1923.[41] Became minister to the United States, August 6, 1924.[42] Left the United States, May 21, 1927.[43] Presented credentials as minister to Latvia on September 16, 1927, remaining until July 28, 1928.[44] Presented credentials as minister to Great Britain on June 1, 1928,[45] simultaneously accredited to The Netherlands, presenting credentials at The Hague on January 22, 1931.[46] Transferred to the

---

[37]   The Hague, January 1, 1936, Sir Hubert Montgomery, FO371/20504-W68/68/29.

[38]   ELI, 1, pp. 278–279.

[39]   Riga, July 12, 1939, C. W. Orde, transmitting dispatch of Thomas H. Preston, Kovno, June 28, 1939, FO371/23609-N3452/3452/59, Records of Leading Personalities in Lithuania.

[40]   Washington, June 3, 1924, Alfred W. Klieforth, USNA701.60m 11/24.

[41]   USDL, December 1923.

[42]   USDL, August 1924.

[43]   Washington, May 21, 1927, Kazys Bizauskas to Secretary of State Frank B. Kellogg, USNA701.60m 11/42.

[44]   LAM, p. 62.

[45]   FOLD, 1929.

[46]   The Hague, January 1, 1932, Sir Odo Russell, FO371/16487-W31/31/29.

Lithuanian Foreign Ministry on October 1, 1931.   Director of the Administrative and Judicial Department of the Foreign Ministry, 1932–1938. While acting secretary-general of the Foreign Ministry in early 1939, again was named minister to Latvia,[47] but appears not to have assumed that post.[48] Deputy prime minister of Lithuania, March 1939–June 1940. His party affiliation was Christian Democrat. Deported, with other Baltic officials, to the Soviet Union. Died in 1941.[49] The last American minister to Lithuania, who departed in 1940 upon Lithuania's Sovietization, included Bizauskas in a list of "Lithuania's greats," writing that Bizauskas "proved a hero during the days of trial when negotiating for the best terms with ambitious Russia in the summer of 1940. He proved himself a man of great courage."[50]

VOLDERMARAS ČARNECKICS

Born in 1893. Drafted into the czarist army during World War I while a student at the Electrotechnical Institute at St. Petersburg.[51] Appointed acting minister of finance, 1918, and, later, served as minister of communications.[52] Participated in negotiations with Poland at Suwalki in 1920 and was a delegate at the League of Nations. Member, Christian

---

[47]   Kaunas, January 14, 1939, Owen J. C. Norem, USNA701.60M 60P/9; Riga, July 12, 1939, C. W. Orde, transmitting dispatch of Thomas H. Preston, Kovno, June 28, 1939, FO371/23609-N3452/3452/59, Records of Leading Personalities in Lithuania.

[48]   One report indicates that he was appointed minister to Latvia but had not arrived, Riga, January 21, 1939, C. W. Orde, FO371/23601-N450/46/59; a later report indicates he had been replaced by Pranas Dailidė, who presented credentials on June 2, 1939, as noted in Riga, July 1, 1939, C. W. Orde, FO371/23601-N3353/46/59.

[49]   Kaslas, pp. 334, 529.

[50]   Norem, pp. 228–229.

[51]   Senn, *The Great Powers*, p. 117, n. 45.

[52]   Senn, *The Emergence*, pp. 237–238; Riga, July 12, 1939, C. W. Orde, transmitting dispatch of Thomas H. Preston, Kovno, June 28, 1939, FO371/23609-N3452/3452/59, Records of Leading Personalities in Lithuania.

Democratic Party.[53] Became the first official representative of Lithuania to the United States as chargé d'affaires on October 11, 1922, serving until September 1923.[54] Thereafter, he served for a short time as a "delegate" in Great Britain,[55] the first official representation having commenced with Ernestas Galvanauskas on December 10, 1924.[56] Čarneckics was foreign minister of Lithuania from June 18, 1924 until his resignation on September 19, 1925.[57] Presented credentials as minister to Italy on December 12, 1925.[58] Held that post until April 1939, when he was named director of the administrative and judicial department of the Lithuanian Foreign Ministry.[59] Among Baltic officials deported to the Soviet Union during 1940–1941.[60]

BRONIUS DAILIDĖ

Born on December 10, 1882.[61] Served as minister to Latvia, September 27, 1928–March 9, 1932,[62] and was, simultaneously, accredited to Sweden, resident in Riga. By 1930, Lithuania decided to reopen the legation

---

[53]   Riga, November 16, 1926, E. H. Carr, transmitting dispatch of C.D. Elphick, Kovno, November 11, 1926, FO371/11736-N5216/5097/59, "Who's Who," Lithuania, November 1926.

[54]   USDL, October 1922, October 1923.

[55]   Riga, July 12, 1939, C. W. Orde, transmitting dispatch of Thomas H. Preston, Kovno, June 28, 1939, FO371/23609-N3452/3452/59, Records of Leading Personalities in Lithuania.

[56]   Noted in biographical sketch of Galvanauskas.

[57]   Senn, The Great Powers, pp. 133, 149.

[58]   Rome, February 15, 1929, Sir R. Graham, FO371/13687-C1338/122/22.

[59]   Riga, July 12, 1939, C. W. Orde, transmitting dispatch of Thomas H. Preston, Kovno, June 28, 1939, FO371/23609-N3452/3452/59, Records of Leading Personalities in Lithuania.

[60]   Hough, pp. 485–487.

[61]   ELI, 2, p. 11

[62]   LAM, p. 62. Dailidė's cousin, Pranas Dailidė, was named minister to Latvia in 1939, Riga, June 10, 1939, John C. Wiley, USNA701.60M 60P/10.

in Stockholm and sent Jurgis Savickis as resident minister, replacing Dailidė in the Stockholm post.[63] It was reported from Riga that Dailidė had been educated at St. Petersburg.[64] Presented credentials as minister to Estonia on February 22, 1933[65] and was accredited, simultaneously, as minister to Finland. He presented credentials in Helsinki on October 30, 1934.[66] The United States minister to the three Baltic states communicated that Dailidė was doyen of the diplomatic corps in Tallinn, and he was considered not only one of the best–informed diplomats in Tallinn but a man of "some influence in political matters which concern Estonia."[67] Died on October 20, 1981, in Chicago.[68]

PRANAS DAILIDĖ

Born on September 29, 1888.[69] Graduate of St. Petersburg University, 1911. Worked as a teacher and held various administrative positions in pre-revolutionary Russia. Entered the Lithuanian Foreign Service in 1918, and his first posting was in the Caucasus region. Served as director of the Lithuanian Telegraph Agency. Presented credentials as minister to Latvia on June 2, 1939.[70] His cousin, Bronius Dailidė, had preceded him as minister to Latvia, September 27, 1928–March 9, 1932.[71] Served in parliament, having been affiliated with the Populist Peasant Union. Taught Slavic languages at

---

[63]   Stockholm, January 2, 1930, Sir H. W. Kennard, FO371/14888-N224/224/42; Stockholm, February 19, 1930, Sir H. W. Kennard, FO371/14888-N1242/224/42.

[64]   Riga, January 10, 1929, Joseph Addison, FO371/13985-N329/329/59.

[65]   Estonia, *Corps diplomatique à Tallin, decembre 1939.*

[66]   Helsinki, November 1, 1934, J. Thyne Henderson, FO371/[number missing]-N6233/452/56.

[67]   Riga, September 14, 1937, Arthur Bliss Lane, USNA701.0060 i/3.

[68]   LEN, 37 (Supplement), p. 119.

[69]   ELI, 2, p. 11.

[70]   Riga, July 1, 1940, C. W. Orde, FO371/24765-N6491/6491/59.

[71]   LAM, p. 62; Riga, June 10, 1939, John C. Wiley, USNA701.60M 60P/10.

Stockholm University, 1945–1947.   Instructor in Russian at Syracuse University from 1951 until his death. Died on September 1, 1965, in Syracuse, New York.[72]

TEODORAS DAUKANTAS

Born on September 8, 1884.[73] Czarist naval background. Studied in St. Petersburg and at naval schools. Served aboard battleships. Chief of operations section of the Baltic Fleet. Awarded the Legion of Honor for successfully organizing the transport of Russian troops to France, 1916. Prisoner of war of the Ottoman Empire, 1918. After World War I, appointed lecturer at Lithuanian Military High School. Lithuanian minister of defense, April 18, 1924–September 24, 1925. Left the military in November 1925, participated in politics, and lectured at Kovno University. Named chief of the General Staff, following the coup d'etat of December 1926, in which he played a prominent role. Appointed Lithuanian minister for national defense, August 9, 1927.[74] He was sent on a diplomatic mission, around 1930, to South America. Arrived in Rio de Janeiro on February 26, 1931,[75] Buenos Aires on September 30, 1931,[76] Asuncion on March 18, 1932, and also was accredited to Uruguay, serving all four posts as chargé d'affaires, resident in Buenos Aires.[77] Recalled in 1935 and made head of the Lithuanian Merchant Marine in 1937.[78] Taught geography at Vilnius University, 1941–1944. Left Lithuania during the second Soviet invasion of 1944 (having been imprisoned during the first Soviet invasion of 1940) and lived in

---

[72]   ELI, 2, p. 11.

[73]   ELI, 2, pp. 36–37.

[74]   Riga, July 12, 1939, C. W. Orde, transmitting dispatch of Thomas H. Preston, Kovno, June 28, 1939, FO371/23609-N3452/3452/59, Records of Leading Personalities in Lithuania.

[75]   Petropolis [Rio de Janeiro], January 9, 1933, Sir William Seeds, FO371/16550-A1049/653/6.

[76]   Buenos Aires, December 27, 1933, Sir H. G. Chilton, FO371/17473-A570/435/2.

[77]   Asunción, March 18, 1932, Post Wheeler, USNA701.60M 32/1.

[78]   Riga, July 12, 1939, C. W. Orde, transmitting dispatch of Thomas H. Preston, Kovno, June 28, 1939, FO371/23609-N3452/3452/59, Records of Leading Personalities in Lithuania.

Germany until 1949, when he went to Argentina. Died on June 10, 1960, in Buenos Aires.[79]

ERNESTAS GALVANAUSKAS

Born in 1882.[80] Prominent Lithuanian. Educated at Jelgava, at the Mining Institute in St. Petersburg, and was a mining engineering graduate of Liege University in Belgium. Participated in the Russian Revolution of 1905 and was imprisoned by the czarist government in 1906. Worked for a French firm in Serbia in railway construction, forestry, and other jobs in 1913. Left for Paris when Serbia was occupied by Austria-Hungary during World War I. While employed in an engineering capacity in France, he was named to the Lithuanian delegation to the Paris Peace Conference following World War I.[81] Returned to Lithuania and served as Prime Minister, October 7, 1919–June 19, 1920 and, again, February 2, 1922–June 10, 1924.[82] Also, served as foreign minister and as minister of finance.[83] Presented credentials as minister to Great Britain on December 10, 1924, holding that position until 1927.[84] Simultaneously, accredited as minister to The Netherlands, presenting credentials on July 23, 1925.[85] It was reported of him, "I do not know what M. Galvanauskas is like when in power, but out of power he is the most charming, intelligent, and polished Lithuanian I have met during my residence in Lithuania. He is a veritable 'encyclopaedia' of knowledge and information on all subjects and seems to be just as fresh at the end of a

---

[79]   ELI, 2, pp. 36–37.

[80]   Bronis J. Kaslas, *The USSR–German Aggression Against Lithuania* (New York: Robert Speller and Sons, 1973), p. 530.

[81]   Riga, July 12, 1939, C. W. Orde, transmitting dispatch of Thomas H. Preston, Kovno, June 28, 1939, FO371/23609-N3452/3452/59, Records of Leading Personalities in Lithuania.

[82]   Rauch, p. 258.

[83]   Albertas Gerutis, ed., *Lithuania: 700 Years* (New York: Manyland Books, 1969), pp. 192, 214; Riga, July 12, 1939, C. W. Orde, transmitting dispatch of Thomas H. Preston, Kovno, June 28, 1939, FO371/23609-N3452/3452/59, Records of Leading Personalities in Lithuania.

[84]   FOLD, 1925–1928.

[85]   The Hague, February 22, 1927, Earl Granville, FO371/12697-W1557/176/29.

four hours' conversation as he is at the beginning."[86] He left political life in 1928[87] but, as a result of a September 1940 meeting of Lithuanian diplomats gathered in Rome, following the Soviet aggression against Lithuania, a Lithuanian National Committee was formed, with Galvanauskas as its chairman.[88] Died in 1967.[89]

STASYS GIRDVAINIS

Born on September 27, 1890. Entered the Lithuanian Foreign Ministry on October 1, 1920. First secretary at the Lithuanian Legation in Berlin, 1922, and sent to Paris, 1923. Posted to the Vatican, 1927, and assigned to the Lithuanian Foreign Ministry, 1930–1931.[90] Served as Lithuanian chief of protocol until being named counselor of the Lithuanian Legation in Paris, July 13, 1933.[91] At the Foreign Ministry, again, 1934–1939.[92] Presented credentials as minister to the Vatican on October 18, 1939,[93] remaining there until his death. It was reported from the Holy See in 1945 that, despite the tragic vicissitudes of his country, he maintained his post, and the Vatican continued to recognize him, a man "whose anxious manner reflects his own anomalous and precarious situation and the tragedy of his native land."[94] Fourteen years later, it was communicated that the

---

[86]   Riga, July 12, 1939, C. W. Orde, transmitting dispatch of Thomas H. Preston, Kovno, June 28, 1939, FO371/23609-N3452/3452/59, Records of Leading Personalities in Lithuania.

[87]   Riga, July 12, 1939, C. W. Orde, transmitting dispatch of Thomas H. Preston, Kovno, June 28, 1939, FO371/23609-N3452/3452/59, Records of Leading Personalities in Lithuania.

[88]   Kaslas, pp. 314–315.

[89]   Kaslas, p. 530.

[90]   ELI, 2, p. 338.

[91]   Kaunas, July 13, 1933, M. L. Stafford, USNA701.60M 91/3.

[92]   ELI, 2, p. 338.

[93]   Holy See/Rome, July 9, 1945, Sir D. G. Osborne, FO371/50096-ZM4428/4428/57.

[94]   Holy See/Rome, July 9, 1945, Sir D. G. Osborne, FO371/50096-ZM4428/4428/57.

Lithuanian Legation was regarded as having legal existence, but, since Girdvainis lacked credentials to give to the new Pope, he was accorded the status of chargé d'affaires, rather than minister.   The communication continued that he looked after the interests of Lithuanian Catholic exiles in Italy.[95] He had attended the gathering of Lithuanian diplomats in Rome, September 19–25, 1940,[96] and is found on the October 30, 1942 list of Lithuanian diplomats still functioning outside the United States.[97] Died on June 15, 1970.[98]

DR. KAZIMIERAS GRAUZINIS

Born on September 14, 1898. Wrote a doctoral dissertation, *La Question de Vilna* [The Vilna Question], published in Paris in 1927.[99] He was "Confidential Secretary to the Lithuanian Ministry of Foreign Affairs"[100] and, then, was assigned chargé d'affaires at the Vatican, summer 1932.[101] Presented credentials as minister to Argentina on November 21, 1939, and, simultaneously, accredited as minister to Brazil, resident in Buenos Aires. It was reported in 1943 that he "lives in relative obscurity on funds believed to be provided by the United States Government, which are often in arrears."[102] An October 30, 1942 list of Lithuanian diplomats still functioning outside the United States cited him as minister to Argentina, Brazil, and Uruguay,

---

[95]   Holy See/Rome, July 8, 1959, Sir Marcus Cheke, FO371/145103-RV1902/1.

[96]   Gerutis, p. 396.

[97]   List prepared by the Lithuanian minister in Washington, Povilas Žadeikis, October 30, 1942, USNA701.60P 00/10.

[98]   ELI, 2, p. 338.

[99]   ELI, 2, p. 375 n.

[100]   Kovno, August 19, 1932, M. L. Stafford, USNA701.60M 66A/1.

[101]   Holy See/Rome, January 2, 1935, Ivone Kirkpatrick, FO371/16805-C336/336/22.

[102]   Buenos Aires, April 8, 1943, Sir D. V. Kelly, FO371/33547-A4135/285/2; Rio de Janeiro, July 24, 1942, Sir Noel Charles, FO371/30367-A7404/4538/6.

resident in Buenos Aires.[103] He moved to Uruguay and lived there for the remainder of his life. Died on June 15, 1962.[104]

VYTAUTUS GYLYS

Born in 1886.[105] Consul in London, 1930. Consul-General in London, from February 16, 1931.[106] Governor of Memel (Klaipėda), 1932. Lithuania established a legation at Brussels, subordinate to the Lithuanian minister in Paris, in 1934. Gylys, counselor of legation in Paris at that time, was assigned, consequently, chargé d'affaires at Brussels.[107] Presented credentials as minister to Sweden on February 16, 1938.[108] Simultaneously assigned as minister to Denmark and Norway, presenting credentials in Copenhagen on April 11, 1938.[109] Became honorary consul general in Toronto, 1949. Died on June 14, 1953.[110]

JUOZAS KAJECKAS

Born on June 17, 1897 at Shenandoah, Pennsylvania. He was taken to Lithuania in 1909, following his father's death. He studied at Kaunas University, received a law degree in 1928 from Montpelier University in France, and received a diploma in diplomatic sciences in 1929 from the School of Political Science in Paris. He began his diplomatic career at the

---

103   List prepared by the Lithuanian minister in Washington, Povilas Žadeikis, October 30, 1942, USNA701.60P 00/10.

104   ELI, 2, p. 375.

105   Kaslas, p. 531.

106   FOLD, 1931–1932.

107   Riga, March 16, 1934, Hughe M. Knatchbull-Hugessen, transmitting dispatch of Thomas H. Preston, Kovno, March 14, 1934, FO371/17626-C1987/736/4; Brussels, April 24, 1934, George N. M. Bland, FO371/17626-C2612/736/4.

108   Stockholm, February 25, 1938, Sir E. Monson, FO371/22302-N1294/243/42.

109   Copenhagen, July 1, 1939, Sir Patrick Ramsay, FO371/23634-N3307/134/15.

110   Gerutis, p. 413.

Lithuanian Foreign Ministry in 1929.[111] Served in London as first secretary, as well as chargé d'affaires, 1930–1934.[112] Thereafter, became director of the Western Section and, subsequently, of the Central European Section of the Lithuanian Foreign Ministry. Counsellor of the legation in Berlin, 1939–1940. Upon the closing of that legation in 1940, he was assigned to Washington,[113] where he was carried as an attaché on the *U. S. Diplomatic List*, from February 1943.[114] Upon the death of the Lithuanian minister, Povlias Žadeikis, on May 11, 1957, Kajeckas, now a counselor, was named chargé d'affaires.[115] He appeared as counselor and chargé d'affaires, for the last time, in the November 1976 *Diplomatic List*. The next *Diplomatic List* showed him succeeded by Stasys A. Backis as chargé d'affaires on January 1, 1977.[116] He died on July 2, 1978.[117]

PETRAS KLIMAS

Born in 1891. Law graduate of Moscow University.[118] Signatory, Lithuanian Declaration of Independence, February 16, 1918. Member, Lithuanian National Council, 1917–1920.[119] Entered the Foreign Ministry, November 11, 1918.[120] As the Lithuanian state was formed, the government based its territorial claims upon his research. He was a prolific writer, and he was credited with being the Lithuanian government's specialist in

---

111   ELI, 3, pp. 20–21.

112   ELI, 3, p. 21; FOLD, 1931–1935.

113   ELI, 3, p. 21.

114   USDL, February 1943.

115   USDL, June 1957.

116   USDL, February 1977.

117   Date of death provided by Arunas Zailskas, Lithuanian Research and Studies Center, Chicago.

118   Senn, *The Great Powers*, p. 12 n. 26.

119   Kaslas, pp. 65, 531.

120   Riga, July 12, 1939, C. W. Orde, transmitting dispatch of Thomas H. Preston, Kovno, June 28, 1939, FO371/23609-N3452/3452/59, Records of Leading Personalities in Lithuania.

"assembling documents." Played a role in the "Vilna question," the once great issue between Lithuania and Poland.[121] Member of the Lithuanian delegation to the Paris Peace Conference following World War I.[122] Appointed minister to Italy on September 15, 1923,[123] and served until he presented credentials as minister to France on July 17, 1925.[124] Simultaneously, accredited as minister to Spain[125] and Portugal,[126] resident in Paris. On May 30, 1940, Lithuanian foreign minister Urbšys informed his diplomats abroad that he had designated Stasys Lozoraitis, Sr., based in Rome, as chief of the Lithuanian diplomatic service, should Lithuania meet with "a catastrophe." Klimas was named first deputy to Lozoraitis, and Jurgis Šaulys second deputy. All Baltic legations were ordered closed by the government of Vichy France on August 15, 1940.[127] But, in a list of Lithuanian diplomats still functioning outside the United States, Klimas was cited as Lithuanian minister to the Vichy government.[128] On several occasions during his career, he discharged the duties of Lithuanian minister of foreign affairs. He also directed the Lithuanian Telegraph Agency "Elta" for some time. His name was submitted to the German government for assignment as Lithuanian minister to Germany, but the Germans "flatly

---

[121]   Senn, *The Great Powers*, p. 12, n. 26, and passim.

[122]   Senn, *The Emergence*, p. 239.

[123]   Riga, July 12, 1939, C. W. Orde, transmitting dispatch of Thomas H. Preston, Kovno, June 28, 1939, FO371/23609-N3452/3452/59, Records of Leading Personalities in Lithuania.

[124]   Paris, January 3, 1936, Sir Joseph R. Clerk, FO371/19868-C105/59/17.

[125]   Madrid, March 3, 1930, Irwin B. Laughlin, USNA701.60m 52/1.

[126]   Lisbon, March 21, 1930, Alexander R. Magruder, USNA701.60m 53/1.

[127]   Hough, p. 430 n. 451; Kaslas, p. 180.

[128]   List prepared by the Lithuanian minister in Washington, Povilas Žadeikis, October 30, 1942, USNA701.60P 00/10.

refused" to accept him, because of anti-German remarks he allegedly made "at banquets in Paris."[129] Died in 1969.[130]

KAZYS LOZORAITIS

Born on July 23, 1929. He was born in Berlin, as was his brother, Stasys. Studied political science and journalism in Rome. Member of the Lithuanian diplomatic service since 1960. Editor of Lithuanian programs on Radio Rome, 1960–1985. Editor of Lithuanian programs on Radio Vatican, 1972–1991. Served as secretary of the Lithuanian minister to the Holy See and, later, as secretary to the chief of the Lithuanian diplomatic service abroad. Chancellor of the Lithuanian Legation to the Holy See, 1985–1991. In 1992, he was appointed ambassador to the Holy See and, in 1994, ambassador to the Sovereign Military Order of Malta. His decorations include the Grand Cross of the Order of Pius IX (Vatican), Grand Cross of the Order *Pro Merito Melitense* (Malta), Order of Grand Duke Gediminas, 2d Class (Lithiania), and Commander of the Order of St. Gregorius (Vatican). His wife is Giovanna Pignatelli di Terranova.[131]

STASYS LOZORAITIS, SR.

Born on October 5, 1898, at Kovno. Studied at Berlin University. Entered the Ministry of the Interior, 1918. Visited Warsaw in 1919 with a special mission led by Dr. Jurgis Saulys. Performed duties for the Lithuanian Cabinet, 1919–1921. Became second secretary of the Lithuanian Legation at Berlin, 1922. Promoted to first secretary, 1924, and became counselor, 1926. Appointed chargé d'affaires at Rome, 1930. Became director of the Political Department of the Lithuanian Foreign Ministry, 1932. Named foreign minister of Lithuania on June 12, 1934—having not yet reached age 36. Resigned in March 1938, but served as acting foreign minister until December, 1938. Posted as minister to Italy, 1939.[132] The Soviet occupation

---

[129]   Riga, July 12, 1939, C. W. Orde, transmitting dispatch of Thomas H. Preston, Kovno, June 28, 1939, FO371/23609-N3452/3452/59, Records of Leading Personalities in Lithuania.

[130]   Kaslas, p. 531.

[131]   Information provided by Vaclovas Kleiza, Honorary Consul, Lithuanian Consulate General, Chicago.

[132]   Riga, July 12, 1939, C. W. Orde, transmitting dispatch of Thomas H. Preston, Kovno, June 28, 1939, FO371/23609-N3452/3452/59, Records of Leading Personalities in Lithuania.

of Lithuania in June 1940 led to the closing of the Lithuanian Legation in Rome by the Italian government.[133] Lithuanian Foreign Minister Juozas Urbšys sent a telegram to Lozoraitis in Rome on May 30, 1940, and to Lithuanian envoys in Berlin, London, Paris, Stockholm, and Washington, that designated Lozoraitis as chief of the Lithuanian diplomatic service if Lithuania should meet "with a catastrophe."[134] Lithuanian diplomats met in Rome, September 19–25, 1940, and this meeting resulted in the Lithuanian National Committee, chaired by Ernestas Galvanauskas, with Lozoraitis as his alternate.[135] Lozoraitis operated out of the Lithuanian Legation at the Vatican, where Stasys Girdvainis was the Lithuanian representative to the Holy See, and Stasys Lozoraitis, Jr. served as a secretary.[136] Lozoraitis' sons, Stasys, Jr. and Kazys, would both serve as ambassadors in Rome, the former son accredited to Italy and the latter son accredited to the Holy See. Stasys Lozoraitis, Sr. died in 1983.[137]

STASYS LOZORAITIS, JR.

Born on August 2, 1924.[138] Birthplace was Berlin, where his father, Stasys Lozoraitis, Sr., served with the Lithuanian Legation.[139] Educated in Lithuania, Germany, and Italy, having studied law at Rome University, 1944–1948. Served with the Lithuanian Legation at the Vatican, beginning in 1943. Achieved rank of attaché in 1947 and first secretary in 1953 and succeeded Stasys Girdvainis as chargé d'affaires when Girdvainis died in 1970.[140] Became counselor of the Lithuanian Legation in Washington in

---

133   Rome, August 13, 1940, Reed, USNA701.60M 65/4.

134   Kaslas, p. 180.

135   Gerutis, pp. 396–397.

136   Anicetas Simutis, *Pasulio Lietuvių Žinynas* [Lithuanian World Directory] (New York: Lithuanian Chamber of Commerce, 1953), p. 30.

137   Obituary of Stasys Lozoraitis, Jr., *New York Times*, June 16, 1994.

138   ELI, 3, p. 426.

139   Noted in biographical sketch of Stasys Lozoraitis, Sr.

140   ELI, 3, p. 426. Obituary in *The New York Times*, June 16, 1994.

1984[141] and chargé d'affaires on November 15, 1987,[142] and was appointed ambassador on December 20, 1991,[143] presenting credentials on March 11, 1992.[144] Became ambassador to Italy, in 1993, holding that position for eight months before his death. He had been an unsuccessful candidate for president of Lithuania, in February 1993. Married to the former Daniela D'Ercole. His brother, Kazys Lozoraitis, was Lithuania's ambassador to the Vatican. Died of liver failure on June 13, 1994, at Georgetown University Hospital, during a private visit to Washington, D.C.[145]

DR. FRIKAS MEIERIS

Born on July 16, 1893.[146] Studied law at Heidelberg, Munich, and Strasbourg. Emigrated to Argentina, when Germany annexed Memel (Klaipėda) in 1939 and settled in Brazil in 1940.[147] One source that claims Lithuanian President Antanas Smetona sailed to Rio de Janeiro on February 14, 1941, and, while there, appointed Meieris minister to Brazil.[148] However, a register of Lithuanian diplomats still functioning outside the United States on October 30, 1942, lists Meieris as "Attaché of the Legation,"[149] while reports from Rio de Janeiro in 1944, 1945, and 1946 list him as chargé d'affaires. The Lithuanian minister to Brazil, 1944–1946, is listed as Dr. Kazimieras Graužinis, also accredited to Argentina and Uruguay, resident

---

[141]   USDL, May 1984.

[142]   USDL, February 1988.

[143]   USDL, February 1992.

[144]   USDL, May 1992. Interestingly, the Russian ambassador, Vladimir P. Lukin, presented credentials on the same day.

[145]   Obituary in *The New York Times*, June 16, 1994.

[146]   LEN, 18, p. 137.

[147]   ELI, 6 (Supplement), pp. 460–461.

[148]   Gerutis, p. 397.

[149]   List prepared by the Lithuanian minister in Washington, Povilas Žadeikis, October 30, 1942, USNA701.60P 00/10.

in Buenos Aires.[150] An American document, dated 1944, marked "secret," now declassified, stated Meieris did not receive a salary from any Lithuanian source and claimed Lithuanian authorities had stated that, if Meieris was "so impoverished," they could find a wealthier person who could maintain "everything" at his own expense.[151] Died on February 6, 1967, in Brazil.[152]

TOMAS NARUŠEVIČIUS [NORUS-NARUŠEVIČIUS]

Born on September 17, 1869.[153] Attended Moscow University. An engineer of the city of Moscow for over 15 years, into the early stages of World War I. Sent to the United States by the Russian government in 1917. Returned to Europe by 1919 to be a representative of American-Lithuanians within the Lithuanian delegation to the Paris Peace Conference, following World War I. Chaired the Lithuanian delegation that negotiated the Treaty of Peace between Lithuania and Russia, in which treaty Russia recognized Lithuanian independence, 1920.   Became unofficial representative of Lithuania in London in 1921, where he previously had organized a Lithuanian information bureau.   Negotiated a loan from the British government to Lithuania for railway construction within Lithuania, 1923. Employed at the Lithuanian Foreign Ministry in Kovno. Chairman of the Memel (Klaipėda) Harbor Board. Lithuanian minister of Communications, 1923–1924.[154] Named minister to the United States in April, 1927,[155] but he

---

[150]   Rio de Janeiro, July 12, 1944, Sir D. Gainer, FO371/37840-AS3978/20/6; Rio de Janeiro, May 24, 1945, Sir D. Gainer, FO371/44818-AS3115/102/6; Rio de Janeiro, June 17, 1946, Sir D. Gainer, FO371/51910-AS4328/61/6.

[151]   [location unknown], February, March, April 1944, [author unknown], USNA701.60M 32/3.

[152]   LEN, 36 (Supplement), p. 381.

[153]   Riga, March 23, 1927, F. W. B. Coleman, USNA701/60m 11/38.

[154]   Senn, The Great Powers, pp. 73, 131; Senn, The Emergence, pp. 85, 178, 213, 235; Washington, April 14, 1927, Secretary of State Frank B. Kellogg to President Calvin Coolidge, USNA701.60M 11/37. Reports regarding the peace treaty can be found in Kaslas, pp. 68–81. Absolutely no mention is made of Naruševičius within the British Foreign Office List. The first citing of Lithuania shows Ernest Galvanauskas having presented credentials as minister on December 10, 1924, FOLD, 1925.

[155]   New York Times, April 24, 1927.

died on September 16, 1927, at Kovno. He never appeared in the pertinent issues of the *U.S. Diplomatic List*, April–October 1927.[156]

DR. LADAS NATKEVIČIUS [NATKUS]

Born on January 19, 1893. Studied mathematics and physics at St. Petersburg University. Drafted into the czarist army, 1917. Later, served as Lithuanian military attaché in Estonia and Latvia. Lived in Paris, 1923-1930, where he served, for a time, as press attaché at the Lithuanian Legation. Earned a doctorate in law at the Sorbonne in 1930[157] and, in the same year, published *Aspect politique et juridique du differend Polono-Lithuanien* [Policy and Jurisdictional Aspects of the Polish-Lithuanian Conflict].[158] Served at the Foreign Ministry in Kaunas, 1930–1934. Counselor of the Paris Legation, 1934–1939.[159] Presented credentials as minister to the Soviet Union on May 16, 1939,[160] serving until 1940 amid the Soviet actions that eventually subjugated his country. Practiced law in Kaunas and taught at Vilnius University during the years of Soviet and German occupation, 1940-1944. Died in Vienna on May 25, 1945, after escaping there during the second Soviet invasion of Lithuania.[161]

DR. JURGIS ŠAULYS

Born in 1879.[162] His appointment as minister to Berlin in 1918 arguably marks the beginning of the Lithuanian foreign service. Traveled from Berlin to Switzerland in December 1918 to open a diplomatic mission. Continued serving in Berlin during the first months of 1919 but was recalled in March 1919 to mediate a government crisis at home. Upon the resolution of the crisis, he was sent to Warsaw to conduct the first official talks with the

---

[156]   Washington, September 17, 1927, Acting Secretary of State Wilbur H. Carr to Lithuanian foreign minister, USNA701.60M 11/44A; Riga, October 10, 1927, F. W. B. Coleman, USNA701.60M 11/46.

[157]   ELI, 4, pp. 39–40.

[158]   Senn, *The Great Powers*, pp. 15 n., 42 n.

[159]   ELI, 4, pp. 39–40.

[160]   Moscow, July 5, 1939, Sir W. Seeds, FO371/23686-N3287/281/38.

[161]   ELI, 4, pp. 39–40.

[162]   Kaslas, p. 535.

Poles. In June 1919, he was named to lead Lithuania's first diplomatic mission to the United States, but was prevented by illness.[163] Posted to Italy, around 1920–1921, as "de facto representative" and not part of the official diplomatic corps.[164] Appointed minister to the Vatican, 1927, and withdrawn from that post, October 1931.[166] Presented credentials in Berlin on December 4, 1931.[167] Reportedly, he was a reasonable man who managed with the Germans as well as could be expected, given the constant tension between Germany and Lithuania.[168] Accredited, simultaneously, to Austria and Hungary, presenting credentials in those countries in May 1932[169] and in Switzerland on December 12, 1934.[170] Transferred to Poland as minister at the end of 1938, presenting credentials on January 11, 1939. Also accredited to Hungary and Switzerland, resident in Warsaw.[171] Posted to Switzerland at the outbreak of World War II, where, in a May 30, 1940 telegram from his foreign minister, Juozas Urbšys, it was ordered that Saulys would become, "in the event of a catastrophe" within Lithuania, second deputy to the Lithuanian minister at Rome, who would assume the role of

---

163   Senn, "The Formation," pp. 501–503, 503 n. 5.

164   Rome, January 26, 1922, Sir R. Graham, FO371/7664-C1465/1465/22.

165   Holy See/Rome, January 1, 1931, G. Ogilvie Forbes, FO371/15253-C233/233/22.

166   Holy See/Rome, January 12, 1932, G. Ogilvie Forbes, FO371/15980-C610/610/22.

167   Berlin, 1938 [author unknown], FO371/21671-C80/80/18.

168   Berlin, 1938 [author unknown], FO371/21671-C80/80/18.

169   Vienna, January 1, 1934, Sir W. Selby, FO371/18359-R229/229/3; Budapest, June 4, 1932, Nicholas Roosevelt, USN A701.60M 64/1.

170   Berne, January 1, 1935, Sir H. W. Kennard, FO371/19750-W125/125/43.

171   Warsaw, June 30, 1939, Sir W. H. Kennard, FO371/23144-C9681/1109/55.

chief of the "residual diplomatic representations abroad."[172] An October 30, 1942 list of Lithuanian diplomats still functioning abroad cites Saulys as minister to Switzerland.[173] Died in 1948.[174]

JURGIS SAVICKIS

Born on May 2, 1890.[175] Appointed to Copenhagen in 1919, where he had been associated with the International Red Cross since 1915.[176] He also was assigned to Norway and Sweden, appearing in a Norwegian diplomatic list in 1923.[177] Denmark, Norway, and Sweden recognized Lithuania de jure in 1921.[178] Savickis was recalled in 1924, when, for financial reasons, Lithuania closed its legation in Copenhagen and lowered its representation in Denmark to the consular level. Reportedly, Danish newspapers expressed "sorrow at his departure" and referred to him in flattering terms.[179] He was sent to Helsinki in early 1924.[180] Left Finland, July 1927, when, for motives of economy, Lithuania closed that diplomatic mission.[181] Returned home and became head of the Administrative Department of the Lithuanian Foreign Ministry. Presented credentials as

---

[172] Petra Klimas was designated as first deputy, as noted in Kaslas, p. 180.

[173] List prepared by the Lithuanian minister in Washington, Povilas Žadeikis, October 30, 1942, USNA701.60P 00/10.

[174] Kaslas, p. 535.

[175] ELI, 5, pp. 81–83.

[176] Copenhagen, January 3, 1924, John Dyneley Prince, USNA701.60M 59/orig.

[177] Norway. *Liste du corps diplomatique à Kristiana, février 1923.*

[178] Kaslas, p. 87.

[179] Copenhagen, January 2, 1924, Lord Granville, FO371/10414-N400/400/15.

[180] Helsinki, January 3, 1925, Ernest Rennie, FO371/10989-N212/212/56.

[181] Helsinki, January 9, 1928, Ernest Rennie, FO371/13925-N569/569/56.

minister to Sweden on February 17, 1930, and also was accredited as minister to Denmark and Norway, resident in Stockholm.[182] Presented credentials in Copenhagen on March 29, 1930.[183] A Copenhagen dispatch mentioned that he spoke Danish well, was a poet, and once served as director of the Lithuanian State Theatre at Kovno.[184] Presented credentials as minister to Latvia on December 15, 1937[185] and was replaced by early 1939.[186] Lived in Roquebrune, France, during, and after, World War II on a small farm that he named Ariogala. Died there on December 22, 1952.[187]

IGNAS ŠEINIUS [IGNAS JURKUNAS-SEINIUS, IURKUNAS, SCHEINIUS, SCHEYNIUS; actual surname was JURKUNAS]

Born on April 3, 1889. Studied at Moscow University. Served as representative of the Lithuanian Central Relief Committee in Stockholm during World War I, 1916–1918,[188] forming the connection between approximately a million Lithuanian emigrants within the United States and their homeland.[189] Assigned as chargé d'affaires in Finland, appearing in the Helsinki diplomatic list for the first time in December 1921 and for the last time in October 1923.[190] Appointed chargé d'affaires for Denmark, Norway, and Sweden, resident in Stockholm. Appeared in the Danish diplomatic list

---

[182]   Stockholm, February 19, 1930, Sir H. W. Kennard, FO371/14888-N1242/224/42.

[183]   Copenhagen, 1932, Sir T. Hohler, FO371/16280-N4/4/15.

[184]   Copenhagen, January 13, 1931, Sir T. Hohler, FO371/15556-N429/429/15.

[185]   LAM, p. 62.

[186]   Riga, January 21, 1939, C. W. Orde, FO371/23601-N450/46/59; Riga, July 1, 1939, C. W. Orde, FO371/23601-N3353/46/59.

[187]   ELI, 5, pp. 81–83.

[188]   ELI, 5, p. 103.

[189]   Stockholm, September 12, 1923, Patrick Ramsay, FO371/9377-N7629/498/42.

[190]   Finland. *Corps diplomatique à Helsingfors, decembre 1921*; Finland. *Corps diplomatique à Helsingfors, octobre 1923*.

as chargé d'affaires, September 1924–July 1927,[191] and in the Norwegian diplomatic list as chargé d'affaires, February 1923–May 1927.[192] Received an *agrément* as chargé d'affaires in Sweden on June 19, 1923, and was withdrawn from that post on June 1, 1927. Remained in Sweden as an employee of private companies, until 1933, when he returned to Lithuania.[193] Editor in chief of the government daily newspaper *Lietuvos Aidas*, 1933–1934, and was press advisor to the Governor of Memel (Klaipėda), 1935–1939. He went to Sweden as a refugee following the Soviet incursion of 1940 and acquired Swedish citizenship in 1943. A writer in Lithuanian and Swedish. His 1913 novel, *Kuprelis* (The Humpback), has been cited as "one of the major works of modern Lithuanian literature." He also wrote the comedy *Diplomatai* [Diplomats] in 1937. Died on January 15, 1959, in Stockholm.[194]

VACLOVAS SIDZIKAUSKAS

Born in 1893. Studied law at Moscow and Berne. Employed at the Lithuanian Ministry of Justice, 1918. Entered the Lithuanian Foreign Ministry at the end of 1919.[195] Appointed chargé d'affaires in Switzerland by November 28, 1921,[196] where he represented Lithuania, simultaneously, at the League of Nations. Continued to render service at the League of Nations upon being posted to Berlin.[197] Presented credentials as minister to Germany

---

[191]   Denmark. *Corps diplomatique accrédité à Copenhague, septembre 1924*; Denmark. *Corps diplomatique accrédité à Copenhague, juillet 1927*.

[192]   Norway. *Liste du corps diplomatique à Kristiania, février 1923*; Norway. *Liste du corps diplomatique à Oslo, mai 1927*.

[193]   Information provided by Bertil Johannson, Senior Archivist, Swedish National Archives, Stockholm, July 15, 1996.

[194]   ELI, 5, pp. 103–104. Bertil Johannson, senior archivist, Swedish National Archives, Stockholm, July 15, 1996.

[195]   Riga, July 12, 1939, C. W. Orde, transmitting dispatch of Thomas H. Preston, Kovno, June 28, 1939, FO371/23609-N3452/3452/59, Records of Leading Personalities in Lithuania.

[196]   Berne, January 3, 1925, R. Sperling, FO371/11101-W89/89/43.

[197]   Senn, "The Formation," pp. 506–507 n. 13.

in 1924.[198] Accredited, simultaneously, as minister to Austria in 1925,[199] and Switzerland on April 22, 1927.[200] Presented credentials as minister to Great Britain on December 9, 1931.[201]   Accredited, simultaneously, to The Netherlands, resident in London, presenting credentials on January 9, 1932.[202]   Tried by the Kaunas Circuit Court and declared guilty of embezzlement while minister in Berlin on October 6, 1939. He was given a suspended sentence of six months in prison and placed on probation for three years.[203] In 1937, he was appointed director in Lithuania of Shell Oil. Elected president of the Lithuanian–British Society on June 12, 1939.[204] Member of VLIK, which is the Lithuanian acronym for the Supreme Committee for the Liberation of Lithuania, serving as its president during the 1960s.[205] He was regarded, at one time, as one of Lithuania's most prominent diplomats, being described as affable, versatile, and intelligent.[206] Died on December 1, 1973, in New York.[207]

---

[198]   Berlin, February 8, 1928, Sir R. C. Lindsay, FO371/12908-C1071/1071/18.

[199]   Vienna, July 7, 1925, Albert H. Washburn, USNA701.60M 63/orig.

[200]   Berne, January 2, 1932, Sir H. W. Kennard, FO371/16516-W114/114/43.

[201]   FOLD, 1932–1934.

[202]   The Hague, June 4, 1934, Sir Hubert Montgomery, FO371/18575-W422/422/29.

[203]   Kaunas, October 11, 1934, M. L. Stafford, USNA701.60M 41/3.

[204]   Riga, July 12, 1939, C. W. Orde, transmitting dispatch of Thomas H. Preston, Kovno, June 28, 1939, FO371/23609-N3452/3452/59, Records of Leading Personalities in Lithuania.

[205]   Gerutis, pp. 349, 418, 425, 430.

[206]   Riga, July 12, 1939, C. W. Orde, transmitting dispatch of Thomas H. Preston, Kovno, June 28, 1939, FO371/23609-N3452/3452/59, Records of Leading Personalities in Lithuania.

[207]   LEN, 37 (Supplement), p. 526.

COLONEL KAZYS ŠKIRPA

Born in 1895. Chief of the Lithuanian General Staff, 1926.[208] Studied at the Royal Belgian Military Academy.[209]   Military attaché at Berlin. Appointed permanent delegate (minister) to the League of Nations, 1937.[210] Presented credentials as minister to Poland on March 31, 1938.[211] Minister to Germany by February 1939.[212] The Soviet occupation of Lithuania, in June 1940, set Škirpa on a path of seeking to regain his country's independence. He was forced to surrender the Lithuanian Legation in Berlin to Soviet diplomats in August 1940.[213]   Attended a conference of Lithuanian diplomats, in Rome, which produced a document on September 25, 1940, creating a Lithuanian National Committee, on which body he served. He organized the Lithuanian Activist Front (LAF) on November 17, 1940.[214] After Hitler attacked the Soviet Union on June 22, 1941, German forces entering the Lithuanian capital on June 25, 1941, found a provisional government of Lithuanians in control. The premier of the provisional

---

[208]   Kaslas, p. 535.

[209]   Gerutis, p. 220.

[210]   Kaunas, July 20, 1937, C. Porter Kuykendall, USNA701.60M 54/2.

[211]   Warsaw, March 31, 1938, A. J. D. Biddle, Jr., USNA701.60M 60C/3.

[212]   Kaslas, p. 535.

[213]   *New York Times*, August 10, 1940; reportedly, Škirpa "tearfully" surrendered the legation to the Soviets, according to *New York Times*, August 15, 1940. Another account contends that Škirpa refused to turn over the legation and was evicted by the German police. Allegedly, he also raised a Lithuanian flag over the building in a way that rendered it almost inaccessible, compelling the Soviets to call the Berlin Fire Department to remove it, as claimed in Kaslas, pp. 307–308.

[214]   Kaslas, pp. 314-316. Reference to the LAF can be found in Gerutis, p. 398 et seq. More on Škirpa is provided in Gerutis, passim.

government was Škirpa, but he had not been permitted, by the Nazis, to leave Germany to participate in the insurrection.[215] Died in 1979.[216]

DR. EDUARDAS TURAUSKAS

Born in 1896.[217] Graduate of a Jesuit high school. Studied at the Fribourg Catholic University in Switzerland. Returned to Lithuania in 1926 and elected as a Christian Democratic member of parliament. Editor of *Rytas*, the unofficial press organ of the Christian Democratic Party. Exiled from Kovno to the provinces, because he published an anti-government article. Declined an appointment as secretary of the Lithuanian consulate at Tallinn but accepted the post of director of the Lithuanian Telegraph Agency, Elta.[218] Presented credentials as minister to Czechoslovakia on October 26, 1934.[219] Simultaneously, accredited as minister to Romania, resident in Prague, and presented credentials in Bucharest on November 29, 1935.[220] Became the first Lithuanian minister to Yugoslavia, resident in Prague, presenting credentials in Belgrade on April 17, 1937.[221] Appointed head of the Political Department of the Lithuanian Foreign Ministry in June 1939.[222] Thereafter, served at the League of Nations and as counselor of the

---

[215]   Romuald J. Misiunas and Rein Taagepera, *The Baltic States: Years of Dependence, 1940-1990* (Berkeley: University of California Press, 1992), pp. 44, 46–47, 351.

[216]   Misiunas and Taagepera, p. 397. An additional interesting report on Škirpa also is provided in Kaslas, pp. 341–342.

[217]   Kaslas, p. 536.

[218]   Riga, July 12, 1939, C. W. Orde, transmitting dispatch of Thomas H. Preston, Kovno, June 28, 1939, FO371/23609-N3452/3452/59, Records of Leading Personalities in Lithuania.

[219]   Prague, January 4, 1938, B. C. Newton, FO434/5-R165/165/12.

[220]   Bucharest, January 1, 1938, Sir R. Hoare, FO434/5-R189/189/37.

[221]   Kaunas, April 22, 1937, C. Porter Kuykendall, USNA701.60M 60F/2.

[222]   Riga, July 12, 1939, C. W. Orde, transmitting dispatch of Thomas H. Preston, Kovno, June 28, 1939, FO371/23609-N3452/3452/59, Records of Leading Personalities in Lithuania.

Lithuanian Legation in Berne.[223] Following the Soviet aggression against Lithuania, became a participant in a meeting of Lithuanian diplomats gathered in Rome in September 1940. The Lithuanian National Committee was created as a result of this meeting, and Turauskas was elected one of its permanent members.[224] However, he does not appear within a 1942 list of Lithuanian diplomats functioning outside the United States.[225] Died in 1967.[226]

JUOZAS URBŠYS

Born in 1896. Served in the Lithuanian army, retiring with the rank of captain. Employed at the Lithuanian Foreign Ministry, 1922–1926. Became head of the consular section of the Lithuanian Legation at Berlin and was promoted to first secretary in 1927. Transferred to Paris, 1927, with the same rank and was promoted, subsequently, to counselor. Presented credentials as minister to Latvia on June 14, 1933. Terminated his tenure at that post by July 12, 1934, having been recalled to become Director of the Political Department of the Lithuanian Foreign Ministry. Made secretary-general of the Foreign Ministry, 1936. Became foreign minister of Lithuania on December 5, 1938.[227] He was in Moscow for diplomatic talks with the Soviet government during June 1940, when, unlike many other high-ranking officials of the Baltic states who were *deported* by the Soviets to the Soviet Union, Urbšys simply was detained and not permitted to return to Lithuania.[228] Interestingly, he had sent a telegram on May 30, 1940, to diplomat Stasys Lozoraitis, Sr. in Rome, and to other Lithuanian diplomats in other capitals, designating Lozoraitis as chief of the Lithuanian diplomatic service "if Lithuania should meet with a catastrophe." Therefore, the diplomatic service would represent "the continuity of the independent

---

[223]   Kaslas, p. 536.

[224]   Kaslas, p. 314.

[225]   List prepared by the Lithuanian minister in Washington, Povilas Žadeikis, October 30, 1942, USNA701.60P 00/10.

[226]   Kaslas, p. 536.

[227]   LAM, p. 62; Riga, July 12, 1939, C. W. Orde, transmitting dispatch of Thomas H. Preston, Kovno, June 28, 1939, FO371/23609-N3452/3452/59, Records of Leading Personalities in Lithuanian.

[228]   Misiunas and Taagepera, p. 22.

Lithuanian state."[229] Urbšys was a rare survivor of Soviet maltreatment, living to tell his story through a tape recording to an audience of approximately 250,000 in Vilnius on August 23, 1988.[230] Died in 1991.[231]

VYTAUTAS VILEIŠIS
Born on November 11, 1887.[232] Former Lithuanian minister of communications. Served as minister to Latvia from September 11, 1934 until his death.[233] Died on July 5, 1937, in Kaunas.[234]

POVILAS ŽADEIKIS
Born on March 14, 1887.[235] Educated as a chemist.[236] Arrived in the United States as Major Povilas Žadeikis on December 18, 1919, as part of a Lithuanian mission sent to express appreciation for American aid rendered to Lithuania, establish economic relations, and secure American recognition of Lithuanian independence.[237] Appointed consul at Chicago, 1923. Promoted to consul general at New York City on February 1, 1928. Served in that capacity until he was elevated to Lithuanian minister to the United

---

[229]   Gerutis, p. 258; Kaslas, p. 180.

[230]   V. Stanley Vardys, "Lithuanian National Politics," *Problems of Communism*, 38, no. 4 (July-August, 1989), p. 62.

[231]   Misiunas and Taagepera, p. 399.

[232]   LEN, 34, p. 85.

[233]   LAM, p. 62.

[234]   Riga, July 12, 1937, Arthur Bliss Lane, USNA701.60M 60P/6. Commentary on his pre-diplomatic days is provided in [Kaunas], January 13, 1931, [author unknown], FO371/15538-N446/273/59, List of Leading Personalities in Lithuania.

[235]   ELI, 6, pp. 285–286.

[236]   Washington, August 20, 1935, Robert F. Kelley, USNA701.60M 11/77.

[237]   Major Žadeikis had been the Lithuanian in charge of an attempt to form an American-Lithuanian Legion, as mentioned in Tarulis, pp. 275, 292.

States, presenting credentials on August 21, 1935.[238] The Soviet-installed Lithuanian government dismissed him, effective July 26, 1940, naming the consul at Chicago, Petras Daudzvardis, as chargé d'affaires, but Žadeikis refused to comply with those instructions.[239] Continued to serve as minister throughout World War II and the Cold War, until his death. Succeeded by Juozas Kajeckas, who became chargé d'affaires. Died on May 11, 1957.[240]

DR. DOVAS ZAUNIUS

Born in 1891 of Lithuanian extraction. Graduate of a German high school and a German university, in law. Served in the German army during World War I. Opted for Lithuanian nationality at the end of the war and entered the Lithuanian diplomatic service.[241] Chargé d'affaires in Latvia, February 13, 1920–December 12, 1921, becoming minister resident on December 12, 1921, and serving until February 13, 1923.[242] Presented credentials as minister to Czechoslovakia on July 12, 1923.[243] Recalled to Kovno, in April 1927, to assume the directorship of the Economic and Administrative Department of the Lithuanian Foreign Ministry. The Lithuanian Legation in Prague was closed, but Dr. Zaunius did not present letters of recall and continued to be carried in the Prague diplomatic list.[244] He reappeared "for a day or two" in Prague during October 1928 to represent Lithuania at the 10th anniversary of Czechoslovak

---

[238]   Washington, January 1, 1936, Sir R. Lindsay, FO371/19832-A309/309/45; Washington, August 20, 1935, Robert F. Kelley, USNA701.60M 11/77.

[239]   Kaunas, July 27, 1940, Owen J. C. Norem, USNA701.60MI 1/92; Washington, July 30, 1940, Loy Henderson, USNA701.60MI 1/93; Washington, August 9, 1940, Povilas Žadeikis to Loy Henderson, USNA701.60MI 1/95.

[240]   ELI, 6, pp. 285–286; USDL, June 1957; Gerutis, pp. 397–426 passim; Kaslas, pp. 229–537 passim.

[241]   Riga, July 12, 1939, C. W. Orde, transmitting dispatch of Thomas H. Preston, Kovno, June 28, 1939, FO371/23609-N3452/3452/59, Records of Leading Personalities in Lithuania.

[242]   LAM, p. 62.

[243]   Prague, January 26, 1924, Sir George R. Clerk, FO371/9677-C1991/1991/12.

[244]   Prague, February 16, 1928, Sir Ronald Macleay, FO371/12867-C1340/1340/12.

independence.[245] He continued to be carried in the Prague diplomatic list until 1931, even while having become secretary-general of the Foreign Ministry in 1928,[246] then foreign minister of Lithuania on November 7, 1929.[247] His successor in Prague, Jonas Aukštuolis, presented credentials on October 27, 1932.[248] While listed as minister at Prague, Dr. Zaunius presented credentials on March 3, 1925, as the first Lithuanian minister to Switzerland — previous Lithuanian diplomatic representatives to Switzerland had been chargés d'affaires. Assigned, simultaneously, as Lithuanian representative to the League of Nations in Geneva.[249] The last American minister to Lithuania, who departed in 1940 upon Lithuania's Sovietization, wrote glowingly of Dr. Zaunius, referring to him as a "brilliant and capable leader" and as a "great leader," concluding a decidedly positive commentary by informing that "death cut short his brilliant career in the winter of 1939–40."[250]

---

[245]   Prague, January 1, 1929, Sir Ronald Macleay, FO371/13579-C118/118/12.

[246]   Prague, January 4, 1932, K. T. Gurney, FO371/15899-C415/415/12; Riga, July 12, 1939, C. W. Orde, transmitting dispatch of Thomas H. Preston, Kovno, June 28, 1939, FO371/23609-N3452/3452/59, Records of Leading Personalities in Lithuania.

[247]   Senn, *The Great Powers*, p. 233 n. 51.

[248]   Prague, January 1, 1933, Joseph Addison, FO371/16659-C396/396/12.

[249]   Berne, February 27, 1925, Hugh Gibson, USNA701.60m 54/orig.; Berne, March 5, 1925, Hugh Gibson, USNA701.60m 54/1; Riga, January 31, 1925, F.B.W. Coleman, USNA701.60m 60f/orig.

[250]   Norem, p. 228. An interesting diplomatic tale about Dr. Zaunius is recounted in Sir Hughe Knatchbull-Hugessen, *Diplomat in Peace and War* (London: John Murray, 1949), pp. 70–71. Sir Hughe was British minister to all three Baltic states, 1930–1934.

Bibliography

Public Records

Australia, Parliament. *Commonwealth Parliamentary Debates*. Senate. August 8, 1974.

Canada. *Royal Commission on Bilingualism and Biculturalism: Final Report*. Hull, QC: Queen's Printer for Canada, 1965.

Denmark, Ministère des Affaires Etrangères. *Liste du Corps Diplomatique accredité à Copenhague*, janvier 1924, septembre 1924, juillet 1927, octobre 1927, juin 1939, octobre 1939.

Estonia, Ministère des Affaires Etrangères. *Liste du Corps Diplomatique à Tallinn*, novembre 1932, decembre 1939.

Finland, Ministère des Affaires Etrangères. *Liste du Corps Diplomatique à Helsingfors*, decembre 1921, avril 1922, octobre 1923.

Italy, Ministero Degli Affari Esteri. *I Documenti Diplomatici Italiani, nona serie 1939-1943*, vol. 4. Rome: *Liberia dello Stato*, 1960.

Latvia, Arlietu Ministrija. *Le Corps diplomatique en Lettonie, 1918-1938*. Riga: Ministère des Affaires Etrangères de Lettonie, novembre 1938.

League of Nations. *Official Journal, 1920–1946*. Records of First Assembly, Plenary Sessions, held November 15 to December 18, 1920. Research Publications (microfilm), pt. 29, 63 reels, 1975.

League of Nations. *Official Journal, 1920–1946*. Records of the Second Assembly, Plenary Sessions, held September 5 to October 5, 1921. Research Publications (microfilm), pt. 29, 63 reels, 1975.

Lithuania, Ministry of Foreign Affairs, State and Diplomatic Protocol Section, *Diplomatinis Korpusas/Diplomatic Corps*. Vilnius: Ministry of Foreign Affairs, 1995.

Norway, Ministère des Affaires Etrangères. *Liste du Corps Diplomatique à Kristiana*, fevrier 1923, janvier 1924.

Norway, Ministère des Affaires Etrangères. *Liste du Corps Diplomatique à Oslo*, novembre 1925, juillet 1926, mai 1927, septembre 1928.

Reno, Edward A., *League of Nations Documents, 1919–1946: A Descriptive Guide and Key to the Microfilm Collection*, 3 vols. New Haven, CT: Research Publications, 1973–1975.

United Kingdom, Foreign and Commonwealth Office. *Foreign Office List and Diplomatic and Consular Yearbook*. London: Harrison and Sons, 1920–1965.

United Kingdom, Foreign and Commonwealth Office. *Diplomatic Service List*. London: Harrison and Sons, 1966–2000.

United Kingdom, Foreign and Commonwealth Office. *London Diplomatic List*. London: Her Majesty's Stationary Office, June 1992.

United Kingdom, Parliament. *Debates of the House of Commons* [Hansard] January 17, 1945.

United Kingdom, Public Records Office. Foreign Office Files 181, 371, 372, 425, 434. London, 1919–1954.

United States, Congress. *United States Congressional Records – Senate*, Vol. 94, part 5, June 1, 1948.

United States, Congress. "Human Rights and the Baltic States," Hearing Before the Subcommittee on International Organizations of the Committee on Foreign Affairs, House of Representatives, June 26, 1979.

United States, Congress. "Joint Resolution of the Senate and the House of Representatives to Direct the President to Issue a Proclamation Designating February 16, 1983 as 'Lithuanian Independence Day,'" H.J. Res. 60. Washington, DC: U.S. Government Printing Office, 1983.

United States, Congress. "Third Interim Report of the House of Representatives Select Committee on Communist Aggression, 83rd Congress, 2nd Session." Washington, DC: U.S. Government Printing Office, 1954.

United States, Department of State. *Papers Relating to the Foreign Relations of the United States, 1920.* Washington: U.S. Government Printing Office, 1936.

United States, Department of State. *Key Officers of Foreign Service Posts.* Washington, DC: U.S. Government Printing Office, 1985–2000.

United States, Department of State. *Papers Relating to the Foreign Relations of the United States: Russia, 1919.* Washington, DC: U.S. Government Printing Office, 1937.

United States, Department of State. *Papers Relating to the Foreign Relations of the United States 1922.* Washington, DC: U.S. Government Printing Office, 1938.

United States, Department of State. *Papers Relating to the Foreign Relations of the United States, 1920.* Washington: U.S. Government Printing Office, 1936.

United States, Department of State. *Papers Relating to the Foreign Relations of the United States: Russia, 1919.* Washington, DC: U.S. Government Printing Office, 1937.

United States, Department of State. *Register of the Department of State.* Washington, DC: U.S. Government Printing Office, 1922–1931.

United States, Department of State. *Papers Relating to the Foreign Relations of the United States, 1922.* Washington, DC: U.S. Government Printing Office, 1938.

United States, Department of State, Office of the Chief of Protocol. *Diplomatic List.* Washington, DC: U.S. Government Printing Office, 1919–2000.

United States, Department of State. Office of the Historian. *Principal Officers of the Department of State and United States Chiefs of Mission, 1778-1990.* Washington, DC: U.S. Government Printing Office, January 1991.

United States, National Archives and Records Administration. *Decimal Files,* record group 59, files 701.60i, 701.60m, 701.60p, 801.60p. Washington, DC and College Park, MD, 1910–1963.

Unpublished Monographs

Jaakson, Ernst. "A Short Biography of Ernst Jaakson," personal to the authors, June 6, 1996.

McHugh, James T. "I the Person: Natural Law, Judicial Decision Making, and Individual Rights." Doctoral dissertation, Queen's University, 1991.

Samts, Jānis A. "The Origins of Latvian Diplomacy, 1917-1925: The Role of Zigfrīds Anna Meierovics in the Formulation of Latvian Foreign Policy." Master's thesis, San Jose State University, 1975.

Sibul, Eric A. "The Origins of Estonian Diplomacy, 1917-1922: The Roles of Kaarel Robert Pusta, Antonius Piip, and Jaan Poska." Master's thesis, San Jose State University, 1989.

Vitas, Robert A. "U.S. Nonrecognition of the Soviet Occupation of Lithuania." Doctoral dissertation, Loyola University, 1989.

Published Monographs

Abell, George, and Gordon, Evelyn, *Let Them Eat Caviar.* New York: Dodge, 1936.

Albinski, Henry S. *Australian External Policy Under Labor.* Vancouver: University of British Columbia Press, 1977.

Ambrose, Stephen E. *Eisenhower,* 2 vols.. New York: Simon and Schuster, 1983.

Andrew, Arthur. *The Rise and Fall of a Middle Power.* Toronto: James Lorimer, 1993.

Andersons, Edgars, *Latvijas Vesture 1920-1940, Arpolitika* [History of Latvia: Foreign Policy], 2 vols. Stockholm: Daugava, 1982-1984.

Andersson, Ingvar. *A History of Sweden*, Carolyn Hannay, trans. New York: Praeger, 1957.

Aron, Raymond. *Peace and War*. New York: Doubleday, 1966.

Bashevkin, Sylvia B., *True Patriot Love: The Politics of Canadian Nationalism*. Oxford, Oxford University Press, 1991.

Bell, Cora. *Dependent Ally*. Melbourne: Oxford University Press, 1988.

Bernard, Andre. *Problèmes politiques: Canada et Québec*. Ste. Foy: Les Presses de l'Université du Québec, 1993.

Bērziņš, Arturs. *Kārlis Zariņš: Dzīvē un Darbā* [*Karlis Zarins' Life and Work*]. London: Ruja, 1959.

Bilmanis, Alfreds. *A History of Latvia*. Westport, CT: Greenwood Press, 1951.

Bilmanis, Alfreds. *Latvia as an Independent State*. Washington, DC: Latvian Legation, 1947.

Bilmanis, Alfreds, ed., *Latvian-Russian Relations: Documents*, 2 vols. Washington, DC: Latvian Legation, 1944 and 1948.

Bilodeau, Rosario, Comeau Robert, Gosselin André, and Julien Denise. *Histoire des Canadas*. Montréal: Editions Hurtubise HMH, 1970.

Birskys, Betty, Birskys, Antanas, Putnins, Aldis L., and Salasoo, Inno. *The Baltic Peoples in Australia*. Melbourne: Australasian Educa Press, 1986.

Burnet, Jean R., and Palmer, Howard. *Coming Canadians: An Introduction to a History of Canada's Peoples*. Toronto: McClelland and Stuart, 1988.

Churchill, Winston S. *The Second World War*. Boston: Houghton Mifflin, 1948.

Clemens, Walter C., Jr. *Baltic Independence and Russian Empire*. New York: St. Martin's Press, 1991.

Clift, Dominique. *Quebec Nationalism in Crisis*. Montreal and Kingston: McGill-Queen's University Press, 1989.

Connor, Walker. *Ethnonationalism: The Quest for Understanding*. Princeton, NJ: Princeton University Press, 1994.

Conquest, Robert, *Stalin and the Kirov Murder*. New York: Oxford University Press, 1989.

Cooper, Andrew F., Higgott, Richard A., and Nossal, Kim Richard. *Relocating Middle Powers: Australia and Canada in a Changing World Order*. Vancouver: University of British Columbia, 1993.

Crowe, David M., *The Baltic States and the Great Powers: Foreign Relations, 1938-1940*. Boulder, CO: Westview Press, 1993.

Dembinski, Ludwik. *The Modern Law of Diplomacy*. Dordrecht, The Netherlands: Martinus Nijhoff, 1988.

Dembkowski, Harry E. *The Union of Lublin*. New York: Columbia University Press, 1982.

Denza, Eileen. *Diplomatic Law*. New York: Oceana Publications, 1976.

Dickson, Peter W. *Kissinger and the Meaning of History*. Cambridge: Cambridge University Press, 1978.

Diefenbaker, John G. *One Canada*, 2 vols. Toronto: Macmillan, 1975.

Dion, Léon. *Québec, 1945–2000: A la recherche du Québec*. Montréal: Editions Québec/Amérique, 1987.

Donnelly, Jack. *Universal Human Rights in Theory and Practice*. Ithaca, NY: Cornell University Press, 1989.

Dougherty, James E., and Pfaltzgraff, Robert L., Jr. *Contending Theories of International Relations*. New York: Harper and Row, 1981.

Doumitt, Donald P. *Conflict in Northern Ireland: The History, the Problem, and the Challenge.* New York: Peter Lang, 1985.

Dunsdorfs, Edgars. *The Baltic Dilemma.* New York: Robert Speller and Sons, 1975.

Entessar, Nader. *Kurdish Ethnonationalism.* Boulder, CO: Lynn Rienner, 1992.

Eversley, George [Lord Eversley]. *The Partition of Poland.* New York: Howard Fertig, 1973.

Fenwick, Charles G. *International Law,* 4th ed. New York: Appleton-Century-Crofts, 1965.

Friedmann, Wolfgang G. *The Changing Structure of International Law.* New York: Columbia University Press, 1964.

Frost, Robert I. *After the Deluge: Poland-Lithuania and the Second Northern War, 1655–1660.* Cambridge: Cambridge University Press, 1993.

Gade, John A. *All My Born Days: Experiences of a Naval Intelligence Officer in Europe.* New York: Charles Scribner's Sons, 1942.

Galbraith, John S. *The Establishment of Canadian Diplomatic Status at Washington.* Berkeley: University of California Press, 1951.

Gammer, M. *Muslim Resistance to the Tsar: Shamil and the Conquest of Chechnia and Daghestan.* London: F. Cass, 1994.

Gerutis, Albertas, ed., *Lithuania: 700 Years,* Algirdas Budreckis, trans. New York: Manyland Books, 1969.

Glendon, Mary Ann, Gordon, Michael W., and Osakwe, Christopher. *Comparative Legal Traditions in a Nutshell.* St. Paul, MN: West, 1982.

Graham, Malbone W. *The Diplomatic Recognition of the Border States.* Publications of the University of California at Los Angeles in Social Sciences, vol. 3, nos. 3-4. Berkeley: University of California Press, 1939 (no. 3, Estonia) and 1941 (no. 4, Latvia).

Graham, Malbone W. *New Governments of Eastern Europe*. New York: Henry Holt and Company, 1927.

Harrison, Ernest J. *Lithuania, Past and Present*. London: T. Fisher Unwin, 1922.

Harvie, Christopher T. *Scotland and Nationalism: Scottish Society and Politics, 1707–1994*. London: Routledge, 1994.

Hazard, John N. *The Soviet System of Government*. Chicago: University of Chicago Press, 1957.

Henkin, Louis, Pugh, Richard C., Schacter, Oscar, and Smit, Hans. *International Law: Cases and Materials*. St. Paul, MN: West, 1980.

Hiden John, and Salmon, Patrick. *The Baltic Nations and Europe*. New York: Longman, 1991.

Hiden, John. *The Baltic States and Weimar Ostpolitik*. Cambridge: Cambridge University Press, 1987.

Hill, Ronald J. *Soviet Politics, Political Science, and Reform*. Oxford: Martin Robertson, 1980.

Holmes, J. W. *Canada and the United States: Political and Security Issues*. Toronto: Canadian Institute of International Affairs, 1970.

Hosking, Geoffrey. *The Awakening of the Soviet Union*. Cambridge: Harvard University Press, 1990.

Hyland, William G. *The Cold War*. New York: Random House, 1991.

Irving, Ronald Eckford Mill. *The Flemings and Walloons of Belgium*. London: Minority Rights Group, 1980.

Jackson, J. Hampden. *Estonia*. Westport, CT: Greenwood Press, 1979 (reprint of 1948 edition published by George Allen & Unwin).

Jacobini, Horace B. *International Law: A Text*. Homewood, IL: Dorsey Press, 1968.

Jasienica, Pawel, *Jagiellonian Poland*, Alexander Jordan, trans. Miami: American Institute of Polish Culture, 1978.

Kacewicz, George V. *Great Britain, the Soviet Union, and the Polish Government in Exile*. The Hague: Martinus Nijhoff, 1979.

Kaslas, Bronis J. *The USSR–German Aggression Against Lithuania*. New York: Robert Speller and Sons, 1973.

Kegley, Charles W., Jr., and Wittkopf, Eugene. *American Foreign Policy: Pattern and Process*. New York: St. Martin's Press, 1987.

Kennan, George F. *Memoirs 1925–1950*. New York: Pantheon Books, 1967.

Kennan, George F. *Measures Short of War*, Giles D. Harlow and George C. Maerz, eds. Washington, DC: National Defense University Press, 1991.

Kennan, George F. *Russia, the Atom, and the West*. New York: Harper and Row, 1958.

Knatchbull-Hugessen, Hughe. *Diplomat in Peace and War*. London: John Murray, 1949.

Lawrence, T. J., *Les Principals de droit international*, Jacques Dumas and A. DeLapradelle, trans. Oxford: Oxford University Press, 1920.

Lerche, Charles O., Jr. and Said, Abdul A. *Concepts of International Relations*. Englewood Cliffs, NJ: Prentice Hall, 1970.

Levi, Werner. *Contemporary International Law*. Boulder, CO: Westview Press, 1991.

Luckett, Richard. *The White Generals*. New York: Viking Press, 1971.

Madar, Daniel. *The End of Containment?* Toronto: Canadian Institute of International Affairs, 1989.

Mägi, Artur. *Das Staatsleben Estlands während seiner Selbständigkeit*, Vol. 1, *Das Regierungssystem*. Stockholm: Almqvist and Wiksell, 1962.

Manning, Clarence A. *The Forgotten Republics*. Westport, CT: Greenwood Press, 1971.

McClanahan, Grant V. *Diplomatic Immunity*. New York: St. Martin's Press, 1989.

McDermott, Geoffrey. *The Eden Legacy*. London: Leslie Frewin, 1969.

McRoberts, Kenneth. *Misconceiving Canada: The Struggle for National Unity*. Toronto: Oxford University Press, 1997.

McHale, Vincent E., ed. *Political Parties of Europe: Albania-Norway*, Sharon S. Skowronski, asst. ed. Westport, CT: Greenwood Press, 1983.

Misiunas, Romauld J., and Taagepera, Rein. *The Baltic States: Years of Dependence*. Berkeley: University of California Press, 1983.

Morgenthau, Hans J., and Thompson, Kenneth W. *Politics Among Nations*. New York: Alfred A. Knopf, 1985.

Murphy, Brian. *The Other Australia: Experiences of Migration*. Cambridge: Cambridge University Press, 1993.

Norem, Owen J. C., *Timeless Lithuania*. Chicago: Amerlith Press, 1943.

Pal, Leslie A. *Interests of State: The Politics of Language, Multiculturalism, and Feminism in Canada*. Montreal and Kingston: McGill-Queen's Universities Press, 1993.

Parry, Clive, and Fitzmaurice, Gerald, eds. *A British Digest of International Law*. London: Stevens and Sons, 1965.

Plakans, Andrejs, *The Latvians: A Short History*. Stanford, CA: Hoover Institution Press, 1995.

Pollis Adamantia, and Schwab, Peter, eds. *Human Rights: Cultural and Ideological Perspectives*. New York: Praeger, 1980.

Putnins, Aldis L. *Latvians in Australia*. Canberra: Australian National University Press, 1981.

Raeff, Marc. *Comprendre l'Ancien Règime Russe*. Paris: Editions du Seuil, 1987.

Rauch, George von. *The Baltic States*, Gerald Onn, trans. Berkeley: University of California Press, 1974.

Rauch, George von. *The Baltic States, The Years of Independence: Estonia, Latvia, Lithuania 1917–1940*. Berkeley: University of California Press, 1974.

Raun, Toivo U. *Estonia and the Estonians*. Stanford, CA: Hoover Institution Press, 1991.

Reese, Trevor. *Australia in the Twentieth Century*. London: Paul Mall Press, 1964.

Rei, August. *The Drama of the Baltic Peoples*. Stockholm: Vaba Eesti, 1972.

Robbins, Keith. *The Eclipse of a Great Power*. London: Longman, 1983.

Robinson, H. Basil. *Diefenbaker's World: A Populist in Foreign Affairs*. Toronto: University of Toronto Press, 1989.

Rodgers, Hugh I., *Search for Security: A Study in Baltic Diplomacy, 1920-1934*. Hamden, CT: Archon Books, 1975.

Royal Institute of International Affairs. *The Baltic States*. Westport, CT: Greenwood Press, 1970.

Sabaliūnas, Leonas. *Lithuania in Crisis*. Bloomington: Indiana University Press, 1972.

Schwartz, Bernard. *American Constitutional Law*. New York: Greenwood Press, 1969.

Sen, Biswanath. *A Diplomat's Handbook of International Law and Practice*. Dordrecht, The Netherlands: Martinus Nijhoff, 1988.

Senn, Alfred Erich. *The Emergence of Modern Lithuania*. New York: Columbia University Press, 1959.

Senn, Alfred Erich. *The Great Powers, Lithuania, and the Vilna Question 1920–1928*. Leiden: E. J. Brill, 1966.

Seton-Watson, Hugh. *The Decline of Imperial Russia*. New York: Praeger, 1952.

Simutis, Anicetas, *Pasulio Lietuviu Zinynas* [Lithuanian World Directory]. New York: Lithuanian Chamber of Commerce, 1953.

Smith, Geoffrey. *British Government and Its Discontents*. New York: Basic Books, 1981.

Snow, Donald M. *The Shape of the Future: The Post-Cold War World*. Armonk, NY: M.E. Sharpe, 1995.

Sprudz, Adolf, and Rusis, Armins, eds., *Res Baltica: A Collection of Essays in Honor of the Memory of Dr. Alfred Bilmanis, 1887-1948*. Leyden: A.W. Sijthoff, 1968.

Stewart, Gordon T. *The American Response to Canada Since 1776*. East Lansing: Michigan State University Press, 1992.

Taagepera, Rein. *Estonia's Return to Independence*. Boulder, CO: Westview Press, 1993.

Tarulis, Albert N. *American-Baltic Relations, 1918-1922: The Struggle over Recognition*. Washington, DC: Catholic University of America Press, 1965.

Tilby, A. Wyatt. *The English People Overseas*. London: Constable, 1912.

Tribe, Laurence. *American Constitutional Law*. Mineola, NY: The Foundation Press, 1988.

Trotter, William R. *A Frozen Hell*. Chapel Hill, NC: Algonquin Books, 1991.

Urban, William. *The Baltic Crusade*. De Kalb: Northern Illinois University Press, 1975.

Uustalu, Evald, *The History of the Estonian People*. London: Boreas, 1952.

Vaksberg, Arkady, *Stalin's Prosecutor: The Life of Andrei Vyshinsky*. New York: Grove and Weidenfeld, 1991.

Vardys, V. Stanley, ed., *Lithuania Under the Soviets*. New York: Praeger, 1965.

Vardys, V. Stanley, and Misiunas, Romauld J., eds. *The Baltic States in Peace and War, 1917-1945*. University Park: Pennsylvania State University Press, 1978.

Vizulis, Izidors, *The Molotov-Ribbentrop Pact of 1939: The Baltic Case*. Westport, CT: Praeger, 1990.

Ward, Russell. *The History of Australia: The Twentieth Century*. New York: Harper and Row, 1977.

Warma, Aleksander, *In the Shadow of Communist Pressure: Finno-Soviet Relations, 1939-1962*. Stockholm: Scandinavian Youth Service, 1962.

Warma, Aleksander, *Lahettilaana Suomessa, 1939-1944* [A Diplomat in Finland, 1939-1944]. Helsinki: Kustannusosakeyhtio Ottava, 1973.

Westwood, J. N. *Endurance and Endeavor*. Oxford: Oxford University Press, 1993.

Williams, Gwyn A. *The Search for Beulah Land: The Welsh and the Atlantic Revolution*. New York: Holmes and Meier, 1980.

Zirakzadeh, Cyrus Ernesto. *A Rebellious People: Basques, Protests, and Politics*. Reno: University of Nevada Press, 1991.

Newspapers

Brīvā Latvija [Free Latvia], Catthorpe, England, and London

The Globe and Mail, Toronto

Laiks [Time], Brooklyn, NY

Lietuvos Aidas [Lithuanian Echo], Kaunas and Vilnius

The New York Times

The Oak Ridger, Oak Ridge, TN

Päevaleht [The Daily Newspaper], Tallinn

Postimees [The Courrier], Tartu

Rahva Hääl [The People's Voice], Tallinn

Rytas ["Morning"], Kovno (Kaunas)

Tallinna Elu [Tallinn Life], Tallinn

Teataja [The Herald], Tallinn

The Times, London

Vaba Eesti Sõna [Free Estonian Word], New York

The Wall Street Journal, New York

The Washington Post

Newspaper Articles and Refereed Journal Essays

"Baltic Community Vote." *Globe and Mail*, Toronto, June 16, 1962, p. A17.

"Phantom Governments Carry on in Britain." *Wall Street Journal*, December 9, 1970, 1:4.

Anderson, Bill. "Ford Assures Baltics: No U.S. Sellout." *Chicago Tribune*, July 29, 1975, Sec. 2, 2:3.

Forde, Steven. "International Realism and the Science of Politics: Thucydides, Machiavelli, and Neorealism." *International Studies Quarterly*, 39, no. 2, June 1995.

Hough, William J. H., III. "The Annexation of the Baltic States and Its Effect on the Development of Law Prohibiting Forcible Seizure of Territory." *New York Law School Journal of International and Comparative Law*, 6, Winter 1985.

Juda, Lawrence. "United States' Nonrecognition of the Soviet Union's Annexation of the Baltic States: Politics and Law." *Journal of Baltic Studies*, 6, no. 4, Winter 1975.

McHugh, James T. "The Quebec Constitution." *Quebec Studies*, 28, Fall/Winter 2000.

McNaughton, James. "Ford Sees 35-Nation Charter as Gauge on Rights in East Europe." *New York Times*, July 26, 1997, 2:3.

Senn, Alfred Erich. "The Formation of the Lithuanian Foreign Office, 1918-1921." *Slavic Review*, 21, September 1962

Sweet, Alec Stone, and Brunell, Thomas L., "Constructing a Supranational Constitution: Dispute Resolution and Governance in the European Community." *American Political Science Review*, 92, no. 1, March 1988.

Vardys, V. Stanley, "Lithuanian National Politics," *Problems of Communism*, 38, July-August 1989.

"X" [George F. Kennan], "The Sources of Soviet Conflict." *Foreign Affairs*, 25 July 1947.

Chapters and Entries in Published Monographs

Aspaturian, Vernon V. "Eastern Europe in World Perspective." In *Communism in Eastern Europe*, Teresa Rakowska-Harmstone and Andrew Gyorgy, eds. Bloomington: Indiana University Press, 1979.

Beaudoin, Louise, "Origines et développement du rôle international du Gouvernement du Québec." In *Le Canada et le Québec sur la scène internationale*, Paul Painchaud, ed. Montréal: Les Presses de l'Université du Québec, 1977.

Bowman, Francis J. Entries on Estonia, Latvia, and Lithuania. *World Book Encyclopedia*. Vol. 5. Chicago, Field Enterprises Educational, 1961.

Breton, Raymond. "Multiculturalism and Canadian Nation-Building." In *The Politics of Gender, Ethnicity and Language in Canada*, Alan C. Cairns and Cynthia Williams, eds. Toronto: University of Toronto Press, 1985.

Cairns, Alan C. "Reflections on the Political Purposes of the Charter: The First Decade." In *Reconfigurations*. Douglas E. Williams, ed. Toronto, McClelland and Stewart, 1995.

Duncan, W. Raymond. "Yugoslavia's Breakup." In *Ethnic Nationalism and Regional Conflict: The Former Soviet Union and Yugoslavia*, W. Raymond Duncan and G. Paul Holman, Jr., eds. Boulder, CO: Westview Press, 1994.

Eidintas, Alfonsas. "The Meeting of the Lithuanian Cabinet, 15 June 1940." In *The Baltic and the Outbreak of the Second World War*, John Hiden and Thomas Lane, eds. Cambridge: Cambridge University Press, 1992.

Gibbs, Hubert S. "The American Alliance System." In *Problems in International Relations*, Andrew Gyorgy and Hubert S. Gibbs, eds. Englewood Cliffs, NJ, Prentice-Hall, 1962.

Haggenmacher, Peter. "Grotius and Gentili: A Reassessment of Thomas E. Holland's Inaugural Lecture." In *Hugo Grotius and International Relations*, Hedley Bull, Benedict Kingsbury, and Adam Roberts, eds. Oxford: Clarendon Press, 1992.

Kaplan, Cynthia. "Estonia: A Plural Society on the Road to Independence." In *Nation and Politics in the Soviet Successor States*, Ian Bremmer and Ray Taras, eds. Cambridge: Cambridge University Press, 1993.

Kelley, David. "British Diplomacy." In *Diplomacy in a Changing World*, Stephen D. Kertesz and M.A. Fitzsimons, eds. Westport, CT: Greenwood Press, 1974.

Khalidi, Rashid. "The PLO as Representative of the Palestinian People." In *The International Relations of the Palestine Liberation Organization*, Augustus R. Norton and Martin H. Greenberg, eds. Carbondale: Southern Illinois University Press, 1989.

Krickus, Richard. "Lithuania: Nationalism in the Modern Era." In *Nation and Politics in the Soviet Successor States,* Ian Bremmer and Ray Taras, eds. Cambridge: Cambridge University Press, 1993.

Leighly, John B. "The Towns of Medieval Livonia." In *University of California Publications in Geography*J. B. Leighly and C.O. Sauer, eds., vol. 6, no. 7. Berkeley: University of California Press, 1939.

Levy, Thomas Allen. "Le rôle des provinces." In *Le Canada et le Québec sur la scène internationale,* Paul Painchaud, ed. Montréal: Les Presses de l'Université du Québec, 1977.

Lyon, Peter. "Britain and Canada Since the Second World War: Two Much Mutually Entangled Countries." In *Britain and Canada in the 1990s,* D.K. Adams, ed. Halifax, NS: Institute for Research on Public Policy, 1992.

Muiznieks, Nils. "Latvia: Origins, Evolution, and Triumph." In *Nation and Politics in the Soviet Successor States,* Ian Bremmer and Ray Taras, eds. Cambridge: Cambridge University Press, 1993.

Plakans, Andrejs. "Russification Policy in the 1880s." In *Russification in the Baltic Provinces and Finland, 1855–1914,* Edward C. Thaden, ed. Princeton, NJ: Princeton University Press, 1981.

Raun, Toivo U. "Russification and the Estonian National Movement." In *Russification in the Baltic Provinces and Finland, 1855–1914,* Edward C. Thaden, ed. Princeton, NJ: Princeton University Press, 1981.

Reinharz, Jehuda. "Chaim Weizmann as Political Strategist: The Initial Years, 1918–1920." In *Essays in Modern Jewish History,* Frances Malino and Phyllis Cohen Albert, eds. East Brunswick, NJ: Association of University Presses, 1982.

Reisman, W. Michael, and Suzuki, Edward. "Recognition and Social Change in International Law." In *Toward World Order and Human Dignity,* W. Michael Reisman and Burns H. Weston, eds. New York: The Free Press, 1976.

Thaden, Edward C. "Reform and Russification in the Western Borderlands, 1796–1855." In *Russification in the Baltic Provinces and Finland, 1855–1914,* Edward C. Thaden, ed. Princeton NJ: Princeton University Press, 1981.

Vardys, V. Stanley. "The Partisan Movement in Postwar Lithuania." In *Lithuania Under the Soviets*, V. Stanley Vardys, ed. New York: Praeger, 1965.

Wagner, Wenceslas J. "Justice for All: Polish Democracy in the Renaissance Period in Historical Perspective." In *The Polish Renaissance in its European Context*, Samuel Fiszman, ed. Bloomington: Indiana University Press, 1988.

Welsh, William A. "Towards an Empirical Typology of Socialist Systems." In *Comparative Socialist Systems: Essays on Politics and Economics*, Carmelo Mesa-Lago and Carl Beck, eds. Pittsburgh: University of Pittsburgh Center for International Studies, 1975.

Index

About the Authors

JAMES T. McHUGH is Associate Professor of Political Science and chair of the Legal Studies Program at Roosevelt University. He has published works in public law, political philosophy, and Canadian and Quebec politics. He also teaches and participates in activities in the area of human and civil rights.

JAMES S. PACY is Professor Emeritus and former Chair of the Department of Political Science at the University of Vermont.